Masterpiece

Masterpiece

America's 50–Year–Old Love Affair
with British Television Drama

Nancy West

ROWMAN & LITTLEFIELD
Lanham • Boulder • New York • London

Published by Rowman & Littlefield
An imprint of The Rowman & Littlefield Publishing Group, Inc.
4501 Forbes Boulevard, Suite 200, Lanham, Maryland 20706
www.rowman.com

6 Tinworth Street, London, SE11 5AL, United Kingdom

British Library Cataloguing in Publication Information Available

Library of Congress Cataloging-in-Publication Data

Name: West, Nancy Martha, 1963–, author.
Title: Masterpiece : America's 50-year-old love affair with British television drama /
    Nancy West.
Description: Lanham : Rowman & Littlefield, [2020] | Includes bibliographical
    references and index. | Summary: "What accounts for Masterpiece's longevity and
    influence? This book offers two reasons: the power of its drama and its aspirational
    appeal. Masterpiece delivers great stories, stories that transport, enthrall, enrich, and
    comfort us. But it also speaks to a uniquely American belief in the possibility of
    self-improvement, even self-transformation, through the acquisition of 'culture'"—
    Provided by publisher.
Identifiers: LCCN 2020008460 (print) | LCCN 2020008461 (ebook) | ISBN
    9781538134474 (cloth) | ISBN 9781538134481 (epub)
Subjects: LCSH: Masterpiece theatre (Television program) | Television programs—
    Great Britain—History. | Manners and customs on television | Great Britain—On
    television. | Great Britain—Foreign public opinion, American.
Classification: LCC PN1992.77.M293 W47 2020 (print) | LCC PN1992.77.M293
    (ebook) | DDC 791.45/72—dc23
LC record available at https://lccn.loc.gov/2020008460
LC ebook record available at https://lccn.loc.gov/2020008461

For Silas

Contents

Foreword

I'll never forget the year when *Masterpiece* ruined my Christmas.

It was 2012, and during a lull in the day's festivities, I made the mistake of checking my Twitter feed only to discover it had blown up with alarming links to British columnists going on about a death relating to everyone's favorite show, *Downton Abbey*. Even more foolishly, I followed the trail to discover, to my (and eventually millions of fans') dismay, that the show's romantic lead, Matthew Crawley—played with smoldering charisma by Dan Stevens—had suddenly been killed off. In the Christmas episode! On the day his beloved Lady Mary gave birth to baby George!!

This calamity was made even worse by the realization that I'd have to keep this terrible news to myself, not breathing a word to family—or to my *TV Guide Magazine* readers—because the episode wouldn't even air for another two months on PBS (which traditionally broadcast the series after its fall run in the UK). What a delicious dilemma, though, to be so caught up once again in a *Masterpiece* phenomenon.

Just as the saying goes, "There'll always be an England" (Brexit notwithstanding), I firmly believe there will always be a *Masterpiece*. As someone whose first memories of being hooked on serialized TV hark back to *Downton*'s Edwardian predecessor, *Upstairs, Downstairs*, in the 1970s, I simply can't imagine TV without it, even in the medium's current fragmented state with seemingly bottomless platforms of content. Like *60 Minutes*, this distinguished anthology has been synonymous with Sunday-night TV for half a century.

A dependable oasis for those seeking intelligent and handsomely produced drama, never as genteel in its period aspects as its critics tend to overgeneralize (*I, Claudius,* anyone?), *Masterpiece* is, to borrow a metaphor, an enduring jewel in the crown that reflects well not only on PBS but on the industry and tradition of long-form storytelling.

It's hard to know where to start, or where to end, in singing *Masterpiece*'s praises. I appreciate how, as a TV-obsessed kid in Indiana, it opened a window into British culture, literature, and history. (Glenda Jackson is still my ideal *Elizabeth R.*) As a lifelong mystery buff, I can no longer read Agatha Christie, P.D. James, or Sir Arthur Conan Doyle without picturing the definitive versions of their legendary creations: David Suchet as the persnickety Hercule Poirot, Roy Marsden as the brooding Adam Dalgliesh, Jeremy Brett as classic Holmes and the dazzling Benedict Cumberbatch as a mercurial contemporary version.

To its credit, *Masterpiece* doesn't just live in the past. Just try to find a more viciously enjoyable contemporary political satire than the original *House of Cards* (so much funnier and certainly more compact than the made-for-Netflix version). Or a more compellingly flawed yet proudly pioneering feminist icon than Helen Mirren as *Prime Suspect*'s embattled Chief Inspector (later Detective Superintendent) Jane Tennison. When NBC tried to adapt it in 2011, you almost had to admire the doomed hubris. What about the word "masterpiece" didn't they understand?

As *Downton Abbey* triumphantly proved, this franchise has lost none of its power to entrance and entertain—or even to ruin one's holiday with a tragic twist. As we relive and appreciate *Masterpiece*'s legacy in the pages that follow, we eagerly anticipate the stories yet to be told.

—Matt Roush, senior television critic for
TV Guide Magazine and former TV critic for *USA Today*

Acknowledgments

I would like to thank all the people at WGBH and *Masterpiece* who helped with this book, especially Steven Ashley, the show's senior producer. I also want to thank Polly Bennell, Averill Murr, and Steven Watts for their whip-smart commentary on drafts of the book. Marie McMullan did a superb job of assembling the appendixes, and Craig Kluever lent his usual pragmatic advice.

I dedicate the book to Silas Kluever, who reminds me that life holds pleasures beyond books and British drama.

Introduction

Masterpiece *and the Allure of Tradition*

*Y*orkshire, England, 1919. In the mellow, disappearing light of an early June evening, two elderly women meet in the entrance hall of a manor house. One is a dowager countess whose every detail of appearance seems to say, "I hate the twentieth century." She wears a high-collared dress, jet beads, and that bizarre crime of Victorian fashion, a corset. The other woman, an American heiress also about eighty years old, wears her dyed red hair in a bob, her makeup and jewelry way overstated. Sporting a jaunty dress and flapper headband, she visibly welcomes the roaring '20s.

Related by marriage, the two women clearly cannot stand each other as they muster small talk, feign politeness. They turn to the subject of their granddaughter's wedding the next day, and the American heiress asks the whereabouts of the husband-to-be, whom she hasn't yet met. The countess explains he will be absent tonight, adding, "The groom *never* sees the bride before the wedding."

Squinting as though to bring the dowager into focus, "Nothing ever alters for you people, does it?" asks the heiress. Revolutions erupt and monarchies crash, and the groom still cannot see the bride before the wedding."

"You Americans. You never understand the importance of tradition," the countess replies.

"Yes, we do," says the heiress. "We just don't give it power over us."

Boom! The heiress flounces away (score one for America), yet the hall's grandeur, the ambient lighting, the whole dressing-for-dinner, butler-attending, sherry-awaiting mien of it suggests otherwise. The heiress may say tradition has no power over Americans, and we may be inclined to agree with her. But at this moment, for the millions of us watching *Downton Abbey*, tradition *does* matter. We find ourselves entranced by the idea that we may be missing something important.

January 2021 marks the tenth anniversary of *Downton Abbey*'s premiere in the United States. More importantly, it is also the fiftieth anniversary of *Masterpiece* (formerly *Masterpiece Theatre*), the broadcast program that brought us *Downton*.

In the world of television, fifty years has a mind-blowing quality, approaching the miraculous. Few programs have achieved this milestone; fewer still will do so in the future. Yet these anniversaries go unnoticed, lost in the pandemonium of today's television world. The countess would disapprove of such neglect, and she'd be right. *Downton Abbey* revolutionized television drama and helped launch our current television renaissance. And *Masterpiece* has been a quiet but powerful influence on American television, winning hundreds of awards and shaping the industry in surprising ways.

Masterpiece's series transport, cheer, enrich, and enlighten us. And many of its characters—David Suchet's implacably principled Poirot, Benedict Cumberbatch's aqua-eyed, slightly Aspergerish Sherlock, Maggie Smith's eyebrow-arching countess—live on in our collective imagination.

To commemorate *Masterpiece*'s jubilee anniversary, this book provides a history of the program and its "sister show" *Mystery!* It traces *Masterpiece*'s evolution from 1971 to the present, exploring its rise, fall, spectacular comeback, and precarious present against watershed moments like the emergence of cable television and streaming. It recounts the reception of individual series and surveys trends in television drama. It explores *Masterpiece*'s relationship with its British affiliates and its American competitors. It delves into Americans' love of mysteries and lavishes attention on the costume drama, *Masterpiece*'s métier and mainstay. Most of all, this book spotlights *Masterpiece*'s best programs. Some of them, like *Upstairs, Downstairs* (1974–1977), *The Jewel in the Crown* (1985), *Prime Suspect* (1991–2006), and *Downton Abbey* (2011–2016), were masterstrokes in their day. Others, such as *Man in an Orange Shirt* (2017), a tender drama about gay identity in two generations of the same family, wait to be discovered, having escaped our notice earlier.

This book is about more than television, however. It is also about the United States of America, about the aspirations and anxieties, desires and confusions that have ensured *Masterpiece*'s longevity. More specifically, it is about America's longing for tradition.

Tradition is something that binds us, guides and settles us. The human soul requires it, craving the comforts of repetition and ritual, familiarity and order. But tradition has a bad rep here in America, where the word's mere utterance can trigger a knee-jerk defense of freedom and change.

Yet as *Downton Abbey* proved with staggering force, Americans want some sense of tradition in our lives. *Masterpiece* answers that yearning. Its shows are based in Britain, but they tap into a deep-rooted American desire for permanence and a human desire for essential truths. With *Masterpiece*, we see ideals like courtesy and kindness, rare in our society and almost invisible on our TV screens, still prevail. So do qualities like charm and wit, qualities we don't even know we miss but that give life its luster. They add sparkle to our days, sweeten our interactions. And in *Masterpiece* we find them.

A PRIMER: WHAT IS *MASTERPIECE*, EXACTLY?

While many people are familiar with *Masterpiece*'s series, few understand the scope of *Masterpiece* productions. How does *Masterpiece* work? Who started it? What keeps it going? Who watches it? And, please, what exactly *is* it?

Masterpiece is the longest-running primetime dramatic production on American television. As an anthology program, *the only one of its kind in the world*, it features a mélange of drama ranging from Austen adaptations to contemporary thrillers. This compendiary nature is key to *Masterpiece*'s identity, for unlike any other show, it offers a kaleidoscopic variety of formats, characters, actors, settings, and storylines.

But where did *Masterpiece* come from, and how is it produced? The where and how are easy. The who, what, when, and why are a bit of a story.

Masterpiece is a unit within WGBH—Boston's public television station and flagship studio for many other PBS productions. About half its funding comes from PBS, itself funded by "Viewers Like You," with the balance coming from a mix of corporate sponsors such as Viking Cruises, home-entertainment license deals, and viewer donations to the *Masterpiece* Trust. The show airs on Sunday nights, at 9:00 p.m. EST, just as it has for fifty years.

Masterpiece's executive producer is Susanne Simpson. She took on the role in 2019 from Rebecca Eaton, who occupied it for thirty-five years, an anomaly in television but fitting for a show steeped in tradition. Simpson's primary job, like Eaton's, is to select the drama for *Masterpiece*, making sure it suits the program's audience while offering a range of storylines, tones, and moods. Sometimes, Simpson looks at already-finished dramas; sometimes, she reads scripts. Sometimes, she just listens to an idea or pitches one herself. She also oversees a team of roughly twenty employees who handle the publicity and promotion for the series' American runs. They make the show's on-air trailers, manage its social media and website, and cultivate reviewers. They are a tightknit and eclectic group that ranges from industry veterans to recent college grads.

Masterpiece's audience is largely the college-educated elite, middle and upper-middle class. Of this group, the majority are women over forty. Older fans of the show—those sixty and up—tend to watch *Masterpiece*'s series on Sunday nights, courtesy of PBS. (Averaging about four million people per week, this audience knows *Masterpiece*'s lineup and appreciates its anthology structure.) Younger audiences, students, millennials, Gens X and Y, tend to stream those *Masterpiece* series that have quicker metabolisms and hot young actors, such as *Grantchester* (2014–) and *Poldark* (2015–2019). These younger viewers watch their media via Netflix, Amazon Prime, Acorn, or BritBox. They like British drama and may even watch a lot of it, but they know very little, if anything, about the dimensions of *Masterpiece* itself. Rebecca Eaton calls them "smart girls."

Masterpiece's programing is 100 percent bona fide British. The shows are produced by a wide variety of UK-based, independent production companies. While it is increasingly a global and multi-platform business, most programs are produced for any of the British television networks: BBC, ITV, Channel 4, and Channel 5. It is these production companies that cast the actors, hire the screenwriters, and shoot the scenes, handling every aspect of production, from leasing castles to finding just the right Edwardian hat.

During its first two decades, *Masterpiece* merely imported every series it ran. It paid a fee, depending on the cost or projected cost of a series, in exchange for distribution rights in the States. Since the late 1980s, however, the program coproduces all its drama. This means that it now will fund a series by as much as 20 percent. It also means that Simpson, like Eaton before her, acts as a consultant on scripts and casting. An unusual arrangement, but it works.

As all this suggests, *Masterpiece* depends on a close relationship with its coproducers, especially these days when competition for British drama is fierce. The program has a far smaller budget than, say, Netflix, which spent $130 million —or thirteen times *Masterpiece*'s total annual budget—on *The Crown*'s first and second seasons. But *Masterpiece* has a long history of fair play and mutual respect with its partners. It also has the advantage of a core audience each week. And in the case of the BBC, it shares a public mission.

Because *Masterpiece*'s investment is small, Simpson takes a hands-off approach once she consults on scripts and casting. Collaborating with *Masterpiece* therefore gives British producers more creative freedom than they might have with partners whose whopping investments might justify a whopping involvement.

Unlike its programming that moves at a leisurely pace, *Masterpiece* originated with breakneck speed. There are various accounts of this origin, the most compelling of which is by Stan Calderwood, the first president of WGBH.[1] According to him, the idea for the show was conceived on a hot

London afternoon in June 1970. Calderwood, an improbable Anglophile hailing from Chugwater, Nebraska, was vacationing in London. Or at least that was what he was supposed to be doing. Trouble was, he couldn't stop thinking about how to fill WGBH's airtime. Calderwood wanted a show with "an air of quality" that would "crown" the station's programming. Lying in his room that afternoon at the Claridge's Hotel (the same hotel in which Winston Churchill holed up for nearly a year after World War II), Calderwood was suddenly struck with an idea.

Like many Americans, he had been hooked on *The Forsyte Saga*, a BBC miniseries chronicling the vicissitudes of an upper-class English family that had aired in the States a year before. What if WGBH imported other miniseries from the BBC? Calderwood wondered. Television had a long history of using imports from the UK. Back in the 1950s, reruns of British period films filled the airwaves, as did cult shows like *The Avengers* and *The Prisoner* during the 1960s. All this programming was driven by a "Brits are better" sensibility, television being the newest frontier in which a cultured England would tame a crude and crass America.[2] Why not do it again? A show importing British drama would give PBS a unique franchise, generate a steady viewership, cost little to produce, and add a dash of class to television.

Calderwood made a cold call to BBC producers with neither a budget nor authority from his station back home. He promised them that if they'd cut him a deal, he'd find a sponsor to underwrite a program that would showcase British programs. The BBC salivated at the prospect of acquiring an American audience for dramas that would otherwise just sit in cans.

Within weeks, WGBH and BBC had made a deal: $390,000 for one season's worth of programming (the final purchase price was $375, 000). "Even then," Calderwood observed years later, "it was a ridiculously low amount of money." Soon afterward, he contacted the heads of over forty companies to see if they would sponsor the program—and was "shown out the executive door every time." He had about given up when he met a man with the unpromising name of Herb Schmertz, who happened to be vice president of public affairs for the Mobil Corporation. Schmertz pounced at the opportunity to associate Mobil with British drama, rightly intuiting that it would distinguish his company from other corporate sponsors of public television.[3]

That fall, Calderwood and a gung ho band of fourteen WGBH affiliates flew to London, locked themselves in a screening room for a week, and picked Season 1's lineup. They selected serious drama, highbrow drama: drama like the 1970 adaptation of Henry James's *The Spoils of Poynton*. Christopher Sarson, who would soon become the program's executive producer, chose the inflated name of "Masterpiece Theatre." He also picked the theme music, "Fanfares for the King's Supper," because he heard it while vacationing at

Club Med and thought it "sounded old and heraldic." In October, he and Calderwood hired the legendary journalist and broadcaster Alistair Cooke to host the series. And *Masterpiece Theatre* was off.

Since its founding, *Masterpiece* has been a model of consistency, resilience, and adaptability. Its mission—to offer the best of British drama—has never varied. It still retains a loyal fan base, some of whom have been watching the show for fifty years. It adjusts to an ever-changing television landscape, nip-and-tucking itself here, taking bold risks there. But *Masterpiece* has had its share of dark days. During the 1990s, its ratings plummeted due to the rise of "reality television" as well as cable networks like HBO. Adding to this was Cooke's retirement in 1992. Then, what seemed like the worst of all blows, in 2002 Mobil withdrew its sponsorship.

Loss of funding, competition, cable television, the decline of television drama: the problems facing *Masterpiece* in the early 2000s seemed insurmountable. Still, the show had the continued support of PBS, which had shepherded more than one program through rocky times, and a faithful, if small, audience. It also had a staff wild about British drama and fervently committed to *Masterpiece*'s public mission.

In the spring of 2006, WGBH hired a straight-shooting consultant who informed them that *Masterpiece* (then, still *Masterpiece Theatre*) needed a facelift. Fast-forward to January 11, 2008. That night, under the racier title *Masterpiece*, the show was re-launched. Audiences tuned in to discover a whole new look and feel about the program. The triumphal fanfare had gone silent. Cooke's wingchair—gone. Viewers discovered that *Masterpiece* would now be divided into three mini-seasons, Classic, Mystery, and Contemporary, each hosted by a glamorous young actor. Gillian Anderson, known to American audiences as Detective Dana Scully in *The X-Files* and to *Masterpiece* fans as Lady Dedlock in the award-winning *Bleak House* (2005), then introduced the first of four new Austen adaptations. Each adaptation was surprising, even shocking, in its strategies to promote Austen as a young person's novelist. A *Masterpiece* promo for Simon Burke's adaptation of *Persuasion* (2008), for example, showed Anne Elliot chasing her beloved down the streets of Lyme Regis to a tune by *Coldplay*. Austenites went into apoplexy. But it created undeniable buzz.

And then *Downton Abbey* came along three years later, dynamizing *Masterpiece*, catapulting PBS to the cool kids table, and revolutionizing the TV industry. Along with shows like *Mad Men*, *Breaking Bad*, and *The Good Wife*, it proved every dreary portent wrong about the supposed death of television drama. Establishing that a country-house drama didn't need to feel quaint, it fostered a new climate in which, as screenwriter Paul Rutman says, "anything goes when it comes to the past."[4] Its unprecedented detail made "world building" a key concept in television, and its happy use of melodrama managed to do the unthinkable: ensure that an average of nine million American viewers sat down with PBS every Sunday night, over the course of six seasons, to discover what would happen next.

Downton Abbey shuttered its windows on March 6, 2016. Since then, *Masterpiece* has been holding its own, trying to survive in a television landscape that, while brimming with excellent drama, is witnessing wholesale disruption from one end of the chain to the other. Traditional business models, artist deals, and viewer experiences: they've all been upended. It's a precarious, perilous time to be in television. But *Masterpiece* is staying the course, doing its best to withstand radical changes in the industry without losing sight of its purpose—not unlike those in *Downton Abbey*.

AN AMERICAN CLASSIC

There is any number of reasons to fall in love with the series on *Masterpiece*, from their finely sketched characters to their swanky real estate. Deep down, it is because they offer something we, as Americans, feel we lack. And that something is best summed up by "tradition." Seemingly abstract, tradition has two concrete definitions: 1) a particular belief or body of beliefs handed down from age to age and 2) a particular custom or set of customs handed down from one age to another. In both cases, tradition isn't abstract nor inherently political, however much right-wing politicians may appeal to it. Rather, it's a way of viewing the world.

The United States certainly has its traditions. Diversity, opportunity, social mobility, freedom of choice, and personal responsibility are among them. So are county fairs. But even though they exist aplenty, these traditions feel less entrenched than those of other countries. One reason is that so many of them—from a two-party system to apple pie—come from England. Another reason is America's diversity and size. "How we spend our time locally may dictate what we care about nationally," says sociologist Frank Russello.[5] Nice sentiment, but one that makes little sense in America, where regions function almost like separate countries. A deeper complication is its origins. Because America was founded as an egalitarian country, there are no remnants of an older social order. There are no castles to tour, no country villages to visit on a Sunday afternoon. And finally, there is this: tradition lacks a strong hold on America because the national mythos forbids it. The theme of liberation is woven so deeply into the country's character that tradition is necessarily seen as *un-American*. "In America, nothing dies easier than tradition," says Russell Baker, one of America's most revered journalists and a former *Masterpiece* host.[6] With aphorisms like these, is it any wonder Americans think tradition has no power over them?

At no time in American history did tradition feel less relevant than in the 1960s. Many young Americans flat out rejected anything that smacked of it, embracing glib shibboleths like "Question authority," "Do your own thing," and "Don't trust anyone over thirty." Older Americans tended to feel differently: wary of, even horrified by, the social ruptures they witnessed (as did many baby boomers, once they hit middle age). *Masterpiece*'s creators targeted this older group, selecting drama they thought would appeal to "more mature viewers." Adding to its conservative appeal was the calming effect of host Alistair Cooke, seated in his signature wingchair, introducing series whose ordered worlds contrasted sharply with 1970s America.

Yet *Masterpiece* has never been just for viewers of a certain age. I watched it as a kid, captivated by the funny accents and costumes. I viewed it in college, excited to see dramas about my favorite authors (*The Tale of Beatrix Potter*, 1983) and adaptations of my favorite novels (*Pride and Prejudice*, 1980; *Crime and Punishment*, 1980). Now I watch it with my college students, who swoon over Shaun Evans in *Endeavour* (2012–) and adore fiery Demelza in *Poldark* (2015–2019). And my son saw all sixty-eight episodes of the original *Upstairs, Downstairs* with my husband and me one summer when he was ten. His favorite character was Hudson, the butler. Later that year, when he met a boy named "Hudson" on a baseball field, Silas asked him if he watched the program, too.

While writing this history, I've listened to dozens of similar stories. "My sister and I used to imitate Alistair Cooke!" my friend Valerie exclaimed to me. She then recounted her memories of watching *The Six Wives of Henry the VIII* (1972) when she was twelve—how it brought alive for her the stories of young women, not much older than herself, subject to the tyrannical whims of their husband and king. Bestselling, thirty-something novelist Lindsay Faye told me she watches *Inspector Morse* whenever she gets writer's block. Pulitzer prize-winning critic Mary McNamara, a *Masterpiece* fan since college, confided that she and her family have watched all eight seasons of *Foyle's War* three times. And Elizabeth McGovern, who played Lady Grantham on *Downton Abbey*, recalls, "When *Upstairs Downstairs* came on, my granny and my mom and I had a ritual of setting up folding chairs in the kitchen, where we had a tiny little black and white TV. We were glued to it every Sunday night."[7] Stories like these convey how *Masterpiece* cuts across all ages and genders. It's family drama in the best sense of the term.

Fifty years after its founding, *Masterpiece* still provides a respite from the grim, gritty realities of much television and American life. "It's a balm to the spirit," one *New York Times* critic says.[8] But its series are also engaging more and more with current issues like racism, drug addiction, homophobia, and sexual assault. They're also casting a much bigger spotlight on young and minority characters, many of whom, like Lady Mary in *Downton Abbey* or Will Davenport in *Grantchester*, are trying to find their own meaning in the concept of tradition.

Masterpiece has made an indelible mark on American culture. Partly, this is because it shares close ties with other institutions—PBS, the *New York Times*, Viking Travel, Ralph Lauren, Audible, Penguin—that promote tradition. Partly, this is because *Masterpiece* has become nearly synonymous in the States with period drama. One happy effect of this is that many people will mistake something—say, *Brideshead Revisited* (1981) or Andrew Davies's adaptation of *Pride and Prejudice* (1995) or Netflix's *The Crown* (2016–)—as a *Masterpiece* production when it is not.[9] But the most important reason is that *Masterpiece* has achieved the status of a classic; in the country's imagination, it seems almost as timeless as the traditions it celebrates. Most Americans may not watch *Masterpiece*, but they appreciate its being here.

The pages ahead draw on a vast archive, from scripts and interviews to tourist brochures and cookbooks. They revolve around nine thematic chapters, each theme vital to the history of the show and its place in American culture. We'll cover wide ground in all of them but stop to consider such delightful tidbits as the graphic novels inspired by *Downton Abbey* or the rise of Spencer Hart suits in America occasioned by *Sherlock*.

We'll also consider the five cornerstones of *Masterpiece*'s traditional appeal: *aspiration, nostalgia, Anglophilia, conventionality*, and *sentimentality*. Each of these is powerful, complex, and risky to build a show around. But *Masterpiece*'s creators, from the producers and screenwriters to the actors and set designers, understand the allure of these qualities. They know how to handle them, making sure to balance each with strategies like irony and satire. They don't always get that balance right, but more often than not, they do.

Most importantly, we'll focus on the *Masterpiece* programs worth watching or rewatching. One aim in writing this book is to illuminate broad cultural and historical themes. But another aim is to stimulate new, and renewed, interest in the program's best or most talked-about shows. I'm writing this book for *Masterpiece*'s fans and those waiting to become them.

So let's begin by going back to the show's origins, to a time when American television was considered a "wasteland," and PBS had just appeared on the scene promising to deliver something better. Something *Masterpiece*.

Mastering Television

$\mathcal{S}$unday night, January 10, 1971. An American couple, let's call them Sharon and Peter, are settling in for a night of television. Uninterested in what the three commercial networks have to offer, they decide to try a new show, a "television playhouse," advertised in the *New York Times* that morning. They turn to PBS, and with a fanfare of trumpets, *Masterpiece* begins. It opens with the elegant and urbane Alistair Cooke, the show's soon-to-be-legend host, greeting them from a wingchair. In his redolent English voice, he introduces a BBC miniseries titled *The First Churchills*, scheduled to run over the next twelve weeks. They can see the creases in Cooke's trousers.

Peter worries the program will be stodgy, pretentious. But Sharon, a former English major, drinks it in. The couple lean back into their sofa and watch. At first, all the political references frustrate them. And there are too many identical wigs. But they love the two leads, a rising star named Susan Hampshire and theatrical giant John Neville, once hailed as John Gielgud's "natural successor." They're also surprised by the show's bawdy humor playfully undercutting the gravitas of the whole thing. At the end of the night, they decide to tune in again next week.

Aspiration comes from the Latin *spirare* (to "breathe") and *spiritus* ("spirit"). It means to be "imbued with spirit," to have a desire for something that takes you beyond yourself and your present life. Though we often confuse the two, aspiration differs from ambition. Ambition is about goals; aspiration is about ideals. That January night, *Masterpiece* arrived in American homes fueled by an aspirational impulse to provide smart, distinctive television. And to viewers like the fictitious Sharon and Peter, fed up with the banalities of American television, *Masterpiece* did. It also encouraged them to aspire themselves—to see television as a gateway to a life filled with books, art, ideas.

But how did *Masterpiece* come to us in the first place? We know it was the brainchild of WGBH president Stan Calderwood, who was chasing the popularity of *The Forsyte Saga*, the blockbuster series that had aired in the States two years before. Behind this story, though, are larger histories that reveal the early ambitions of PBS, the theatrical origins of television drama, and the spectacular arrival of the miniseries on American shores.

CULTIVATING THE WASTELAND

In a way, *Masterpiece* began on May 9, 1961, in Washington, DC, in the ballroom of the Sheraton Hotel, with a speech that has gone down in history as the most searing indictment of television ever made. That day, Newton Minow, the mild-mannered, newly appointed chair of the Federal Communications Commission, shocked his audience of over three thousand broadcasters by denouncing television as a "vast wasteland." Sitting before a microphone in a dark gray suit, with his wide forehead, glasses, and receding hairline, he looked more like a mid-level accountant than someone who commanded America's interstate communications. Less than a minute into his speech, he said:

> When television is good, nothing—not the theater, not the magazines or newspapers—nothing is better.
>
> But when television is bad, nothing is worse. I invite each of you to sit down in front of your television set when your station goes on the air and stay there, for a day, without a book, without a magazine, without a newspaper, without a profit-and-loss sheet or rating book to distract you. Keep your eyes glued to that set until the station signs off. I can assure you that what you will observe is a vast wasteland.
>
> You will see a procession of game shows, formula comedies about totally unbelievable families, blood and thunder, mayhem, violence, sadism, murder, western badmen, western good men, private eyes, gangsters, more violence and cartoons. And, endlessly, commercials—many screaming, cajoling and offending.

The room fell silent, everyone stunned by the unexpected slap in the face delivered so gently, almost paternally. One station manager would remark a week later, "Minow alienated the whole goddamn industry that day." But Minow's words had their impact. Within six weeks, six thousand letters, lopsidedly favorable, flooded the FCC office. "Your speech is still reverberating!"

Adlai Stevenson exclaimed to Minow three months later in a memo. Social commentators like Howard Zinn, Marshall McLuhan, and Margaret Mead blasted commercial TV for its "barefaced, unprincipled obsession with capturing the largest possible number of viewers during the broadcast day." They pointed out that a decade earlier, each network had dedicated portions of its schedule to cultural and news programming. Such efforts had not commanded high ratings, but they had satisfied those viewers who wanted programs that enlightened them. "All that is dried up now," Mead lamented.[1]

Reflecting on the speech's significance fifty years later, one critic remarked, "Whatever else Mr. Minow did with that sublime phrase the 'vast wasteland,' he set up an extremely productive tension in television that has greatly enlivened the art form."[2] This is not to say that "unbelievable families" and "formula comedies" suddenly disappeared from the TV landscape. They didn't. *Gilligan's Island*, that flapdoodle of a TV show, debuted on CBS in 1964, the island's castaways coming from the wreck of a boat named the *SS Minnow*.

Pressure was mounting, however, for American TV to smarten up. Driving this effort was a worry that ran deeper than television. For many, the indolent allure of the "idiot box" wasn't just about the failure to deliver quality entertainment. It was a symptom of America's growing disinterest in culture and politics. Commentators regularly compared television to other "sad and soulless" forms of American life. Television was a "shopping mall," a "freeway," a "billboard to be driven past," all of them signifying the country's woeful slide into mindless conformism. It was anything but aspirational.

In response, a clutch of smart shows began to appear. *Firing Line*, a public affairs program, debuted in 1966. Its host was the legendary William F. Buckley, who brimmed with brains and confidence as he interviewed one compelling personality—Muhammad Ali, Groucho Marx, Hugh Hefner—after another. In 1968, CBS launched *60 Minutes,* a "thoughtful, progressive" news magazine for television. Balancing this sober fare were lighter, "smart" shows like *Mission Impossible, The Mod Squad*, and a new sitcom scheduled to air on January 12, 1971, that would tackle social problems like unemployment and racism by featuring a "lovable bigot" named Archie Bunker. He would be the first character on American television to flush a toilet, two days after Cooke launched *Masterpiece Theatre* in his gentlemanly fashion.

The biggest breakthrough was the hard-won establishment of the Public Broadcasting Service (PBS). A clarion call for public television had been sounded ever since television first made its way into American homes in the late 1940s. National Educational Television (NET), founded in November 1952 by a grant from the Ford Foundation, was a reputable gesture toward the concept. But it focused solely on educational issues and offered only five hours' worth of daily programming. Dubbed the "university in the air," it also had a reputation for being too academic, prompting one commentator to remark, "Educational television today is like oatmeal: vaguely good for you, but a little hard to take."[3]

By the mid-1960s, the Ford Foundation had pulled much of its funding for NET. Meanwhile, more and more people—politicians, educational leaders, cultural commentators, and scores of America's professional elite—were pushing for the establishment of a government-funded public network. In 1962, John White, president of NET, published *The True Fourth Network: Why and How*, arguing "America must have a fourth network—a strong, free noncommercial network whose only purpose, whose very reason for being, is to supply in abundance, for people in every region of the country and at the most convenient viewing hours, the fine cultural and informational programming that goes to their homes in such small quantity today."[4]

Faced with increasing pressure to act, President Lyndon Johnson arranged in 1966 for the Carnegie Foundation to conduct a study on the "future of public broadcasting." Four months later, the twenty-member Carnegie Commission recommended that the government institute a public broadcasting station that would "educate viewers on national and international affairs, provide a forum for the exchange of political opinions, and offer an abundance of cultural programming."[5] Reading excerpts from the report, written with all the fervor of a manifesto, one easily discerns the commission's belief that public television would transform America's airwaves. No wonder Congress passed the Public Broadcasting Act of 1967 in record-breaking time or that President Johnson immediately signed it. Johnson was not altogether sure what he wanted broadcasting to look like, but he was convinced that Americans needed an alternative to commercial television. That same year, Congress also founded the Corporation for Public Broadcasting (CPB) to facilitate the production and distribution of programming. Two years later, CPB established PBS—and on October 5, 1970, just three months before the opening night of *Masterpiece Theatre*, PBS aired on televisions around the country.

At a time when cynicism caked nearly every aspect of American culture, PBS's vision was lofty and high-minded. It aimed to inform and educate, and from the outset, its British influence was evident: it modeled itself on the BBC. Founded in 1922, the BBC's mission was to "present the best of music, theater, political debate, and conversation, all of which will further the education of British citizens, sharpen their minds, and enlarge their expectations."[6] Those at PBS imagined a similar role for the station: it would feature live programming of ballets and operas but it would also broadcast "intelligent and vigorous debates about the key issues of the day."[7]

Aspiration thus defined PBS. There was the aspiration to provide quality television. But underlying this aim was a more grandiose, starry-eyed one: to create a better America by creating better citizens. In her book on aspiration, philosopher Agnes Collard tells us, "Aspiration is about change. It is not only about becoming a different person but also about appreciating the values distinctive of that kind of person."[8] Vital to PBS's founding was its promotion of certain values—education, artistic appreciation, social awareness, civility—that audiences would not only come to cherish but also enact.

The BBC's first director-general was John Reith, the son of a Scottish Presbyterian minister and an engineer by training. Reith had all the charm of a plate of haggis. But he did have zeal. Reith believed the BBC had a twofold purpose: 1) to uphold British life and its virtues and 2) to launch a process of public education and challenge. How seriously did he take this purpose? Enough to exhort the British public to wear evening dress whenever they listened to the BBC's nightly radio programs.

PBS used a less Scottish approach, to be sure. But it adopted a similar gravity. Some employees even imagined PBS would come to best its British exemplar. In their view, the BBC had gone over to the dark side by producing sitcoms and talk shows to compete with its commercial rival, ITV.

Within a few months, lavish descriptors not commonly ascribed to television—"quality," "excellence," "thoughtful," "sophisticated," "intelligent"—encircled PBS like a halo. Others, however, feared PBS's mission was doomed from the start. Unlike the BBC, arriving before household TV was a twinkle in anyone's eye, PBS emerged late in the game. It didn't have, nor ever could have, the pathfinder status of its British model. PBS's budget was also scrimpy compared to its British model. Then as now, the BBC charged a licensing fee (at present, about $230 per year) to all who purchased a television in Britain. By contrast, PBS money came in the form of discretionary government grants, therefore exposing the station to political horse trading and cuts by unsympathetic incumbents. The BBC had ample resources to create and distribute its content, while PBS was merely a handler for other people's programs. In 1970, many Americans may have fantasized about PBS becoming a star-spangled BBC, but few would have put money on it.[9]

PBS needed a program to bolster and stabilize it: a sparkling, surefire series with big-time aura. Stan Calderwood tried to fill that need. But when he pitched the idea of *Masterpiece Theatre* to those at WGBH, many people pooh-poohed it. They bristled at the notion of using British imports rather than native drama, and they doubted the appeal of period pieces in America's climate of social fracture. Calderwood, however, knew a program specializing in productions from the BBC, the very institution PBS was striving to emulate, was just what America's new public station needed.

As Calderwood imagined it, *Masterpiece* would be glittering proof PBS was poised to fill American television's need for quality programming. He was right. Responses to *Masterpiece* those first several weeks were downright gushy—and not because *The First Churchills* was masterpiece drama. The series had fine acting and sparkling dialogue, to be sure. But it was really a lot of huggermugger, cluttered with troops of actors you couldn't identify and plot lines you couldn't follow. Rather, what viewers like Sharon and Peter loved was the idea behind *Masterpiece*. They wanted to be transported to England, to hear its accents and breathe its history. They wanted to see actors like Derek Jacobi and Glenda Jackson perform right in front of them, as if they had third-row seats at London's Prince Edward Theatre. And they wanted to be the kind of people who enjoyed high culture. "We aspire by doing things," says Agnes Callard, "and the things we do change us so that we are able to do the same things, or things of that kind, better and better."[10] In the minds of many Americans, watching *Masterpiece* every Sunday night would lead to learning more about British history, reading good literature, attending plays, maybe even traveling to England.

Over the next several weeks, reviews and fan letters were giddy with gratitude to PBS for bringing *Masterpiece* to television—and inspiring viewers to pursue their own liberal education. John O'Connor of the *New York Times* called *The First Churchills* a "revelation on the potential of television to combine intelligence with solid entertainment" even as he noted the series' confusions and contrivances. Another reviewer praised the program's "gifts of subtlety and nuance" in a "world of pow and blam, which equates reality with a sledgehammer." And dozens of letters thanked PBS for a show that, as one fan put it, "now has me checking out books from my local library on the Duke of Marlborough and Charles II. I would never have done so without it."[11]

Quickly pronounced a hit, *Masterpiece* gave PBS an identity, imbuing it with an air of quality, confidence, and tradition. It piqued the curiosity of those who hadn't yet turned their dials to PBS and raised its primetime audience by a whopping 30 percent between 1971 and 1972. It also exerted an undeniable influence on television in general. By the mid-1970s, WNET was producing a blockbuster historical drama called *The Adams Chronicles*; NBC was adapting Dickens and Austen; and several miniseries soon to become television masterworks—*Rich Man, Poor Man*, *The Holocaust*, and *Roots*—were under way. Meanwhile, a bevy of other British series, such as *Monty Python's Flying Circus*, were airing on PBS, prompting Larry Grossman, the network's president from 1976 to 1984, to remark, "I can't imagine where American public television would be if the British didn't speak English."[12]

On the night of its premiere, Newton Minow watched *Masterpiece* with his wife and three daughters in their Chicago home on Lakeshore Drive. For years afterward, his family would affectionately grumble that, with the exception of *The Rocky and Bullwinkle Show*, PBS was the only station they were allowed to watch. It was, after all, the very kind of television Minow had urged broadcasters to aspire to. But PBS and *Masterpiece* were not only committed to an aspiration for quality. They also wanted to recapture a lost era of television.

RESTORING THE GOLDEN AGE

Not long ago, before our present era of television splendor, people talked about another "Golden Age of Television." Like all golden ages, this one evoked awe for a glorious past and dismay over a crummy present. The "age" in question was roughly 1948 and 1960, the early years of television when American viewers could tune in any night of the week to watch live performances of plays via programs called "anthology dramas." Now consigned to the dustbin of history, these dramas were an essential part of early television. They were also the forerunners to *Masterpiece*. Presenting a variety of drama with award-winning scriptwriters and method-trained actors, they suggested that a natural intimacy existed between the new, uncertain medium of television and the centuries-old, venerated medium of theater.

As a self-described "television playhouse," *Masterpiece* sought to revitalize the anthology drama and return American television to its "golden age." It entwined nostalgia for television's past with an aspiration for its future. Following writer Svetlana Boym, we might say that *Masterpiece* was a product of "restorative" nostalgia—a type of nostalgia that aims to rebuild the past rather than simply wallow in its loss. Restorative nostalgia is at the core of all revivals, evoking a collective vision for the future as well as a collective memory. It gets things done.[13]

In America, the first anthology drama was NBC's *Kraft Television Theatre* (1947–1958). Others quickly followed, including *Studio One* (1948–1958), *The Philco Television Playhouse* (1948–1955), the *Goodyear Television Playhouse* (1951–1960), and *Lux Video Theatre* (1950–1957). Airing between 7:00 and 9:00 p.m. EST on different nights, they typically ran for an hour to an hour and a half. Many of them had corporate sponsors eager to link their product—cheese, soap, gas, tires—with quality entertainment. And they rocked TV ratings. A 1954 poll, for example, revealed that 86 percent of television's audience regularly viewed anthology dramas, and 72 percent claimed to have watched four to six shows per week. Statistics like these lend credence to the story told by an employee of the J. Walter Thompson agency, who handled the *Kraft Theatre* account: while at a bar one night in the Bronx, he requested the TV set be tuned to the program. A vote was taken, with *Kraft Theatre* defeating basketball fifteen to three.

Anthology dramas were a product of New York City, whose rich theatrical culture would shape American television for its first ten years. As Fred Coe, producer of the weekly Philco *Television Playhouse* (1948–55), remarked, "All of us were convinced it was our mission to bring Broadway to America via the television set."[14] With their air of high culture, these programs soon became the darlings of critics and cognoscenti who thought they possessed a quality other shows lacked. In their eyes, anthology dramas aspired to the standards of "legitimate" theater; everything else on TV dumbly imitated Hollywood or vaudeville. Reviewers applauded their live format. They extolled the talent of performers like James Dean, Charles Bronson, Marlon Brando, Paul Newman, Jack Lemmon, Rod Steiger, and Grace Kelly, who all cut their teeth on anthology dramas. Most of all, critics praised the scripts. Some of these were classic adaptations like *Alice in Wonderland* and *A Christmas Carol*. Many others were original plays by people like Rod Serling and Paddy Chayefsky, playwrights determined to use television as a means of raising social consciousness. These dramas include titles many of us recognize today, such as *Marty, Twelve Angry Men, Requiem for a Heavyweight*, and *The Days of Wine and Roses*, all of which became award-winning movies.

If we look at the anthology drama from an operational point of view, it's a wonder the form lasted a year. One problem was that it required a different production each week, putting it wholly at odds with the serialized programming that dominated television. As early as the mid-1940s, station owners and managers had figured out the profit of creating TV series that ran indefinitely. All three networks therefore began churning out sitcoms, westerns, and police stories that had years of life in them, offering more or less the same thing week after week. A series was every producer's dream. But a play? It was a one-shot—something that had to be drummed up out of nothing every time. And it was *live*, subject to any and every kind of catastrophe. As TV scholar David Thomson says, "The process of live drama was fiendishly, comically difficult in an age that still worried about a clear picture and audible sound."[15]

Americans, however, loved the anthology drama. It satisfied their desire for good entertainment and their aspirational itch. With the intimacy provided by television, viewers could also see an actor's performance up-close and personal. They could watch Rod Steiger, for example, inhabit his role as a "fat little guy" in *Marty*, witnessing the subtle nuances in expression, gesture, and inflection that his performance comprised. Sometimes the cameramen goofed, obscuring a view or drawing unwanted attention to some object or character onstage. But these mistakes were golden, too. Viewers sensed that a new language for a new medium was being worked out right before their eyes—

and for many, this uncertainty trumped all the prerecorded, pre-scripted stuff on the air.

Television's technical constraints limited the possibilities for anthology dramas, but their directors knew how to turn limitation to advantage. Confined studio space and restricted camera movement were two of the genre's signature traits, as they would be for the early *Masterpiece*. By 1971, film cameras were sophisticated enough to move fluidly and freely, even to venture outdoors. Yet many of the series that aired on *Masterpiece* during the 1970s still employed single sets and stationary cameras. Why? To focus on the details of an actor's performance, just as anthology dramas had done. Detail was paramount to anthology dramas, making close-ups *the* television shot. Such punctilious camerawork also ensured *Masterpiece*'s success, whose programs even today hold our attention through the facets of character and situation rather than the suspense of plot. We pay more attention to the elements of Maggie Smith's performance in the TV version of *Downton Abbey* (her declarative use of a cane, her high-pitched harrumphs) than we do the film version.

The very idea of an anthology also determined audience response to these dramas. The *Oxford Dictionary* tells us that the word entered the English language in the mid-seventeenth century to define those books that collected the "flowers of verse": "small choice poems by a variety of authors." Whether a book of verse, *Studio One*, *Masterpiece*, or that Norton tome undergraduates lug around for their lit courses, an anthology presents material presumed to be exceptional. At the same time, it depends on an implicit agreement to take the parts of a work for the whole—for it is based on the assumption that a bounty of other material like it exists. *Masterpiece* collects and coheres British drama while exalting it. Little surprise, then, that American viewers often admire its shows more than their British counterparts do, who lack their own *Masterpiece*.

What happened to the anthology drama? It died out partly because of its impracticality. It also ended when American television left New York. Recognizing that its manifest destiny lay out West, television packed up the truck and headed for Hollywood. Live drama was soon replaced by filmed sitcoms, talk shows, quiz shows, crime dramas, and westerns. Almost immediately, a pining for television's "Golden Age" began. Critic after critic in the 1960s wrote threnodies to the anthology drama. Television would "never again" offer such a wealth of original writing. Scriptwriters would "never again" enjoy such authority and freedom. And actors would "never again" deliver such "superlative performances." Americans had left the Golden Age of television and entered its Dark Ages.

In the weeks and months that followed *Masterpiece*'s debut, however, many people, including Newton Minow, praised PBS for "restoring that vital tradition of the anthology drama" to American culture. "I'd forgotten how much television could feel like theater," wrote one grateful viewer in a letter to the station.[16]

But *Masterpiece* was a far cry from its precursors in many ways. The old anthology dramas featured American scripts engaged in the here and now. They depicted a fractured America with stark realism, and their focus was on the working class. By contrast, *Masterpiece* specialized in period drama that transported viewers to a stable, more orderly Britain populated by toffs. There seemed to be no agitational push to its drama, no call to social consciousness. This choice of content would haunt *Masterpiece* over the years, linking the program with a kind of fuddy-duddy escapism. But it was also what millions of American viewers wanted in 1971—and judging by the phenomenon of *Downton Abbey*, still want today.

Another difference separated *Masterpiece* from its predecessors. Most of its dramas weren't one-offs at all. They were *miniseries*, designed to entice viewers by providing long, immersive stories delivered in weekly installments. It was a form of storytelling dating back to Charles Dickens. But it was new to television. And just like Dickens's novels, many of these miniseries combined highbrow appeal with the low-end allure of soap opera.

INTRODUCING THE MINISERIES

What is a miniseries exactly? This question has spawned some ridiculous answers, with pedants insisting a miniseries can't include fewer than {insert first arbitrary number here} or more than {insert second arbitrary number here} episodes. A more useful approach is simply to say that a miniseries tells a complete story in a predetermined, limited number of episodes. Entwining itself in the daily lives of audiences while offering the certainty of an end, a miniseries gets its impact partly from its unique duration.

Serialized storytelling had gone out of fashion by the early twentieth century. The BBC singlehandedly revitalized it. In the 1930s, it began airing abridged versions of novels like *Jane Eyre* in weekly radio installments. Starting in the early 1960s, it adapted classic novels like Charles Dickens's *Barnaby Rudge* and Jane Austen's *Persuasion* in a limited number of dramatic episodes. And then in 1967, the BBC produced *The Forsyte Saga*, the Queen Mother of the miniseries, and the single biggest inspiration for *Masterpiece*.

The Forsyte Saga derived from John Galsworthy's bestselling trilogy by the same name. Much like *Upstairs, Downstairs* and *Downton Abbey*, it chronicles the vicissitudes of an upper-class British family between 1879 and 1926. Its original principal characters are the antagonistic cousins, Soames and Jolyon

Forsyte. Soames is a rapacious lawyer who falls hopelessly in love with the captivating but reluctant Irene, only to condemn them both to a miserable marriage. Jolyon is a frustrated artist who causes a scandal when he leaves his wife and child for their German governess. The story rapidly expands to explore the romantic and financial chaos that Soames's and Jolyon's disagreements cause over the next forty years.

The Forsyte Saga was unlike anything American viewers had seen before. To be sure, serial dramas had been a TV staple since the late 1940s. By the 1960s, they made up nearly 50 percent of primetime programming, with shows like *The Fugitive* and *Peyton Place* topping the American ratings list. But *The Forsyte Saga* combined a deliciously long storyline (twenty-six episodes) with the promise of a definite end. That combination meant that characters and the worlds they inhabited would develop and age. TV critic David Bianculli captures the importance of this shift when he writes, "The moment shows and characters began to reflect their own history, that's when TV in the USA truly mattered."[17]

In England, where it aired between January 7 and July 1, 1967, *The Forsyte Saga* caused a national shutdown every Sunday night. Pubs closed early. Streets cleared. Ministers across the country had to reschedule vespers in order to appease parishioners torn between Christ's agonies and those of the Forsytes. British newspapers were full of this subject during the fall of 1968, quoting horrified Church leaders who worried about "the new, dangerous addiction" to television. One pragmatic member of the clergy, Canon Ernest Corbell, said, "I am not saying that worship is less important than television, but there is no reason why we cannot enjoy both."[18] By the end of 1968, *The Forsyte Saga* had become a record-breaking wonder in Britain, attracting a total of seventeen million viewers. It had also appeared in dozens of countries around the world, with an estimated viewership of 160 million.

Those nations did not include the United States, whose three commercial networks scoffed at the idea of a "high-toned" historical drama shot in black and white. The only outlet that was interested, it turns out, was an ailing NET. It purchased rights to the series in 1969 for the bargain price of $140,000, about $50,000 less than what it cost to produce a single episode of *Star Trek* at the time.

The Forsyte Saga debuted in the United States on October 5, 1969, airing on NET. At its peak, the series attracted a weekly audience of fourteen million viewers (that's five million more, by the way, than *Downton Abbey*'s average American audience). Americans loved the show's down-to-the-dinnerware recreation of Victorian England, its stage-trained actors, its sumptuous interiors. And although many wouldn't admit it, viewers reveled in *The Forsyte Saga* because it was high-lather soap opera. They delighted in its stories of betrayal and revenge, its secrets and seductions, all those heaving emotions beneath the characters' cravats and corsets. When Soames, drunk and sick with rage, raped his wife, Irene, in episode 4, "a gasp was heard across the country," according to TV critic Molly Haskell. She praised *The Forsyte Saga* as "grand soap opera." In fact, American commentary on the show identified many connections between the British import and American shows like *The Guiding Light* and *As the World Turns.*[19]

To praise *The Forsyte Saga* for its soapy qualities was A-1 irony, given that cultural critics had been besmearing television soap operas for nearly two decades. One critic grumbled that soap opera threatened to "inundate and poison American culture" by "its sheer pervasiveness, its brutal overwhelming *quantity.*" Another harangued his magazine readers with exhortations on what he called the "lowest, trashiest form of entertainment," pointing to soap operas as "American television's single greatest shame."[20] Why, then, were American critics so dotty about *The Forsyte Saga*'s use of soap opera? The answers are clear. *The Forsyte Saga* had a top-shelf cast and an exquisitely written script, penned by an award-winning team of screenwriters that included Donald Wilson, the cocreator of *Dr. Who.* It was based on a trilogy of novels that had won its author the Nobel Prize for Literature. And it was British! And old! In American minds, *The Forsyte Saga* wasn't guilty television at all. It was aspirational.

And so it goes with many of the dramas airing on *Masterpiece*—*Upstairs, Downstairs*; *I, Claudius*; *The Jewel in the Crown*; *Bleak House*; *Downton Abbey*—all of which milk soap opera conventions while seeming far superior to it. This muddling of high and low forms is far more common to *Masterpiece*'s period drama than one might think; screenwriters use it to punctuate the genre's heaviness with the levity of other genres, modes, or styles. Consequently, viewers can pursue the hard work of aspiration—reading good books, learning history, appreciating the craft of theater-trained acting—while enjoying such low-grade delights as sudden plot reversals and last-minute rescues.

The Forsyte Saga was also the first drama to earn the title "television event." Soames's and Irene's misbegotten marriage became a matter of national debate, dissected on talk shows, editorialized in opinion pieces, and lampooned in cartoons. When Irene's smoldering lover, Bosinney, got dragged to his death by a runaway horse and carriage, hate mail poured into NET. And when episode 15 ended with the death of the affable, young Jolyon, viewers suffered through the interminable days of the following week to see how his lover, Fleur, would react on Sunday. For the first time in twenty years of television, millions of Americans felt connected by a story, goosed by that narrative device we both love and hate: the cliffhanger.

Undoubtedly, one reason for viewers' addiction to *The Forsyte Saga* was their desire to escape the American nightmares of 1969. Only a few weeks after *The Forsyte Saga* debuted, revelations came to the surface about the My Lai massacre, in which 340 to 500 Vietnamese civilians were brutally killed by American soldiers during March 1968. Americans heard about how women were gang raped and mutilated, children slaughtered. They learned about systematic attempts at cover-ups. By March 1970, murder charges would be brought against Captain Ernest L. Medina for killing twenty-six Vietnamese people himself. Is it any wonder, then, that expressions of raw sentiment poured into NET praising *The Forsyte Saga* as a palliative to American chaos? One viewer, writing on a note attached to a hundred-dollar check for NET, remarked, "What a wonderful thing to do for our country, particularly at this unsettled time." A Minnesota professor wrote about how he and "other regular viewers in his town" discuss the Forsytes "as if we know them, relieved not to be talking, for once, about the war." And a critic for *Life* magazine observed, "In our own time, we have more or less stopped believing in the continuity of anything. As behavior becomes more generally erratic, our own erratic actions provoke fewer ripples on our society. What does one more rip mean to a tattered fabric? But in *The Forsyte Saga*, rips matter."[21]

In 2002, *Masterpiece* aired ITV's remake of *The Forsyte Saga*, starring Damian Lewis (*Wolf Hall*, 2015), Ioan Gruffudd (*Great Expectations*, 1999), and Gina McKee (*Inspector Lewis*, 2007). In coproducing a new *Forsyte* adaptation, *Masterpiece* was returning to its roots—and at a time when its future could hardly have seemed more precarious. This was the year when ExxonMobil announced it would be withdrawing its support for *Masterpiece*. What's more, the BBC was still cutting way back on classic miniseries, convinced there was too small a market for them. The new *Forsyte Saga* was made as a gesture of faith. It turned out to be a whopping success, earning a solid viewership here of seven million weekly. Critics praised its acting, production values, and the "bold choice" to depart from the original series by developing new plotlines that would resonate with contemporary audiences, such as the striving of Irene and June Forsyte to reinvent themselves as women in a changing England. Still, its success did little for *Masterpiece* and virtually nothing for period drama. The program staggered along, doomed by market wisdom that said no one except bookish old Anglophiles were interested in stories about the past. Who would have thought that ten years later, thanks to *Downton Abbey*, *Masterpiece* would reach its zenith—and that a new television landscape, sparkling with classic miniseries, would be born?

KEEPING THE DRAMATIC FLAME

"How did the wasteland get so beautiful?" asked one TV critic in 2016, wowed, as we all are, by the variety and excellence of our current television landscape. One wonders what Newton Minow, in his mid-nineties at the time of this writing, must think of it. In 2018, nearly 350 scripted shows were released in America alone, many of them teeming with energy and ambition. Meanwhile, new adaptations of great literature, from Hulu's *Catch 22* to Amazon's *Good Omens*, hasten apace. And television drama—popularly perceived to be on life support only fifteen years ago—is better than ever. "We're living through a renaissance of ambitious television," writes the *New Yorker*. "The vast wasteland of television has been replaced by an excess of excellence," pronounces the *New York Times*. And the *Guardian* reflects, "Today, US television is where cultural debates are sparked, and where popular culture renews and reinvigorates itself. TV has slowly seized the creative initiative from the movies and run with it, all the way to the Emmys—and to the bank. Today, television is at the center of culture in ways that its inventors likely never imagined."[22]

Amid the overwhelming now of television, it's easy to forget what came before. One critic describes television as a "medium without a past," observing that in its relentless drive to keep its content fresh and flowing, television has built an antipathy to its own history.[23] This observation is especially true today, when critic after critic seems unwilling to go any further back, says Adams, than 1999, the year when *The Sopranos* debuted and Television Got Good, to discuss the advent of quality TV.

But thirty years before HBO came along, *Masterpiece* introduced viewers to a new world of television excellence. It got there first. It planted the flag. And as the book you're holding in your hands will show, *Masterpiece* exerted a strong influence on the industry. It pioneered and developed long-form drama. It pushed the limits of small-screen sex and violence with *I, Claudius* (1977). It gave us television's first broken female detective in the form of *Prime Suspect*'s Jane Tennison. It conditioned a climate where television now enthusiastically adapts good literature. And it revolutionized period drama. Throughout its fifty years, as American television sitcomed and reality-TVed us to death, *Masterpiece* quietly championed the value of well-scripted, well-acted drama. As Rebecca Eaton, its former executive producer, says, "We're the keepers of the dramatic flame."

To date, *Masterpiece* and its sister show, *Mystery!*, have aired nearly four hundred series, many of them among the best dramas television has ever produced. But two series eclipse all others. *Upstairs, Downstairs* and *Downton Abbey* each came out of nowhere, at a time when *Masterpiece*'s ratings were less than robust, to recharge *Masterpiece* and redefine television. And each show became a worldwide wonder, watched in places as unlikely as South Korea and Cambodia, where viewers wouldn't know a baronet from a bondsman. Americans especially loved these series. And why not? Along with all their aspirational attributes, the two series satisfied America's dirty little secret: an ages-old, telltale, incongruous fascination with Britain's class system. Let's look at them now.

Upstairs, Downstairs and *Downton Abbey*

Everyone knows *Downton Abbey* was a record-breaking, addiction-forming, franchise-making phenomenon in America. But in what ways? The questions and answers below will give you some idea.

1. Over its six-year run, *Downton Abbey* received a total of how many Emmy nominations?
   A) 11, B) 37, C) 59
2. At its peak, *Downton Abbey* attracted approximately how many viewers worldwide per week?
   A) 40 million, B) 80 million, C) 120 million
   And in how many countries and regions?
   A) 100, B) 182, C) 203
3. Who got advance copies of *Downton Abbey*?
   A) Michelle Obama, B) Katie Couric, C) Oprah Winfrey
4. Which superstar actor requested a cameo role on *Downton Abbey*?
   A) Nicole Kidman, B) Harrison Ford, C) Tom Cruise
5. Which of these American musicians publicly stated he had a crush on Lady Sybil?
   A) Puff Daddy, B) Bruce Springsteen, C) Winton Marsalis
6. Which American designer based a fashion line on the show?
   A) Ralph Lauren, B) Marc Jacobs, C) Naeem Khan, D) all of the above
7. A US politician was forced to resign after the discovery that he spent _____ of public funds to redecorate his office in the lavish style of *Downton Abbey*.
   A) $10,000, B) $25,000, C) $100,000

Answers: 1 (C), 2 (C and C), 3 (A), 4 (B), 5 (A), 6 (D), and 7 (C).

Downton Abbey garnered fifteen Emmys, three BAFTAs, and eleven Golden Globe awards. It also earned more Emmy nominations—fifty-nine—than any other British series in TV history. It aired in 203 countries worldwide, attracting over 120 million viewers weekly. Among its fans were American celebrities Tom Hanks, Taylor Swift, Matt Damon, Conan O'Brien, Dustin Hoffman, Reba McEntire, rappers Jay Electronica and Puff Daddy, Harrison Ford, and George Clooney. Michelle Obama got advance copies delivered to the White House, where she watched them with her teenage daughters while her husband binged on *Game of Thrones*. Harrison Ford loved the show so much he requested (and got turned down for) a cameo role in it. Puff Daddy—the "Bad Boy" rapper turned entrepreneur and lifestyle coach—admitted "crying his eyes out" when Lady Sybil died. Ralph Lauren, Marc Jacobs, and Naeem Khan all built fashion lines around the show, making 2013 the "season of Harris tweed." And Illinois Congressman Aaron Schock kissed his career goodbye when news leaked that he spent $100,000 of taxpayer money patterning his office on *Downton Abbey*'s "Red Room."

Four decades earlier, *Upstairs, Downstairs* swept America with similar velocity, attracting eleven million weekly viewers at its peak. It spawned cookbooks, novelizations, spinoffs, a clutch of Edwardian dramas, and a disastrous American remake, *Beacon Hill*. By the late 1980s, *Upstairs, Downstairs* had reached one billion viewers worldwide, including the Shah of Iran, and generated more commentary than any TV show to date. When the final episode aired on May 1, 1977, Boston's mayor pronounced it "Upstairs, Downstairs Day." The *New York Times*, meanwhile, joked that President Carter had submitted a joint resolution to Congress for a national day of mourning.

What made these two shows such megahits in America? Both boasted a long, immersive storyline, a dazzling ensemble of actors, finely sketched characters, and lavish attention to historical detail. Each also married period drama to soap opera, appealing to our aspirational desires and our love of lowbrow. And in classic *Masterpiece* style, both celebrated a vanished world of tradition, with its distinct social mores and lovely accouterments.

But most powerfully, *Upstairs, Downstairs* and *Downton Abbey* made the human dilemma—the perennial problem of how to live a satisfying, meaningful life in a world beyond one's control—just as important to their portrayal of servants as to their portrayal of the upper classes. Each series invited us to compare one way of living with another, and to recognize that we're all in the business of trying to figure out who we are—class be damned.

This essential theme underlies much of *Masterpiece*'s programming. It draws on sentimentality, the quality of having or appealing to tender feelings. Far more pervasive and powerful than people think, sentimentality celebrates the emotional connections between people. At the core of every sentimental tale, then, is a desire for love, friendship, and belonging. That's why sentimentality—whether that of *Downton Abbey* or *It's a Wonderful Life* or a Ken Burns documentary—moves so many of us, especially in its suggestion that differences between people can be overcome.

But sentimentality is risky, always in danger of simplifying the human experience it purposes to represent. And when it comes to depicting historical subjects charged with controversy, such as Britain's class system, sentimentality can sometimes be downright offensive. How is it, then, that Americans loved these shows as much as they did?

UPSTAIRS, DOWNSTAIRS

Airing on *Masterpiece Theatre* between January 6, 1974, and May 1, 1977, *Upstairs, Downstairs* is one of several series, along with *I, Claudius*, *The Jewel in the Crown*, *Prime Suspect*, and *Downton Abbey*, that changed television. It arrived just as *Masterpiece*'s ratings had begun to drop and wound up garnering twenty-five TV awards, among them two BAFTAs, one Golden Globe, and four Emmys, including the Primetime Emmy Award for Outstanding Dramatic Series in 1974, 1975, and 1977. Contemporary reviews teemed with the sense that *Upstairs, Downstairs* had brought "a new kind of television excellence" to America. "Stylish, literate, and witty, the series is unlike anything we've seen on television before," said the *New York Times*. "It's about old times," observed the *Washington Post*, "but it is not old hat."[1] And as *Downton Abbey* would do forty years later, *Upstairs, Downstairs* put *Masterpiece* and PBS in the center of a national conversation. The decline of manners, class relations, America's "indifference" to history: the series generated fervent commentary about all of these subjects.

Upstairs, Downstairs offered a very different experience from previous *Masterpiece* dramas. Unlike *Vanity Fair* and *The Golden Bowl*, it was an original series created for television. It was also the first *Masterpiece* series to be produced for Britain's commercial network, ITV, rather than the BBC. And it merrily employed lowbrow forms like broad comedy and soap opera. These aspects furrowed the brows of several WGBH producers, including Cambridge-educated Christopher Sarson, a textbook image of a British "gentleman." He liked the show but deemed it "very un-Masterpiece," at odds with the program's aspirational mission to deliver drama based on great literature or history. Sarson voted "no" to airing it—and almost blew PBS's chance of landing its most popular series until *Downton Abbey*.

Luckily, *Masterpiece*'s new executive producer, Joan Wilson, thought otherwise.[2] A Wisconsin native who drove a Mustang and believed in the occult, Wilson was a woman of guts and good instinct. In her first purchase for the program, she gambled that *Upstairs, Downstairs* would free *Masterpiece* of its top-lofty associations and raise its ratings. It was a ballsy move for a new producer, especially a woman working in a male-dominated industry, but she ran with it. With her creative input, Mobil's public relations agency, Frank Goodman Associates, designed a campaign featuring photos of the cast looking prim and starchy with the caption "Behind these sober faces lurk 13 weeks of sex, intrigue, jealousy—and just plain fun." Clearly, this show would be a whole different can of worms from *The Golden Bowl*.

Running for sixty-eight episodes over the course of five seasons, *Upstairs, Downstairs* is epic drama. (In America, Upstairs, Downstairs aired fifty-five episodes over four years.) It begins in 1903, during the bright morning of the Edwardian era and ends in 1930, at the twilight of England's domination as a world power. Along the way, the series covers historical events like the sinking of the *Titanic*, the suffragette movement, World War I, and the Wall Street crash. It also boasts a cast of thirty-four characters. In their day, some of these characters were as adored by Americans as *Downton Abbey*'s Carson and the countess are now. The "upstairs" cast includes:

- Richard Bellamy, a conservative member of Parliament (David Langton);
- Marjorie, his impeccably mannered wife who dies on the *Titanic* (Rachel Gurney);
- Virginia, Richard's second wife and a feisty war widow (Hannah Gordon);
- Richard and Marjorie's shiftless son, James (Simon Williams);
- James's long-suffering wife, Hazel, who dies of influenza (Meg Wynn Owen); and
- James's cousin, Georgina, a party girl with flashes of depth (Lesley-Anne Down).

The "downstairs" contingent includes:

- Rose Buck, the dutiful parlor maid (Jean Marsh);
- Angus Hudson, the stiff-necked yet endearing butler (Gordon Jackson);
- Mrs. Bridges, the grumpy but warmhearted cook (Angela Baddeley);
- Edward Barnes, the Bellamys' chauffeur (Christopher Beeny);
- Daisy Barnes, Edward's shrewish wife (Jacqueline Tong); and
- Ruby Finch, the comically inept kitchen helper (Jenny Tomasin).

In a true television first, all these characters received equal narrative treatment. This democratic approach nicely countered the snooty hierarchy of *Upstairs, Downstairs* while making for a rich variety of subplots. It also reinforced another feature pioneered by the series: the ensemble cast. *Upstairs, Downstairs* was the first series to showcase the art of ensemble acting. Watch almost any episode, and you can see the synergy, personal chemistry, and camaraderie that come when a tightly knit group of actors perform together.

Publicity highlighted this aspect of the show, stressing its novelty while sentimentally underscoring the "deep friendships" among actors. Press releases noted that Simon Williams (James Bellamy) was a "careful and loving care-taker" of Angela Baddeley, the aging actress who played Mrs. Bridges, and that all the cast strove to cheer Gordon Jackson (Hudson), who suffered from chronic anxiety on the set. When Jean Marsh, who played Rose, discovered she wouldn't be present for the final cast party, she claimed in interviews that she cried for a week. Such publicity reinforced the series' sentimental depic-tion of the Bellamy household, suggesting a strong emotional bond existed among the actors as well as their characters.

A "Forsyte Saga turned upside down" is how Alistair Cooke, *Master-piece*'s host, introduced *Upstairs, Downstairs* to American audiences when it debuted. Cooke's phrasing was nicely calculated. PBS wanted viewers to link *Upstairs, Downstairs* with BBC's smash hit but to appreciate this difference: while *The Forsyte Saga* dwelt in the lofty world of the aristos, *Upstairs, Down-stairs* went below, depicting the poor commoners who had to blacken their boots and cook their food. This approach was also a first in television, and *Masterpiece* publicity mined it. Rose became the face of *Upstairs, Downstairs*, her frilly capped head plastered on buses all over New York and Boston. Along with downstairs dwellers Mr. Hudson and Mrs. Bridges, Rose was a viewer favorite, inspiring a string of American novelizations. Hudson, the deeply proper butler, had his "secret diaries" published by Random House. And Mrs. Bridges graced dozens of cookbooks, instructing American readers on how to make such English meals as spotted dick and toad in the hole.

The populist strain to *Upstairs, Downstairs* goes back to the summer of 1969, when Jean Marsh and actress Eileen Atkins were lolling beside a pool by the Mediterranean, broke and unemployed. Having just seen *The Forsyte Saga*, they were furious about how the servants had been airbrushed out of it. "We went apeshit," says Marsh. "It was disgusting, the way there were no downstairs people in it at all."[3] Marsh, whose mother had been a maid, and Atkins, whose father had been an underbutler, knew the upstairs/downstairs life from the basement up: the shoe-blacking, grate-cleaning, rising-at-dawn slog of it all. They decided to write a comedy about two parlor maids and call it "Below Stairs," and they'd spare none of the mucky details.

Heady with ideas, Marsh and Atkins wrote a treatment in one night, which soon made its way to the illustrious John Hawkesworth. A TV pro-ducer of prodigious talent and energy, he had taught history at Oxford, served as captain in the British army, and designed sets for British costume director Alexander Korda. Hawkesworth loved the idea of a series that would portray servant life. "This was the pearl in the oyster," he explained in an interview. "Up to then servants had really just been mobile props in period drama."[4] Still, he thought the series would "pack more conflict" with a dual structure featuring masters and servants, and he insisted the show be a stylish interplay of humor and drama rather than strictly a comedy. His proposed changes effectively shifted Marsh and Atkin's emphasis on social satire to a more sentimental treatment of the Bellamy household, stressing human connections rather than class differences.

Hawkesworth then hired Alfred Shaughnessy, reputed in the 1970s to be the best script editor in British television. A tall, silver-haired man who wore an ascot and went by the name of "Freddy," Shaughnessy became the driving force behind the series. It was he who decided *Upstairs, Downstairs* needed to be character driven, "keeping its eye, always, on rendering the essential humanity of these people."[5] And as a former writer of British anthology dramas like *Armchair Theatre*, Shaughnessy also insisted that the script, not the camera, be the star of the series (he phrased it in a memo to Hawkesworth: television should be an "electronic form of theatre and not some cheap imitation of film").

Shaughnessy therefore convinced his partner to locate most of the story within the Bellamy home at 165 Eaton Place. This was a bold and backward move for the early 1970s, when television was beginning to take its drama outdoors. But Shaughnessy bucked the trend. Under his stripped-down approach, *Upstairs, Downstairs* paid no heed to the hubbub of London streets. It rarely ventured to a country estate. And even though its entire fourth season focused on World War I, there wasn't a single battlefield scene. Instead, the series portrayed an inside-out history, conveying real forces and events through how they affected a fictional household.

With money saved on camera equipment and shooting, Hawkesworth and Shaughnessy were able to hire twelve of England's hotshot writers. Having a troupe of authors would ensure a "rich variety of perspectives" on each character. To ensure script continuity, the two men wrote the basic storyline and invented all the characters themselves. The other writers simply took turns picking up the narrative thread: ensemble authorship! Shaughnessy also devised a list of fifteen decrees. Topping the list was the directive that all episodes had to include an upstairs and downstairs plot, "so we make sure to give equal humanity to both worlds."[6] To add realism, Shaughnessy also insisted that each episode be set in an exact month and year.

This last point brings us to one of the series' greatest strengths: its authenticity. "*Upstairs, Downstairs* offers a historical and social reality unprecedented in TV drama," observed one critic in 1974. Other commentators went so far as to call the series a "social history," praising *Upstairs, Downstairs* for "breathing life into the past by portraying it with such exactness."[7] Social history concerns itself with the tangible and everyday. It prefers real life to abstractions, ordinary people to exalted figures, and the commonplace to big events. Miniseries are perfectly poised to provide social history, given their expansiveness and capacity for detail. One undeniable contribution of *Upstairs, Downstairs*—and by extension, *Masterpiece*—is how it discovered this television truth.

Having grown up in households much like 165 Eaton Place, Hawkesworth and Shaughnessy knew all about upper-class life, and they insisted on a rigorous accuracy of presentation. That rigor applied to everything, from political history to the popular tunes Edward the chauffeur hummed, inspiring future creators, such as *Downton Abbey*'s Julian Fellowes, to "get the little details right."[8] Hawkesworth hired a food historian, for example, to make sure that the props department knew that "no Edwardian cook would lift a spatula until the scullery maid had laid out the worktable 'properly'—sixty implements, as precisely placed as a surgeon's operating instruments."[9]

More importantly, *Upstairs, Downstairs* captured the patterns of Edwardian behavior, at once minutely exacting and subtly nuanced. The guiding principle, always, was to be faithful "to how the characters would have behaved." So when Lord Bellamy visits Hudson in his bedroom after the butler suffers a heart attack, he asks permission to sit down. Why? Because this is what "a gentleman of his standing would have done," according to Shaughnessy's notes. Similarly, when Virginia Bellamy's little boy goes off to boarding school, he hugs Rose, the parlor maid, rather than his mother because "the upper-classes simply didn't touch each other in public."[10] The series portrays its characters with a combination of empathy and distance. In this way, it's very different from *Downton Abbey*, whose characters are entirely relatable because they're wholly modernized.

At nearly fifty years old, *Upstairs, Downstairs* is still absorbing drama—witty, comforting, and rip-your-heart-out sad. It moves slowly at times, and whatever Shaughnessy believed about the value of filming indoors, it could use a bit of fresh air. But despite these limitations, the show is consistently rated as one of the top three television series ever made. One reason is its unapologetic use of soap opera. "A thinking person's *All My Children*" is how one American critic described it in 1975. Proving that PBS could beat commercial television at its own game, *Upstairs, Downstairs* went a long way toward undoing the fusty reputation of period drama. Its soapy elements added sentimental warmth to the genre, suggesting that rich or poor, master or servant, we all laugh, suffer, and screw up.

How is it that period drama and soap opera came to be such distinctly British bedfellows? It turns out that soap opera is a vital British tradition stemming back to Charles Dickens, the genre's grandee. A virtuoso of the cliffhanger, master of multiple plotlines, and unabashed believer in full-on emotional indulgence (no writer made Victorian readers cry more), Dickens would have been the showrunner for *Game of Thrones* had he been alive in the 2010s. He wrote fifteen novels in serialized installments, making his readers wait in breathless agony to see if Little Nell in *The Old Curiosity Shop* would die (she did) or Lady Dedlock's terrible secret in *Bleak House* would be revealed (it was). And he loved sentimentality, casting it against the forces of industrialization, mechanization, and even science. For Dickens, sentimentality was a moral and civilizing force, put to use so people might live more harmoniously.

Most British soap operas are patterned on the techniques Dickens originated. *Coronation Street* and *EastEnders*, for example, employ a Dickensian combination of humor and pathos. And like Dickens's novels, they put their spotlight on the working classes and the gritty, everyday trials and tribulations that affect them—aiming for realism even as they indulge in melodrama's improbabilities and absurdities. American soaps, by contrast, love the sheen of wealth and beauty. Airing in the evenings, soap operas also attract a far larger audience in Britain than the stay-at-home mothers and retirees that make up America's audience.

The freewheeling plotlines and unregulated emotions of soap opera eventually proved unsuitable for *Upstairs, Downstairs*, however. By the end of Season 3, Hawkesworth and Shaugnessy knew they wanted to shift the series in a darker direction. They ditched much of the melodrama and veered more toward realism, using it to depict mounting tensions between the Bellamys and their servants. And with a psychological naturalness that could pass the scrutiny of Henry James, they also examined the emotional ramifications of living in a new, uncertain world.

What of the show's sentimentality? *Upstairs, Downstairs* retained some of it, to be sure. But its sentimental moments in Seasons 4 and 5 are offset by scenes portraying the ugly realities of Britain's class system. In Season 5, Georgina goes out with her highborn friends for a drunken joy ride and accidentally hits—and kills—a local farmer. It's one of the series' most shattering moments, appalling in its portrayal of upper-class recklessness. Yet even more appalling is how quickly she recovers from the experience, giddily planning her wedding to the son of a duke months afterward.

Upstairs, Downstairs also gradually fastened its drama onto one character, James Bellamy. By Season 4, he becomes the story's protagonist, though there is not much pro about him. Arrogant and rude, James Bellamy is the character most marked by the sins of his class. When he goes off to war, he finds purpose for the first time in his life. But he returns home only to feel more lost than ever. In the penultimate episode, he recklessly invests the family fortune and Rose's savings, losing it all in the stock market crash. And then, in one of the most heart-wrenching sequences in television history, he retreats to his bedroom, meticulously arranges his belongings, and takes off for a supposed weekend in the country—only to shoot himself in a nearby hotel.

Lord and Lady Bellamy leave Eaton Place in the final episode, forced to pay off James's debts. The house goes to strangers, and the staff disperses, moving into the brave, new world of 1930s England. Rose walks around the house she has tended for thirty years, its rooms reverberating with the voiceovers of characters in former scenes. It's a sentimental touch, but one the show has earned. Oscar Wilde once described a sentimentalist as someone "who wants to have the luxury of an emotion without paying for it." Wilde was being his cynical self, but the observation bears truth. For sentimentality to work as art, it must be accompanied by its own critical awareness: a kind of second layer that asks us to interrogate the very feelings it draws from us. *Upstairs, Downstairs* has that awareness, determined, in the end, to faithfully capture the era it represents.

The show's somber progression didn't keep audiences from forming sentimental attachments to its characters, however. Far from it. The week before *Upstairs, Downstairs* ended, a critic for *Prime Time* magazine said, "It doesn't feel like a television series is ending. It feels like our best friends are moving away, far away." The *Los Angeles Times* proclaimed, "It will all be over May 1. And we're taking it hard." And the *Washington Star* observed, "Fans will be mourning the end of a superb television series, the end of an era, and the departure of a marvelous troupe of actors who have become real people in the eyes and hearts of millions of viewers."[11] Such comments convey the powerful connection many Americans felt to these characters. In the months ahead, some of them even traveled to Eaton Place to see the building in which the Bellamys lived, as if looking for some lost, spiritual home.

In the spring of 2011, *Masterpiece* aired a BBC sequel to *Upstairs, Downstairs* starring Keeley Hawes, Claire Foy, and the two actresses who conceived of the show forty years earlier, Jean Marsh and Eileen Atkins. But the series received tepid reviews, failed to capture a sizeable audience, and was canceled after nine episodes. One reason for this was Season 1's truncated length; BBC producers had unwisely decided to limit the number of episodes to three, thereby cramming too much story into too little time. What's more, the series betrayed an almost palpable uncertainty over how or even why the BBC wanted to revisit the story. And in a fateful twist that must still niggle at BBC executives, the new *Upstairs, Downstairs* aired the very same season as *Downton Abbey*.

DOWNTON ABBEY

As Rebecca Eaton explains in her memoir, *Making Masterpiece*, she originally passed on the script of *Downton Abbey*. It was the summer of 2009, and she was sitting on the front porch of her Maine vacation home, reading a book, when the phone rang. A program executive at ITV was calling with news of a sensational script by Julian Fellowes, the same man who wrote the Oscar-winning film, *Gosford Park*. Was she interested? Eaton paused, thought about the upcoming remake of *Upstairs, Downstairs*. "Did *Masterpiece* really need another aristocratic-family-charming-servant miniseries at this point?" Eaton wondered to herself. "Probably not." She declined politely and went back to her book. When she heard a year later that Dame Maggie Smith had been cast in the part of the dowager countess, Eaton immediately called ITV to see if they had found an American coproducer. They hadn't. By the end of the day, Eaton had secured the script. As she says, "I have been very, very lucky in my career despite myself."[12]

Like *Upstairs, Downstairs, Downton Abbey* is a richly textured and sumptuous drama, spanning fourteen years (1912–1926) and six seasons with a cast of nearly fifty characters. In contrast to *Upstairs, Downstairs'* "urban" locale, its setting is a sprawling manor house in Yorkshire. That house is "Downton Abbey," and its fate (Who will inherit it? How will it survive amid changing times?) forms the center of the series' drama. The residing family are:

- Lord Grantham (Robert), a kindly but slow-to-adapt patriarch (Hugh Bonneville);
- Lady Grantham (Cora), Lord Grantham's resilient American wife (Elizabeth McGovern);
- Lady Mary, their eldest and haughty daughter (Michelle Dockery);
- Lady Edith, their middle daughter (Laura Carmichael);
- Lady Sybil, their free-thinking daughter who marries the chauffeur and dies after childbirth (Jessica Brown Findlay);
- Lady Violet, Lord Grantham's quip-quick mother (Maggie Smith);
- Matthew Crawley, the heir apparent to Downton Abbey who dies shortly after marrying Lady Mary (Dan Stevens);
- Rose Aldridge, cousin of the Crawleys and full-fledged modernist (Lily James); and
- Isobel, Matthew Crawley's goodhearted but annoyingly earnest mother (Penelope Wilton).

Among the Downton servants are:

- Tom Branson, the Irish chauffeur/socialist who marries Lady Sybil (Allen Leech);
- Anna Bates (nee Smith), the good-souled head housemaid (Joanne Froggatt);
- Mr. Bates, Anna's luckless husband and Lord Grantham's valet (Brendan Coyle);
- O'Brien, Lady Grantham's malicious maid (Siobhan Finneran);
- Thomas Barrow, the scheming gay footman who finds a conscience (Rob James-Collier);
- Mrs. Hughes, housekeeper and sage pragmatist (Phyllis Logan);
- Mrs. Patmore, the crotchety cook (Lesley Nicol);
- Daisy, the meek kitchen maid who learns to stand up for herself (Sophie McShera); and
- Carson, a butler more loyal than Lord Grantham's Labrador (Jim Carter).

The series premiered in America on January 9, 2011, one day before *Masterpiece*'s fortieth anniversary and two weeks after the end of its spectacular run in the UK. A critic gloomily predicted it would die on the vine in the United States. "Chances are you won't get to see the show. The reason? It's been relegated to PBS, and shoehorned into the dreary *Masterpiece Theater* slot where it's likely to disappear among the Jane Austen and Charles Dickens adaptations the network endlessly churns out."[13] He was wrong. *Downton Abbey* was an overnight, out-of-the-blue sensation in America, galloping in to refresh *Masterpiece*, PBS, and the waning belief that a scripted family drama could still attract a wide demographic crossover. It generated immediate praise from American critics. "Compulsively watchable from the get go," declared the *Wall Street Journal* that first week. "It's a juicy soap opera in Edwardian clothing—and that's not a criticism," pronounced *Slant* magazine.[14] Reviews everywhere—*Vanity Fair, Newsweek,* the *New York Times*—were similarly breathless, expressing wonder that a period drama could be so compelling. Those at *Masterpiece* couldn't believe their good fortune, especially given *Sherlock*'s stupendous debut just a few months before.

  Downton Abbey didn't have a team of writers like *Upstairs, Downstairs.* It had one guy, a genius in his way: Julian Fellowes. Now seventy-one, Fellowes is a late bloomer whose every feature, from his twinkling manner to the unwavering courtesy he shows journalists, exudes gratitude for his belated success. He had twelve screenplays rejected before he hit gold with *Gosford Park*, a 2001 British murder mystery for which he won an Academy Award. Directed by Robert Altman, the film features an ensemble cast that includes *Masterpiece* actors Eileen Atkins, Stephen Fry, Helen Mirren, and Michael Gambon.

Since 2001, Fellowes has scripted *Vanity Fair*, with Reese Witherspoon; *The Young Victoria*, with Emily Blunt; *The Tourist*, with Johnny Depp and Angelina Jolie. He also wrote the book for the musical theater adaptation of *Mary Poppins* and the bestselling novel *Snobs*. He recently finished writing the first season of HBO's *The Gilded Age*, an "American *Downton Abbey*" about wealth and class in turn-of-the-century New York. And he also scripted the *Downton Abbey* film, which took in $31 million on its opening weekend in September 2019: nearly twice as much money as Sylvester Stallone's *Rambo*.

"He made all this up," remarks Rebecca Eaton, referring to *Downton Abbey*. "Their backstories, their future, all of it. How does he know how those characters think or talk? He hasn't been an Edwardian undermaid, or a gay footman, or a farmer."[15] Although Eaton knows Fellowes well, she asks this with genuine wonder, even awe, as if she were talking about J. R. R. Tolkien. The comparison bears thinking about. Like Tolkien, whose books we enjoy for their nerdy minutiae, Fellowes loves ferreting through history. "I believe the little details are terribly important," he says in interviews.

But perhaps the better comparison is with Dickens, Fellowes's hero. Like Dickens, Fellowes's greatest talent is inventing characters, and even the most cartoonish of them—Molesley, Carson—radiate a certain kind of truth, just like the characters of Dickens. Fellowes also conveys an unmistakable joy in storytelling, somehow imparting it to us, his audience. Despite our better judgment, we root for him to add another subplot, introduce another baddie, slip in yet another revelation about a character's past. Why? Because we know that Fellowes, like Dickens before him, is cheerfully working to entertain us.

Most of all, Fellowes shares Dickens's love of sentimentality. His writing extols the values of kindness, decency, and generosity; it teems with a hopefulness that seems absolutely sincere. And as with Dickens, this quality makes his work reviled by some critics and beloved by millions. Reflecting on how we love and hate Dickens for his sentimentality, the writer John Irving remarks, "And when we writers—in our own work—escape the slur of sentimentality, we should ask ourselves if what we are doing matters."[16] Clearly, for millions of people around the world, Fellowes's and Dickens's writing *does* matter.

Following *Upstairs, Downstairs*, Fellowes refused to make any character the star of *Downton Abbey*. "The series' appeal, from the first, was its company feel," says Dan Stevens, who played Matthew Crawley. "There was no main character."[17] *Downton Abbey* directs its attention to masters and servants alike, though its world is far more fluid than that of the earlier show. Guest actors—Shirley MacLaine, Richard E. Grant, Paul Giamatti—breeze in and out. American characters pop up frequently. Servants spend far more time upstairs than poor Rose or Hudson ever did. And a bunch of characters die (eleven altogether, including Isis, the dog).

Almost all the actors in *Downton Abbey* earned critical acclaim for their performances. Seven of them received multiple Emmy nominations, and Maggie Smith won Best Supporting Actress three times. A good many of them—Joanne Froggatt (Anna), Jim Carter (Carson), Elizabeth McGovern (Cora), Michelle Dockery (Mary), Hugh Bonneville (Lord Grantham)— achieved celebrity status in the States, appearing on talk shows, late-night comedies, and *Masterpiece*-sponsored tours. Bonneville even topped the guest list at a White House state dinner for former British prime minister David Cameron. And Michelle Dockery won over many a Stateside heart when, at the request of Stephen Colbert on *The Late Show*, she did the hoity-toity Lady Mary with a Jersey accent.

When Fellowes sat down to write the first season of *Downton Abbey* in 2008, neither he nor anyone else involved in the project had any idea that the show would revitalize, even transform, long-form drama. But that's precisely what happened. In 2008, the genre had become a relic. No one wanted to invest in it anymore because 1) it was expensive, 2) young people didn't have the attention span for it, and 3) television drama itself seemed to be on life support, the perceived victim of reality TV and the smartphone revolution. So beginning in the early 2000s, the BBC started cramming stories like *Dr. Zhivago* (2002) into two or three episodes, dooming them to fail. But executives at ITV took a chance with *Downton Abbey* and committed to an opening season of six episodes. The show's success proved all market wisdom wrong, blowing demographics away like a house of straw. One consequence is that long-form drama is now the locus of serious entertainment, attracting educated audiences of all ages.

Employing its length to full effect, *Downton Abbey* didn't just give us a story; it gave us a world. Rarely has any television drama been as densely detailed or as expansive. The show was as layered as a *mille-feuille*, carefully constructed by Fellowes and a bevy of experts—set designers, costume specialists, a historical consultant—committed to "getting the details right." Of course, creators of other period dramas on TV also went to great lengths to re-create a past era. But they didn't have the resources Fellowes and his team had. Every one of Lady Grantham's breakfast trays, for example, contained a cooked meal, a facsimile of a period newspaper, and specially created letters, "written on the correct paper for the era, by either a man or woman as appropriate, using a fountain pen and ink and even containing the right sentiments."[18] The effect, according to media scholar Henry Jenkins, was to create "a fictional universe far bigger than what we saw on the screen. It was an elaborate mythology, really."[19]

Downton Abbey also mixed high- and lowbrow more gleefully than any period drama before it. It's not news to say that the show was grand soap opera. "The classiest soap opera in television history," *Rolling Stone* called it.[20] But *Downton Abbey* was impenitent in its use of the genre. It indulged in every kind of melodramatic device, from medical tomfoolery involving dropsy to a bar of soap carefully arranged to cause a miscarriage. And while *Upstairs, Downstairs* cut out its soapy business by the end of Season 3, *Downton Abbey* did just the opposite. With each new season, its plots grew wackier and more delinquent. Not a few critics, here and in Britain, threw up their hands at this. But this was precisely what so many American viewers found appealing. "I'd sit in a corner, checking my cell phone while my wife and girls watched the show," says one male fan from Vermont. "But my ears perked up when that Turk died in Lady Mary's bed. After that moment, I was all in."[21]

With all these attributes, it's no wonder that *Downton Abbey* has enjoyed a richer cultural afterlife than any other period drama in history: "The Downton Effect," as commentators call it. The publishing industry made a cottage industry of tie-ins to the series. Penguin and Knopf furiously promoted histories of subjects featured in *Downton Abbey*, such as the *Titanic* and World War I. St. Martin's Press recommended John Steinbeck and Ford Madox Ford as "chroniclers of the Downton age." And myriad publishers printed "Downtonesque" romances or reissued memoirs written by servants. Other tie-ins included scripts, cookbooks, graphic novels, behind-the-scenes accounts, travel essays, novelizations, children's stories, histories of household management, biographies, and novels that consciously revisit the themes of the show while focusing on other characters and plots. *New York Times* bestselling author Sera Belle even wrote the series Downton Abbey Historical Erotica.

And there were scores of *Downton Abbey* parodies, including *Downton Tabby*, a children's book. An edgier parody was *Downton Zomby*, a video in which all the characters killed off in the show return as zombies. A naughty one was *Down on Abby*, starring Lord Grabhem, his butler, Smallcock, and Master Bates. An entire TV series parodied *Downton Abbey*: Comedy Central's *Another Period*, whose aristocrats name their servants "Chair" for convenience sake. Americans didn't need to be fans of the show to enjoy these parodies; *Downton Abbey* had become such a part of our cultural imagination that everyone was in on the joke.

DOWNTON DENIGRATORS

But not everyone was enamored. "That is why I left England," said the actor Daniel-Day Lewis of the show, appalled by its "rosy" depiction of the country's class system. British historian Simon Schama called *Downton Abbey* "a steaming, silvered tureen of snobbery." And Benedict Cumberbatch, the star of *Masterpiece*'s *Sherlock*, denounced it as "fucking atrocious . . . a nostalgia trip." On this side of the Atlantic, hostile critics condemned the series as a "toxic import," a "theme park," and "an anachronism from start to finish."[22]

For these detractors, the cardinal sin of *Downton Abbey* was its sentimental depiction of an era rife with injustice. Critics particularly objected to how the show rendered master/servant relations "anodyne" and "cozy," pointing out that Edwardian servitude involved cleaning grates, scrubbing floors, heaving coal, cooking round the clock, or hauling forty gallons of water upstairs just for one toff's bath. With no time (or water) to themselves, domestics were sooty and dirty. They smelled of sweat. And employers were typically not the nice people of Eaton Place or Downton Abbey. They could be smug and arrogant, snickering at their servants and dismissing them for the slightest infraction.

Downton Abbey's creators defended the show by saying that this sort of thing would be the province of a completely different kind of project. Rebecca Eaton flatly stated that the series is "not a documentary" while Fellowes maintained, "The power of the show is that people are people. Some aristocrats are very nice and some are not."[23] Fellowes has repeatedly expressed his belief that we need television drama celebrating our shared humanity. His portrait of the Downton household, he maintains, wasn't meant to whitewash history but to show how people can form connections despite class differences.

Upstairs, Downstairs also had sentimental appeal. But it blended that sentimentality with a realism that grew harsher as the series progressed. *Downton Abbey* lacked this critical edge, which is why many British viewers stopped watching it. By Season 4, the show's weekly ratings had plummeted in the UK from 12 million viewers to 5.6 million, and they never recovered. But American fans loved *Downton Abbey* from its first episode to its last. And with each new season, a torrent of intense if slightly sheepish meditations would appear, speculating on why this was so. "Why are Americans, who fought a revolution to free themselves from the British crown, so enchanted by a honeyed look at wealthy lords and ladies and the butlers and maids who look after them?" asked one journalist.[24]

Any number of answers to this question exist. One is Americans' conflicted feelings about the rich. We're appalled by the exorbitant wealth of movie stars and other celebrities. Yet we devour information about their lifestyles, poring over images that picture them lounging poolside or couchant on beds. Do we hate these people, or do we love them? The answer is both. It's a rich ambiguity that has long defined American culture. No wonder, then, that millions of us loved seeing highborn and low brought together in one household, happily coexisting.

We also enjoyed watching *Downton Abbey* because it gave us a world where the pressures of social mobility were gone—everyone knew their place and seemed more or less happy with it. That's not to say social climbing didn't occur. It did, and with blessed frequency: Daisy got educated; Molesley rose from footman to teacher; Mrs. Patmore landed her own bed and breakfast; and Branson, the Irish chauffeur, wound up as manager of Downton Abbey (and in the film, its future owner!). But these upward moves all happened as if in a fairy tale, with Father Fellowes waving his magic wand over them all. We didn't believe any of it, exactly. But we took comfort in inhabiting a world not overburdened with questions of ambition and self-invention. For six balmy years, *Downton Abbey*'s sentimentality helped ease the anxiety of American individualism, even if we didn't quite realize it.

★ ★ ★

From our look at these two series, we can see how easily television, even period drama, can trigger issues that run deep: upper-class privilege, quarrels over history, class resentment, and America's weird fascination with the rich. *Masterpiece* has sparked similar controversies over the years because its classical bent raises thorny issues about class, gender, and race. These dustups are vital to the show's history, key to consider before we dive into more glamorous topics like the show's award-winning actors and luscious locales. Let's examine, then, the politics of being *Masterpiece*.

The Politics and Culture of Being *Masterpiece*

THE GENTLEMAN HOST

$\mathcal{F}$rom 1971 to 1992, one person embodied *Masterpiece*'s aspirational promise of cultural refinement: Alistair Cooke, the show's original, inimitable host. It was he, silver haired and debonair, sitting in that library, whom people thought of when they thought of the show.

Alistair Cooke is slowly slipping into the vast limbo where the once famous but now nearly forgotten reside. In most cases, this is no great tragedy. In Cooke's case, it is. He made a brilliant career of navigating between America and Britain, illuminating each country to the citizens of the other. Cooke was a cicerone, a cultural interpreter, and a smoother of transatlantic tensions. Born in the working-class town of Salford, England, he came to the States in 1932 to study theater at Yale. He intended on staying two years, but the following summer he rode across country and, amazed by the contrast between Britain's postwar weariness and America's "tremendous vitality," abandoned theater for a journalistic career.

In 1946, Cooke began broadcasting a weekly radio show for British audiences called *Letters from America*. A strong flavor of anti-American sentiment pervaded England at the time, stirred by Roosevelt's open condemnation of Britain's rule over India and the perceived arrogance of American soldiers stationed in England. Cooke thought a radio program could help bridge the fissure between the countries. Pitching his show to the BBC, he imagined it as "a weekly personal letter," written for his native countrymen, about American life and people and places." *Letters from America* aired for fifty-eight years, breaking every broadcast record because of how Cooke unfailingly charmed his listeners with peerless observations of American life.

Stan Calderwood and Christopher Sarson, the men most responsible for *Masterpiece*'s conception and early design, wanted Cooke from the start. Savvy and intuitive, like all good producers, they knew the show needed an authority on British history and culture, someone smart and affable who could set each episode in an informative but entertaining context. Cooke was "the only choice," Sarson said. But when he called to offer him the job, the producer was turned down flat. Hearing a few weeks later that his quarry was in Boston, Sarson invited him to a favorite local restaurant and lured him with his favorite scotch. When Cooke politely declined again, Sarson persuaded Cooke's daughter, Susan, to work on her father. Cooke agreed to a thirteen-week contract one month before the show's premiere, never imagining he'd stay longer—certainly not for twenty-two years.

All Alistair Cooke was hired to do was deliver weekly introductions and closing remarks spanning thirty seconds to four minutes. But those accompanying words, and the persona he created, would discernibly link *Masterpiece* with the ideal of high culture.

Cooke's contribution to *Masterpiece* was to invert *Letters from America*, his across-the-pond agility now illuminating Britain for Americans. And in keeping with the show's aspirational bent, he did so with extraordinary erudition. A man who could distill the story of the English Civil War into a paragraph or tell you what color geraniums (red) Dickens planted in his garden, Cooke was a living footnote, the Lord Google of his era. And his grammar was impeccable. Yet for all his learnedness, there was no academic tweediness about him, nothing of the prig or snob. Vigorous and agile, possessed of a mischievous grin and puckish sense of humor, Cooke would have had undergraduates flocking to his courses.

"In the United States he was the very model of the English gentleman," writes the *Encyclopedia Britannica*. Cooke might have chuckled at the description, but it's true nonetheless—and it was paramount to his success on *Masterpiece*. The British gentleman possesses, among the usual attributes of gentility and refinement, a relaxed relationship to knowledge. He is versatile and responsive to a variety of subjects, drawn to them by feeling rather than professional necessity. It was this eclectic bent, this approach to learning in an inductive and miscellaneous way, that gave Cooke his own gentlemanly charisma. His passion for knowledge inspired fans of *Masterpiece* to be articulate, better read, well traveled, and above all, curious about the world. It didn't hurt that he wore suits by Hawes and Curtis, outfitters to the Duke of Edinburgh.

Cooke always wrote the introductions and closing remarks for *Masterpiece* himself, banging them out on an old manual typewriter as he sat at his desk, in his red-walled study overlooking Central Park. On the day of the taping, he would retreat to a small corner of the *Masterpiece* studio to memorize his script ("No Teleprompters; No Makeup" were his inviolate broadcasting rules). And because he had the memory of a dolphin, it took him no more than a half hour to commit five pages to heart. Once the filming began, he would recite his script as if he had just thought of it all, flubbing on purpose or improvising every once in a while to make the whole thing seem natural. "It's an old-fashioned prescription, tougher on the memory and the nerves," he wrote.[1] But the effect was to make his audience feel as if he were speaking directly to them.

Cooke wrote over nine hundred scripts for *Masterpiece* loaded with sharp, witty, and often profound observations about British history and culture. If culled, they'd make a sprightly collection. From them, we learn the details of Dostoyevsky's gambling addiction, Thomas Hardy's bouts of depression, George Eliot's peculiar education at her father's side, and Dickens's disastrous reunion in midlife with his first love. We also get memorable encapsulations of figures such as these:

> Of Noel Coward: "Glib in a grim time, he was the twenties dude in a poor post-war society."
> Of Dickens: "He was egocentricity incorporated."
> Of *Vanity Fair*'s Becky Sharp: She is "poor but pretentious, genteel but on the make, one of the most accomplished bitches in fact or fiction between the fall of Rome and the rise of Las Vegas."

Alistair Cooke retired in 1992, the same year Johnny Carson, another ace conversationalist and TV institution, stepped down as host of the *Tonight Show*. *Masterpiece* considered over 150 candidates to replace him, finally landing on Russell Baker, the esteemed *New York Times* columnist. But Baker never seemed comfortable in the role. How could he? No one could ever quite embody the aspirational bent of *Masterpiece* like Cooke, the working-class boy who got a full ride to Cambridge and, at twenty, changed his name from Alfred to the much more elegant Alistair. He embodied the British ideal of the gentleman *and* achieved the American ideal of a self-made man. To play off his own words, he was Aspiration, Inc.

But not everyone was a fan of Alistair Cooke. To some, he connoted a troubling image of white male authority. No matter that he was a liberal-leaning humanitarian who wrote often and eloquently about the sins of sexism and racism. His age, gender, and old-world style of imparting knowledge turned off many Americans. They certainly did *Masterpiece*'s critics, who frequently noted how the show's cultural conservatism was embodied in its host (one hilarious expression of this is *Saturday Night Live*'s parody of *Masterpiece* with a Rastafarian sitting in a wingchair, introducing a period drama to a reggae beat). In his twenty-two years as *Masterpiece*'s "emcee," as he humbly called himself, Cooke was an aspirational model for millions of American viewers. But he also represented an ideal that was quickly coming to an end.

PBS, *MASTERPIECE*, AND THE IDEAL OF HIGH CULTURE

Masterpiece was initially founded on the widespread assumption that American television was hopelessly uncultured. Many high-profile writers, among them Daniel Boorstin, a Pulitzer-prize-winning historian, charged television with creating a nation of increasingly isolated people, in mindless thrall to whatever they were watching on the screen. "Of all the forces which have tempted us to lose our sense of history," he wrote in 1969, "none has been more potent than television . . . it fills the present moment with experience so engrossing and overwhelming, it dulls our sense of the past, cutting us off from history as it cuts us off from one another." Portentous and gloomy, Boorstin's rhetoric typifies that of many commentators who agreed that under the pull of television, America had achieved the feat of "national self-hypnosis, . . . forgetting about the pleasure of reading books, attending concerts, engaging in good conversation." (One can only wonder what they would say about American culture now.)[2]

Within such a climate, the establishment of PBS felt to many like the arrival of a different television altogether: "Un-TV," as some people in the 1970s called it. PBS made no bones about promoting itself as such. Its original slogans were "Television Worth Watching," "The New Face of Television," and "For Viewers Like You." Such catchphrases distinguished PBS from the commercial networks while also creating an imagined community of viewers keen on high culture and public affairs. PBS therefore emerged on the American scene not only as an alternative network but also as a tastemaker—much like the Book-of-the-Month Club during the 1920s or HBO in the 1990s.

To fill its cultural programming and promote its highbrow appeal, PBS relied, still relies, heavily on WGBH. A public television and radio station, it produces *Masterpiece* and many other PBS programs—*Nova, Frontline, American Experience*—that combine edification with entertainment.

WGBH is located in Boston, the original cultural capital of the United States, the home of the Boston Brahmin, a city of sixty-three museums and thirty-five institutions of higher learning. Samuel Adams dubbed it the "Athens of America." E. B. White blessed it as "the perfect state of grace" in his poem "Boston." And Mark Twain distinguished it as the city where people ask "How much does he know?" rather than "How much is he worth?"

Harvard University was WGBH's home for many years, and employees still grumble about having had to move to a corporate locale with nary a student nor spire in sight. All the same, *Masterpiece*'s studio, located in a big blue can of a building in the business district of Brighton, has a warm, inviting vibe. Posters of old series hang on walls like family portraits. Life-size cutouts of Benedict Cumberbatch, Mark Rylance, Jenna Coleman, and Rufus Sewell populate hallways and offices, some sporting 3-D glasses. In one producer's office is a snapshot of her daughter dressed as Little Dorrit for Halloween.

A cosmopolitan city, a TV studio that doesn't feel like one, a kid who identifies with Dickens rather than Disney: it all fits a program that, as Rebecca Eaton would claim, "purveys culture."

Eaton's phrase recalls English poet and critic Matthew Arnold's notion of "high culture, which he described as "the best that has been thought and said in the world." In our day, it also encompasses the best that has been composed, painted, sculpted, filmed, and multi-media-ed. Following this ideal, a cultured person dedicates herself to a lifelong pursuit of knowledge, guided by the principles of tradition, beauty, and excellence. Reading literature, visiting museums, watching quality television: these are regarded as vital activities because they enlarge the mind and feed the soul. In this manifestation of culture, the arts are a set of beliefs.

Masterpiece has always been based on this appeal. But as the program's history reveals, America has a vexed relationship with high culture. On the one hand, we have made it an aspiration ever since the colonial period, a key component in the great American Quest for Self-Improvement. Become cultured, so the idea goes, and you gain class, resist the temptations of vulgarity, improve your character. On the other hand, we hate what we perceive as its strong whiff of snobbery. High culture mocks our populist values. Its emphasis on history and tradition checks the emphasis we put on innovation. Its elitism counters our democratic spirit. And since the 1980s, it has come to be linked with a promotion of dead white men over female artists or artists of color. These days, it seems hopelessly inessential to many Americans, old-fashioned at best, reactionary and racist at worst. Yet it still exerts a pull.

No wonder, then, that *Masterpiece* has been the show critics love to hate now and then. Or that over the course of its fifty-year history, the program has wisely learned to blend highbrow and low. Or that in recent years, *Masterpiece* has begun to confront the troubling politics that has lurked behind its offerings.

However different now, the original aim of PBS and *Masterpiece* was to shift American tastes toward the highbrow. Taste is a system, though not a very systematic system, of preferences. With a menu of "quality" programs that "furnished both artistic and social value," PBS aimed to cultivate American taste away from shows like *Get Smart* and *Gunsmoke* to something more as-pirational. Its first-year lineup included *Evening at Pops*, featuring the Boston Pops Orchestra; *Washington Week*, a political roundup still on the air; and *Masterpiece*.

Sound elitist? It certainly did to some critics, who blasted PBS for what they called its "snob appeal." These curmudgeons refused to acknowledge, however, that PBS's vision was also democratic, openly inviting anyone who wanted cultural uplift to tune in. It's true that in PBS's early years, the station attracted mainly East Coasters, many residing in ritzy urban areas or suburbs. But its audience also included women like Mary Cashman, whose story is recounted by a relative in the *Masterpiece* files. Cashman lived in the tiny town of Menlo, Iowa, where she taught English at the local high school and played organ for the Catholic church. She had a house full of books and never watched what she called "dummy TV." But she did tune in to PBS every evening. She'd curl up on her aged sofa, tuck her legs underneath an afghan, and watch shows like *Firing Line* as she chain smoked and drank a beer. Elit-ism thus isn't synonymous with wealth or cosmopolitanism. Nor is it the same thing as snobbery, even though many PBS detractors would insist otherwise.

The story of Mary Cashman also captures how PBS functioned as a mid-dlebrow venue, aiming to bring intelligent entertainment to a mass audience. Admittedly, *middlebrow* is a touchy term. Originating in the 1920s, it designates a category of the arts that occupied the intermediary space between highbrow and lowbrow. Although never intended to be derogatory, the word quickly assumed pejorative meanings. According to modernist snoots like writers Virginia Woolf and Dwight MacDonald, "middlebrows" were either paltry purveyors of highbrow culture or social-climbing audiences who mindlessly selected the art they were told was best.[3]

But middlebrow, like sentimentality, has value. And like sentimentality, it has been consistently misunderstood and misrepresented by people anxious to defend their own cultural status. PBS, BBC, and *Masterpiece* are all middle-brow forms, as are HBO, the Oprah Winfrey Book Club, and Wikipedia. The venues are devoted to the high: to that which achieves artistic excellence. But they are also intent on making the high accessible to many, bringing ideas that might remain trapped in high-art scenes or scholarly books within reach of all Americans.

That said, these high/middle/low distinctions no longer make the same sense they did when *Masterpiece* arrived in 1971. American culture has changed since then—and in massive, mind-blowing ways. "High culture" once implied a certain degree of inaccessibility. To see a live performance of British theater, you traveled to London; now you visit YouTube. *Everything* is accessible now, making concepts like highbrow and lowbrow much more fluid than they used to be. And much less resonant.

Fifty years ago, though, high culture still exerted aspirational force. And no PBS show exuded it more than *Masterpiece*. To begin, there was its bent toward history. The ideal of culture hinges on a felt sense of continuity with the past; in fact, one way of describing an uncultured person is to say he or she lives solely in the present. *Masterpiece* sought to bring viewers into the past every Sunday night, providing the thrill of discovering that centuries-old characters had thoughts and emotions akin to their own. That historical emphasis gave even its more popular shows—for example, *Upstairs, Downstairs*—high-class cred, especially compared to the dross that made up most programming.

If its concentration on the past helped to high tone *Masterpiece*, so did its British imports. A British is Better ethos has influenced this country ever since the colonial period, but the 1960s witnessed a powerful wave of it. It began with the Beatles' arrival in New York on February 7, 1964, cleverly dubbed by a CBS correspondent as "The British Invasion." Two days later, on Sunday, February 9, the Beatles appeared on the *Ed Sullivan Show*—and before anyone could say "Yeah yeah yeah!," Beatlemania took hold of our country and opened the floodgates for other British influences. Almost immediately, UK bands like The Rolling Stones, The Honeycombs, The Hollies, The Kinks, and the Yardbirds were topping American charts. James Bond, with his martinis and gadgets and offhand conquests, soared in popularity. Hipster shows like *The Prisoner* and *The Avengers* attracted a cult following. Mod fashions from London designers made their way into stores like J.C. Penney and Sears.

The "Hail Britannia" atmosphere pervaded America through most of the 1960s, striking everyone from twelve to ninety-two. *Masterpiece* and the Beatles were therefore two strains of the same phenomenon, united in America's love affair with the UK. But the strains couldn't have been more divergent. That of the Beatles was countercultural and inclusive, embracing influences that included Indian raga and rhythm and blues. Its Anglophilic appeal was marked by crosscurrents of every kind, while that of *Masterpiece* was far more traditional—experienced, if not conceived, as a counterbalance to the other strain. That would come to serve a political purpose, as we'll see now.

PLAYING POLITICS

Viewed naively, the ideal of culture seems detached from politics. Yet the two are very much entwined. To understand *Masterpiece*'s cultural mission and appeal, therefore, we need to consider the political pressures that vexed and *still* vex PBS.

From the start, PBS's government funding (about 15 percent of its overall budget) has been contingent on politics, always in danger of withdrawal should a particular administration find public programming offensive or dangerous. This is not to say there are no protective measures against such a possibility; a three-year buffer, for example, exists between Congress's appropriation of funds and their receipt by the Corporation for Public Broadcasting (CPB). Yet as Trump's persistent quest to gut public-media funding reveals, PBS has always been a political football. During the 2012 presidential election, Mitt Romney vowed to cut funds to public broadcasting—despite insisting, "I like Big Bird!" Before Romney, there was Ronald Reagan, who contemplated eliminating the National Endowment for the Arts (NEA). And before him, there was Richard Nixon, whose threats to cut CPB funding prompted a moving and effective defense from PBS personality Fred Rogers, dressed in his signature cardigan sweater, before the US Senate Commerce Committee in May 1969.

Under such menacing conditions, PBS had to balance its attention to public affairs with safer kinds of programming. *Masterpiece* seemed especially harmless, for however progressive some of its series were, it possessed an unmistakable conservatism. In this way, it counterbalanced the station's leftist, even radical, shows. PBS brimmed with such programs in its early years. Among them were *Black Perspectives on the News*, *Soul!*, and WGBH's *Say Brother, Say Brother*, the first program credited with saying "fuck" on the air. Focusing on aspects of black life most white Americans knew little about, they interviewed figures far outside the mainstream, such as Amiri Baraka, Louis Farrakhan, and Ellis Haizlip, an openly gay African American closely associated with the Black Arts movement. Not surprisingly, the shows' viewership in the African American community was enormous (close to 65 percent).

Nixon, who worried constantly that the liberal-leaning network would torpedo his administration, hated PBS's more radical shows. To counter their effect, *Masterpiece* became PBS's trump card, assurance for a hostile administration that even when the network took up hot-button issues, it was also fulfilling its mission of cultural enlightenment. For leftist critics, *Masterpiece* was glaring proof that PBS's emphasis on cultural programming was not only cowardly but also white and elitist. That charge has been leveled at PBS ever since. A similar indictment, voiced on both sides of the Atlantic, has been made against period drama in general. From this viewpoint, the lavish and nostalgic dramas airing on *Masterpiece* divert viewers' attention from the political urgencies of the present. *Downton Abbey*: the opiate of the people.

Fueling such criticism was *Masterpiece*'s sponsorship by Mobil Oil. During the 1970s, Mobil Oil, Texaco, and Shell, the trinity of companies pejoratively known as "Big Oil," were targets of American outrage. The trouble began in the mid-1960s, when tremors about a potential oil crisis had started to surface, triggered by reports that the United States seemed to be reaching its geological peak of oil production. Aware of the shrinking domestic supply and growing demand, and nervous about the looming presidential election, Nixon lifted import prohibitions in 1971. All seemed well again. But in 1973, peeved by America's support of Israel in the Yom Kippur War, the Organization of Arab Petroleum Exporting Countries (OAPEC) issued an embargo on exports. It ordered Mobil, Texaco, and Shell, each with drilling machinery in the Middle East, to cut off all shipments to the United States. They complied, cut way back on their overall supply, and quadrupled prices. The result? An indelible crisis that in many ways defined the decade. In cities like Los Angeles and Dallas, lines at gasoline stations reached two miles. Hundreds of stations shut down, posting cardboard signs that read "Pumps Closed." For many Americans, life as they knew it—oversized cars, sprawling suburban neighborhoods, limitless consumption—seemed over. According to polls, 75 percent of the public insisted that "Big Oil" had created a phony shortage in order to turn a profit.

Mobil operated at ground zero of this crisis. Between 1968 and 1979, it remained in the media's crosshairs, often as a representative of greed and unbridled capitalism. Bombs exploded in front of Mobil headquarters on at least two occasions. An aggressive PR man, Herb Schmertz, vice president of public affairs for Mobil, countered criticism with hardball tactics, working under the logic that if companies don't actively participate in discussions that affect them, they deserve what they get. Under his regime of "creative confrontation," Schmertz bought space in the *New York Times* and wrote "advertorials" on the oil crisis and other related issues. More importantly, he sponsored *Masterpiece*. Schmertz called this "affinity-of-purpose marketing," where audiences associate successful ventures with the companies that sponsor them. "Cultural excellence implies corporate excellence," he would later write in his autobiography *Goodbye to the Low Profile*. History proved Schmertz right. By 1982, a public opinion poll found Mobil to be the most respected oil company in the world, with the highest public reputation in the arts and culture area. And in 2018, as part of a *New York Times* obituary that cast Schmertz in remarkably heroic terms, Rebecca Eaton eulogized him as a "modern-day Medici."

Mobil's sponsorship gave *Masterpiece* the funding it needed—close to $350 million over thirty-three years—but it came at a price. To critics, *Masterpiece*'s alignment with Mobil was further proof of the constraints and compromises under which the program and its network operated (PBS long suffered the joke that it was the "Petroleum Broadcasting Company"). Today, *Master-*

piece's corporate sponsors are Raymond James, a financial services company, and Viking River Cruises. Neither of these shows carries the controversial charge Mobil did. But they do cater to white, affluent, older Americans: the very people who tend to watch *Masterpiece*. This isn't a criticism as much as an observation, alerting us to how the politics of class and race continue to trouble the show—though as we'll see in the remaining sections, *Masterpiece* has taken big strides to address that problem head-on.

MASTERPIECE AND THE "GREAT BOOKS" DEBATE: OR, HOW SHOULD CULTURE REPRESENT ITSELF?

Anna Karenina, Bleak House, Cranford, David Copperfield, Madame Bovary, Middlemarch, Oliver Twist, Pride and Prejudice, A Room with a View, Vanity Fair, War and Peace: over the years, *Masterpiece* has featured adaptations of these and many other classic novels. They make up roughly 30 percent of *Masterpiece*'s overall programming, and yet they are immediately what comes to mind when people think of *Masterpiece*. As John Irving, Pulitzer-prize winner and long-time fan of the show says, "*Masterpiece* is the Great Books on the small screen."[4]

This was the original vision behind the series, in fact. As Alistair Cooke explained in one of his introductions, "Our show is designed to please a reading audience that would like to recall the life and work of favorite authors and of authors forgotten or never attempted." From its first year on, *Masterpiece* offered adaptations of many nineteenth- and early-twentieth-century novels— and it didn't shy away from obscure or difficult ones, either. Among its 1970s lineup were favorites like *Madame Bovary* (1976) as well as Henry James's *The Golden Bowl* (1973), Richard Llewelyn's *How Green Was My Valley* (1977), and Dickens's utterly lugubrious novel *Our Mutual Friend* (1978). It was a lineup born of the assumption that *Masterpiece* viewers were serious readers. During the 1970s, these readers included young people who still thought a taste hierarchy was the ladder you climbed to be a grownup.

A decade or so later, the idea that reading the classics was vital to one's education came under violent attack. It started at Stanford University in August of 1988, when a handful of students and faculty protested against a freshman course called "Western Culture" and the list of fifteen books it deemed "necessary reading for all educated human beings." Arguing that the course represented an "outdated philosophy of the West," protestors objected to the list's omission of minority writers and non-Western cultures. Over the next several months, Stanford found itself in the national news on a regular basis. *Newsweek*, for example, published a full-page report on Stanford's deliberations under the headline "Say Goodnight Socrates: Stanford University and the decline of the West." Secretary of State William Bennett entered the controversy, berating Stanford in public speeches for even considering a change in the course.[5]

How did one class spark so much national interest? Certainly, the publication of Allan Bloom's *The Closing of the American Mind* and E. D. Hirsch's *Cultural Literacy* had something to do with it. Published the year before, each book argued for the preservation of "traditional cultural values," decrying what its author saw as a shift toward relativism and "contempt for the past."

Interest in the Stanford controversy was no doubt also fueled by America's conservative turn in politics during the 1980s. Under the paternal aura of Ronald Reagan and his moderate administration, the rejection of a classical reading list was interpreted as a sign that the feminists and ethnic minorities who gained political consciousness since the 1960s were now taking over the universities. Their influence on the curriculum threatened the cultural values articulated by Hirsch and Bloom. They also seemed to jeopardize the stability and peacetime prosperity that many felt had been achieved during the 1980s.

Against this backdrop, *Masterpiece* emerged as a cultural touchstone. Its proponents routinely described it as a program that "inspired the right kinds of values—humanism, respect for tradition, contact with our intellectual past—through its superior rendition of timeless stories." Its detractors accused it of "dumbing down" the classics. "The closest we Americans get to reading the great novelists," wrote Bloom, "is watching bastardized versions of them on PBS." Radical critics attacked the show for promulgating racist notions by showcasing novels whose subject was "the faded glory of the British empire."[6] "Master Race Theatre," they called it. Timothy Brennan, a Marxist professor at MIT, published an essay on *Masterpiece* in 1989 that strongly influenced academic thought about period dramas for years to come. Calling *Masterpiece* a "tawdry fabrication of a BBC education," he argued the program purported to educate Americans while "really schooling them in the upper-class manners of white supremacists." Like other critics, Brennan delighted in bashing Alistair Cooke, "whose image of posh, white intellectualism is appalling."[7]

The "canon wars," as they came to be called, played no small role in shutting down period drama production. By 1990, the BBC and *Masterpiece* had shifted their dramatic focus to contemporary fiction like *Traffik* (1990) and *House of Cards* (1991). They also ventured into producing adaptations of American classics, such as Edith Wharton's *The Buccaneers* (1995). But while these new series earned acclaim, they undermined the program itself. Longtime fans of the program, while expressing admiration for the stories, nevertheless wanted the "old *Masterpiece Theatre* back." As one fan put it, "I tune into *Masterpiece Theatre* to see Elizabeth Bennett, not Huck Finn. And if I want a slick modern-day drama, I'll go to cable television, thank you very much."[8] Another lesson: the delivery of British classics is the heart and soul of *Masterpiece*; get rid of them, and you've gutted the show.

It was Andrew Davies's cheeky adaptations that saved period drama and reenergized *Masterpiece*. His bold rewriting of *Pride and Prejudice* in 1995 almost singlehandedly created "Austenmania" both here and in the UK. He would soon go on to popularize many classic authors, including Dickens, Elizabeth Gaskell, George Eliot, and the improbable Anthony Trollope. The key to his success? Davies made classic fiction into what he called "stories about you and me." Adapting Austen was no longer about getting culture; it was about finding personal relevance. Other screenwriters followed suit, rewriting classics like *Oliver Twist* (1999), *The Hound of the Baskervilles* (2002), and *Jane Eyre* (2007) by adding sequels, shock effects, and sex. As one *Boston Globe* critic put it, "This new drama isn't your mother's *Masterpiece*."[9]

By the late 1990s, *Masterpiece* was actively responding to the cultural changes taking place in America and elsewhere, trying to target a younger audience, loosen up its cultural appeal, and make period dramas *au courant*. But it had yet to tackle what was becoming more and more obvious to critics: the whiteness of its characters and cast.

IN BLACK AND WHITE

In April 2019, *Masterpiece* aired Davies's full-on, bet-the-house adaptation of Victor Hugo's 1862 novel *Les Misérables*. If ever a novel had the heft of high culture, it is Hugo's. To begin, there is the sheer, staggering length of it; *Les Misérables* is five volumes, 365 chapters, and roughly 1,500 pages long. Adding to its highbrow creds is the novel's historical and thematic sweep. Spanning 1817 to 1832, *Les Misérables* covers the history of France, religion, politics, slavery, the Battle of Waterloo, moral philosophy, and antimonarchism, taking Moby Dick–like detours to meditate on topics like street urchins and Paris sewers. Upton Sinclair called it "one of the half-dozen greatest novels of the world" and G. K. Chesterton pronounced it "a masterpiece of historical fiction."

If *Les Misérables* had aired on *Masterpiece* in the 1970s, it would have followed the book with painstaking fidelity. Alistair Cooke would have introduced it with a five-minute lecture each week, making sure to tell us how, during the Civil War, Confederate soldiers carried around installments of the novel and renamed themselves "Lee's Miserables." Critics, no doubt, would have rhapsodized about how *Les Misérables* was smartening up the television landscape. If a version of the novel had aired in the 1980s or 1990s, it might well have come under attack for perpetuating the dead-white-men club. And if an adaptation appeared in the early 2000s, the critical buzz might have been on its bold departures from the original story.

In a Brexit/Trump era where reports of racial tension come up daily in Britain and America, it's no surprise that the talk about *Les Misérables* was all about race. Director Tom Shankland helped engineer that. He insisted on incorporating a range of dialects and accents into the series. Dominic West used his thick Yorkshire accent to play the hero, Jean Paul Valjean, while Lily Collins employed her Cockney accent to portray Fantine. This calculated use of dialect markedly departs from previous period dramas, where "received pronunciation," or "the Queen's English," has dominated dialogue ever since the invention of sound. And yet less than 3 percent of the country's population speaks this way. "In Britain," Shankland says, "there are class divisions that we perceive on the basis of accents. I thought a costume drama should address this head-on for once." Shankland's bolder change was to populate the series with actors of color. "We live in a society that looks like this, so therefore to make a 150-year-old novel feel like it's relevant to everyone here you want to see yourself in it," he said.[10] His most radical decision was to cast Nigerian-born actor David Oyelowo, a classically trained stage actor, as Javert, the novel's police chief and principal antagonist.

Shankland's choice of Oyelowo followed the BBC's highly publicized commitment to casting 15 percent more black and ethnic-minority actors by 2020. No doubt, the BBC is responding to the fact that many black actors have spoken out against the dearth of opportunities afforded them in period drama. In an interview with the *Telegraph* in 2017, *Westworld* star Thandie Newton lamented that she has been forced to look to Hollywood because she can't find enough rewarding work in Britain. "I can't do *Downton Abbey*, can't be in *Victoria*, can't be in *Call the Midwife*—well, I could, but I don't want to play someone who's being racially abused," she said.[11]

One answer to this dilemma is "color-conscious casting:" the practice of using an actor's skin color as an intentional, strategic part of a performance's meaning. Theater has been doing color-conscious casting for years (Denzel Washington as Hickey in *The Iceman Cometh*, Jordan Donica as Freddy in *My Fair Lady*, and the entire cast of *Hamilton* are recent examples). It seems film and TV are finally catching up. The 2018 film *Mary Queen of Scots* features a racially diverse cast as does the BBC's new adaptation of *David Copperfield* (2020) starring Dev Patel, a Brit of Indian heritage, in the titular role.

Color-conscious casting can open up stories in exciting ways, reinterpreting characters and expanding roles beyond how they may have been written or traditionally portrayed. As one actor says, the practice "acknowledges the differences that we see and experience daily and asks, how can these differences enhance the story?"[12] But it also raises questions about period drama's and *Masterpiece*'s mission to maintain continuity with the past. There is no question that assigning a black actor to a historically white role misrepresents history, as critics of *Les Misérables* have maintained. And in an era increasingly defined by its disconnection from the past, can we really afford such misrepresentations? Can *Masterpiece*?

The answer must be yes. Seeing Oyelowo play Javert is to watch a brilliant actor inhabit a complex role, and to feel thrilled by—and grateful for— the experience. (Isn't that the point of acting, after all: to suspend audience disbelief to the point of personal reinvention?) At the same time, watching Oyelowo play Javert also means witnessing a profound reversal of power that adds another layer to our appreciation of the story; here a black man tyrannizes a white one, assuming all the accoutrements of authority that would never have been his in early nineteenth-century France. It's a fascinating turnaround. And on another level, seeing Oyelowo star in *Les Misérables* is to recognize, viscerally, the deep-dyed whiteness of period drama. This effect brings a new critical awareness to the genre, promising to redefine *Masterpiece* in important ways.

At the same time, it would be a mistake not to proceed script by script, considering all factors before settling on the use of color-conscious casting. Period drama has a duty to history as well as to storytelling, as its creators well know. And as we'll see in chapter 5, the genre has recently become America's most promising venue for teaching people, especially young people, about the past. That responsibility matters, especially when the drama is produced by public television.

HEADING DOWNSTREAM

What does this overview tell us? One answer is that even quiet venues like *Masterpiece* can become front-page arenas for political battles. Who'd have thought that a show specializing in British period drama could join with so many red-hot American issues, from the oil crisis of the 1970s to debates about curricula in the 1990s to our current conversations about racial inclusion? *Masterpiece* may have emerged in 1971 as an escape from politics, but politics found it nevertheless.

Several years ago, conservative publisher and writer Andrew Breitbart remarked, "Politics is downstream from culture," by which he meant that the two are always entwined—and that if you wish to change politics, you change the culture first. In our current moment, politics *is* culture, informing every aspect of our arts-and-entertainment industry, from standup comedy to sculpture. *Masterpiece* is now part of this phenomenon, as the intentions behind *Les Misérables* clearly suggest. And while this is a positive development in many ways, it can also subvert the program's traditional call to find our shared human values—those that cut across racial, class, and gender divides—in the stories we tell and experience. How do you reconcile these two? It's a Gordian challenge, one not only facing *Masterpiece* but the whole of American society as the former works upstream of the latter.

The censures and blowups behind *Masterpiece*'s appeal are crucial to its history, reminding us that tradition has its dark sides. But for the rest of this book, we'll focus on sunnier matters. We'll explore what delights, moves, and inspires viewers about *Masterpiece*, looking at the program's most winning aspects—from its blue-chip performances to its spectacular locales. So let's begin with *Masterpiece*'s beloved adaptations of classic literature, jumping back to shortly before the show's relaunch in 2008, when everything was resting on Jane Austen.

Loving Literature

TWO SCENES ADAPTED FROM LIFE (MORE OR LESS)

*L*ondon, 2006. As he picked up his copy of the script for *Sense and Sensibility*, British actor Dan Stevens was nervous. A few days before, he had been cast as Edward Ferrars, the diffident love interest of Austen's heroine, Elinor Dashwood. Stevens had been over the moon about the role, but now that it was time to settle down and learn his lines, he could feel himself getting anxious.

Watching television in his redbrick home in the English midlands, seventy-year-old Andrew Davies was nervous, too. He was worrying about the script he sent off to the BBC a few weeks before. This was his first adaptation of an Austen novel since *Pride and Prejudice* in 1995, and he was competing with director Ang Lee's 1996 film version of *Sense and Sensibility*, scripted by the brilliant Emma Thompson and beloved by millions.

At twenty-eight, Stevens was only two years into his acting career, and a lot was riding on this adaptation. The BBC had high hopes it would outshine every one of the three Austen adaptations produced one year before by its competitor ITV. What's more, Rebecca Eaton at *Masterpiece* had selected *Sense and Sensibility* as part of a showcase series, *The Complete Jane Austen*. And Edward Ferrars was a tough role. Hugh Grant had played him in Lee's *Sense and Sensibility* and had come across as stiff and stuffed, causing one reviewer to quip, "a taxidermist could not have done better."[1]

In writing *Sense and Sensibility*, Davies's instinct had been to ramp up the sexual tension between the main couples and "fix the men," addressing head-on the problem of Austen's male protagonists not being romantic or virile enough for modern audiences. It had worked for *Pride and Prejudice*. But with *Sense and Sensibility*, Davies had taken bigger risks, such as putting an explicit seduction scene right at the beginning of the story and inventing a clutch of new, testosterone-charged scenes for the male characters. He'd boasted to the press about how his goal was to "make people forget the Ang Lee version." But could he really do it?[2]

As Stevens read through the screenplay, he was surprised by how much of the dialogue came straight from Austen without feeling staid. He smiled when he saw that Davies had added a wood-chopping scene for Edward. And he was especially struck by Davies's stage directions, indicating that the screenwriter, unlike Austen, thought Elinor recognized Edward's weaknesses, felt her compromise in loving him, and hoped he'd man up. In one direction Davies wrote, "Elinor looks at Edward as if to say, 'Oh, for fuck's sake.'" Stevens laughed aloud when he read it, his nervousness subsiding.

Davies's *Sense and Sensibility* fared well in the UK and America, capping off *Masterpiece*'s winter-long homage to Austen with solid ratings. It won high marks for Stevens, whose "sexy and redeeming performance" of Edward Ferrars would land him the role of Matthew Crawley in *Downton Abbey*. The adaptation also earned praise for its "frankness," "spontaneity," and the way it told a "truly dark tale of poverty and desertion" while capturing the ordered loveliness of Austen's world.[3] But Davies's *Sense and Sensibility* also nettled some viewers and enraged others. Many bristled at his invented scenes, finding them a "presumptuous addition." And many more grumbled over how Davies had "sexed up" the novel generally. Pronouncing it "raunchy," the Jane Austen Society accused Davies of doing nothing less than "degrading the canon of fine English literature."[4]

Over the years, *Masterpiece* has featured many adaptations of beloved novels like *Sense and Sensibility*. These dramas reinforce *Masterpiece*'s traditional appeal. They align television with the hallowed medium of British literature, and they allow us to experience, or re-experience, a classic story. In remaking these stories for television, adaptations blend the comfort of conventionality with the stir of surprise. Watching them, we indulge in the pleasures of remembrance while witnessing the changes that one writer, confronting the work of another, must make to suit his medium and audience. But adaptation is a tricky and dangerous road to navigate, beset by industry pressures, fan prejudices, nationalist concerns, and cultural debates. It's enough to make any writer, even Davies, throw up his hands and say, "Oh, for fuck's sake."

MASTER ADAPTERS

Since its beginnings, British television has enjoyed an enviable aura of literary respectability, especially when compared to its American counterpart. One reason for this is the BBC remit to feature "great literature" in order to further the public good. A deeper reason is that the Brits have a profound respect for written language, priding themselves on having produced much of the world's most celebrated fiction, poetry, and drama. Literature is vital to the country's heritage, just as the pursuit of liberty is to ours. Originating from this tradition, British television has inevitably assumed its own literate status and proclivities.

Unlike America, England possesses a distinct canon of authors—Shakespeare, Austen, the Brontës, Dickens, Hardy—whose writings are as essential to its national identity as a stiff upper lip. This solid substratum continues to retain its cultural force, even as more and more authors (Hilary Mantel, Zadie Smith, J. K. Rowling) are recognized as representative voices, too. With its big-budget, epic adaptations, especially those produced by the BBC, television has played no small role in this phenomenon.

Given this rich ancestry, it's natural that so many of television's screenwriters have an uncanny knack for adapting literature, even the longest, knottiest, most lugubrious of novels. They also enjoy more respect from the studios and companies that employ them than do their poor American peers. In Britain, screenwriters tend to be cosseted and indulged, sometimes even solicited for their suggestions on what to adapt. This is especially true now, as television enjoys unprecedented prestige. American screenwriters, while faring better than they did before television's renaissance, still have to submit to endless review committees and interference by know-it-all producers and directors. By contrast, screenwriters in the UK enjoy an almost auteur-like status.

Several writers have strongly influenced the success or development of *Masterpiece*. Among them are Heidi Thomas, who adapted *Masterpiece*'s *Cranford* (2007–2009) and *Little Women* (2018) as well as PBS's *Call the Midwife*; Sandy Welch, who has authored a string of *Masterpiece* series based on classic novels, including *Our Mutual Friend* (1998), *Jane Eyre* (2006), and *Emma* (2010); Clive Exton, who adapted twenty-one episodes of the *Poirot* miniseries for *Mystery!* (1989–2001) and twenty-three episodes of *Jeeves and Wooster* (1990–1993); Jack Pulman, whose adaptations for *Masterpiece* include *The Golden Bowl* (1973), *I, Claudius* (1977–1978), and *Crime and Punishment* (1980); Sally Wainwright, who adapted *The Amazing Mrs. Pritchard* (2006) and *Unforgotten* (2018) and wrote her own biopic of the Brontë sisters, *To Walk Invisible* (2016); and, most important, Andrew Davies, who has written a whopping twenty-four classic adaptations, nineteen of which have appeared on *Masterpiece*. Like Davies, most of these writers are also authors of original plays and novels. And a goodly number of them "read English," as the Brits say, for their undergraduate or graduate degrees. Books are in their bones.

This literary bent is fundamental to *Masterpiece*'s appeal. Though it features original series like *Downton Abbey* and *Beecham House* (2020), *Masterpiece*'s bulwark has always been the literary adaptation. In fact, the program averages 60 percent more adaptations than original dramas. Roughly two-thirds of these adaptations are based on literary classics; the rest are retellings of contemporary novels like Julian Barnes's *Arthur and George* (2015), Ian McEwan's *The Child in Time* (2017), and Jesse Burton's *The Miniaturist* (2018). Some *Masterpiece* series, like *Poldark* (2015–2019), adapt popular fiction. But just as many, if not more, adapt "literary" fiction—prize-winning, critically acclaimed novels known for their complex probing of inner psychology. These adaptations, such as Peter Straughan's *Wolf Hall* (2017), lend *Masterpiece* an aura of literary artistry and intelligence. When these novels happen to be classics, *Masterpiece*'s adaptations also offer continuity with the past.

Over the years, some critics have grumbled that *Masterpiece*'s heavy reliance on adaptations is a sign of its snobbery. Others wonder about the enterprise of adapting literature rather than promoting original drama. Some question the value of producing another version of a well-worn novel when so many excellent, unadapted stories are out there. And some individuals regard adaptations as simply drama, a derivative retelling of someone else's story.

Adaptation, however, is always an interpretive and creative act. It can revitalize a novel or give us new ways of thinking about it—and sometimes, it even improves the original story. Sandy Welch adapted *Masterpiece*'s *Jane Eyre* (2006) by releasing the repressed, sexual tensions of the novel, using flashbacks that show Jane and Rochester kissing on Jane's bed and Bertha Mason, Rochester's libido-charged wife, committing vigorous adultery. Andrew Davies heard about a scrap of paper tucked away in E. M. Forster's desk that imagined a sequel to *A Room with a View*. In a few sentences, Forster had sketched out how the novel's hero, George, dies in World War I, leaving his young and ebullient wife, Lucy, devastated. Forster never wrote the sequel. Davies did, and his *Masterpiece* adaptation of *A Room with a View* (2007) adds a layer of sad fragility to one of literature's most radiant but immature romances.

No medium adapts literature, especially the long, detailed novels of the nineteenth century, better than television. Novels have to be shoehorned into two-hour movies. But a TV series can run for multiple episodes over weeks, even months. Davies's adaptation of *Masterpiece*'s *Bleak House* (2005), for example, retells Dickens's ambitious story, with its cast of nearly one hundred characters and intertwined subplots, over the course of sixteen thirty-minute episodes.[5] Davies made the episodes short to speed up the pace, intensify the cliffhangers, and keep audiences hooked. "The thing that was uppermost in our minds," he explained in an interview, "was to tell the story in a way that made people absolutely die to know what happens next."[6] That ambition is a very Victorian one, given how most nineteenth-century novels were serialized over weeks and months, leaving readers "dying to know" what would happen in the following installment. In this way, too, *Masterpiece*'s adaptations provide continuity with the past.

Contrary to common wisdom, the success of an adaptation doesn't hang on how faithful it is to the book. It depends on finding its own, sure point between fidelity and innovation. From its beginnings, *Masterpiece*'s series have leaned toward fidelity, in keeping with the program's traditional appeal and the BBC's remit of providing educative value. But this doesn't mean we can't see a radical shift over the years in *Masterpiece*'s approach to delivering the classics. During the 1970s, *Masterpiece* adaptations tended to be scrupulously faithful to the novels, sometimes to the point of drowning them in formaldehyde. Series like *Jude the Obscure* (1974) or *Our Mutual Friend* (1978) reproduced plotlines and scenes exactly. Their dialogue came verbatim from the books, with no effort to update language for a modern audience. Actors declaimed their lines as if onstage, rarely moving their bodies, apart from their hands and heads. No one watches these adaptations anymore, and no one should.

During the 1980s, with the help of bigger budgets and new technologies, classic adaptations assumed a whole new look and feel. *Brideshead Revisited* (1981) is a far more extroverted adaptation than any of those we see from the 1970s, borne on cumulus clouds of big budgets and cinematic-style filmmaking. It also goes outdoors, showing Britain's great real estate and scenery; it gives us a classic novel and a mini-travelogue of England. And thanks to writers like Davies, adaptation started taking more liberties with classic novels by the mid-1990s. It had to. By this point, classic adaptations had fallen out of favor as viewers turned to more contemporary, darker, pumped-up fare. This was also the decade that saw a vigorous protest against the canon of "dead white men." If the BBC was going to adapt a novel by Dickens or Austen, it needed to inject it with a modern feel.

Since then, a floodtide of new dramas has emerged that takes bold, often audacious approaches to adaptation. HBO, Netflix, Hulu, Starz: they're all in the game now, releasing their own retellings of classics like *Vanity Fair* (2018), *Catch-22* (2019), *The ABC Murders* (2019), and *Lord of the Rings* (2021). The guiding principle in these dramas isn't fidelity; it's *relevance*, the idea being to make classic stories as relatable to our lives as possible.

Within this new climate, *Masterpiece* still maintains a conservative position. It certainly has produced some cheeky retellings: witness *Sherlock* (2010–2017) or *House of Cards* (1991), the BBC miniseries whose audacious breaking of the fourth wall inspired the Netflix version twenty-three years later. But to veer too far from the novels would undermine the humanist, traditional values the program celebrates.

The essayist Phillip Lopate asks, "Is there something unstoppably human about wanting to see a book faithfully represented onscreen?"[7] For many *Masterpiece* viewers, the answer is yes. Partly, this has to do with the traditional idea that our best books need to be re-experienced, intact, for the future. But it also has to do with love. Faithful adaptations are acts of love, reminding us that the world of books is a deeply romantic one. Sure, we respond to novels intellectually. But deep down, it is our emotional connection to literature that matters most to us. We "fall in love" with our books, describing them in language of infatuation, seduction, intimacy, and devotion. It's almost impossible to imagine the act of reading without such words.

In her astounding cultural history *Loving Literature*, Deidre Shauna Lynch shows us that this wasn't always the case. "Loving literature," it turns out, has a history. For a long time, people didn't love literature; they *used* it—to court women, make speeches, persuade would-be allies, dodge creditors. Literature was part of a civic-minded sensibility that depended on effective rhetoric, so people turned to books for advice, wisdom, and lines they could steal. They read with their heads, not their hearts. It was the establishment of the literary canon in the nineteenth century that changed all this, making literature into an object of tender regard for the first time. No passage captures this new view of reading better than the one below from Dickens's *David Copperfield*, itself one of the most beloved novels of all time. Here, David writes tenderly about how his dead father's "small collection of books" eased the pain of his lonely childhood:

> From that blessed little room, Roderick Random, Peregrine Pickle, Humphrey Clinker, Tom Jones, the Vicar of Wakefield, Don Quixote, Gil Blas, and Robinson Crusoe, came out, a glorious host, to keep me company. They kept alive my fancy, and my hope of something beyond that place and time. . .
>
> This was my only and constant comfort. When I think of it, the picture always rises in my mind, of a summer evening, the boys at play in the churchyard, and I sitting on my bed, reading as if for life.[8]

Passages like this one transformed reading into a deeply nostalgic act, with readers "striving," as Lynch puts it, "to bridge the distance" between themselves and others, present and past. In this new age of loving literature, the most important books were those that endured beyond the era in which they were produced. And their most devoted readers were sensitive, soulful sorts like David Copperfield.[9]

Following this tender tradition, *Masterpiece*'s scriptwriters are careful not to alter original novels too much, for fear not only of alienating viewers but also destroying the whole romance of reading. That's why *Masterpiece* leans toward faithful retellings, indulging in the pleasures of nostalgia and conventionality. It knows that whatever it may lack in originality, it makes up for in love. (*Masterpiece*, by the way, aired a very traditional adaptation of *David Copperfield* in 2000, starring Maggie Smith, Bob Hoskins, and a ten-year-old Daniel Radcliffe. Replete with delightfully comic and heartbreaking performances, it plays like one long love letter to Dickens.)

There are two bodies of classic English fiction that American audiences particularly revere. We reread them regularly, join their fan clubs, parade around as their characters, make pilgrimages to the places they feature, and write fiction inspired by them. And when a new adaptation of them arrives, we approach it with a truly weird mixture of wild ecstasy and deep skepticism. One is Arthur Conan Doyle's collection of Sherlock Holmes stories; the other is the novels of Jane Austen. These works offer a wealth of traditional appeals. In Doyle's stories, we escape into a cozy world of Victorian crime, always assured justice will triumph in the end. In Austen's novels, we find the old-fashioned pleasures of sociability, decorum, and romance. Yet for all their old-fashioned elements, Holmes and Austen are remarkably easy to modernize. And in their long adaptational history, few productions, if any, have rivaled those done by *Masterpiece*.

THE CASE OF SHERLOCK HOLMES

Ever since the Philadelphia-based magazine *Lippincott's* first published *The Sign of Four* in 1890, Sherlock Holmes has attracted a huge American fan base. Just ask basketball great Kareem Abdul-Jabbar, a self-proclaimed Sherlockian, who published his own novel, *Mycroft Holmes*, in 2018. Reading the Holmes stories for the first time on a San Diego beach when the Lakers were playing the Rockets, Abdul-Jabbar says the detective taught him how to become a courtside sleuth. "Holmes saw clues where other people saw nothing. I try to do the same thing, figuring out a player's weaknesses. I make deductions."[10]

Abdul-Jabbar loves the BBC adaptation *Sherlock*, which aired on *Masterpiece* from 2010 to 2017. Winner of seven Emmy awards and a string of others, its claim to the "best-ever Holmes adaptation" is challenged only by another PBS production: the *Sherlock Holmes* series, which aired on *Masterpiece*'s sister show *Mystery!* between 1984 and 1995. Produced by Granada Television in conjunction with *Mystery!*, that series also won a heap of awards and attracted millions of American fans, including the improbable crew of Gloria Steinem, Barbara Bush, Jimmy Carter, and Hugh Hefner. Adaptations *extraordinaire*, each of these series took its own pioneering approach to reinventing Holmes for the TV screen.

VICTORIAN VERACITY

When director/producer Michael Cox got the idea to create a Sherlock Holmes series in 1981, he knew one thing: he wanted it to be the "definitive version." His first thought was to hire John Hawkesworth, the writer/producer whose scrupulous attention to period detail in *Upstairs, Downstairs* had made him an industry legend. Sherlock enthusiasts both, Cox and Hawkesworth sat down one rainy afternoon in Cox's London flat, and over the course of several hours and "endless rounds of Darjeeling tea," worked out their vision for the series. They would shoot all fifty-six original stories and four novellas over the course of ten years, aiming to provide a visual equivalent to the Holmes canon. And making use of television's bigger budgets and new technologies, they would achieve what Cox called "a whole new level of historical authenticity."[11]

In truth, Cox's attention to period detail (a term that includes setting, location, props, costume, styling, dialogue, speech, diction, music, and the deportment and movement of actors) bordered on the fanatical. Choosing 1890 as their historical anchor, he and his team did a whole-hog investigation into the London of that year, studying maps, contemporary photographs, old street directories, and Harrod's catalogues. They closely followed the architectural principles of the 1890s in constructing the houses and shops of their Baker Street set (maybe the largest and most expensive TV set to date), even to the point of choosing tarmacadam over the more picturesque cobblestone because, as Cox explained, "it was what was being used that year." Holmes's rooms were an almost exact reconstruction of how they appeared within the pages of *The Strand* magazine during the 1890s, right down to the unanswered letters Holmes nailed to his mantelpiece with a dagger. Cox even wrote a handbook, *The Baker Street File*, of twelve hundred items related to the stories and their era. He distributed it to every member of the cast and crew, insisting they consult it regularly. Now housed in the British Library, it contains items as arcane as "dottle" (the foul-smelling, charred tobacco found at the bottom of a smoked pipe) and "Dewar flask" (an insulating storage thermos invented in 1892).[12]

Historical accuracy was paramount for Cox. The more important goal for Hawkesworth was to retell the Doyle stories faithfully while adding plenty of dramatic punch. The screenwriter flatly rejected the idea of pastiche, choosing instead to adapt the Holmes canon tale by tale. And he instructed writers to keep a good balance between action and inaction. For example, they chose scenes where Holmes carefully studies a new visitor to his rooms and then tells Watson, in extraordinary detail, what he has deduced about the person. Other writers might have shuttled these scenes, but as Jeremy Brett, the actor who played Sherlock Holmes, explained, "They underscore why Holmes is still unsurpassed as a detective."[13] More importantly, they are a key convention in the Holmes canon, stamping each and every story. Audiences love these scenes because, like adaptation itself, they blend repetition with variation.

To balance such dialogue-heavy moments, the writers chose to dramatize those sensational events that Doyle left off the printed page. One example is the climactic struggle at Reichenbach Falls, Switzerland, where Holmes and his arch-nemesis, Dr. Moriarty, fall to their apparent deaths in "The Final Problem." Using the big budget available to him (augmented by *Mystery!*'s coproduction funding), Cox chose to film the scene on location. He hired England's two best stuntmen to fall from a height of 430 feet, suspended only by a thin steel cable. Even today, it is a breathtaking moment. Back in 1985, it was widely hailed as one of the most astonishing stunts ever seen on film or television. Byron Rogers of the *New York Times* called it "the best fall ever filmed, much better than Butch Cassidy and Sundance, whirling arms in the spray, capes flapping. God knows how they did it."[14]

But let's be honest: the stories themselves matter little in the end. A Holmes adaptation lives or dies by the portrayal of its star detective and his sidekick. In the case of both, as the *Chicago Tribune* put it, the series was a "revelation."[15] Teed off by Watson's buffoonish treatment in earlier versions, Cox and Hawkesworth resolved that their series would restore the good doctor to his original characterization as a solid, reliable fellow of considerable intelligence and no small amount of courage. And so it did. Played by David Burke in Season 1 and Sir Edward Hardwicke for subsequent seasons, Watson is a kind and caring man who tried to keep Holmes off cocaine (*A Scandal in Bohemia*) and who would stand in for him at a moment's notice (*The Hound of the Baskervilles*), even if it meant having to scale a wall while running from the police (*The Master Blackmailer*). Using just the right mixture of sentimentality and reserve, the portrayal of Watson and Holmes's friendship may be the single best part of the series. It set a template for many British detective dramas to come, including *Inspector Morse*, *Endeavour*, *Grantchester*, and *Sherlock*, all of which are essays on male friendship.

On January 25, 1996, four months after he died at age fifty-nine, Jeremy Brett appeared on *Mystery!* for the forty-first and last time. Obituaries running in the States all spoke to how the actor had emerged in America's cultural imagination as *the* Sherlock Holmes. The *New York Times* pronounced him "The actor that wiped the memory clean of all previous portrayals of Sherlock Holmes." The *Los Angeles Times* concurred, saying, "He will go down in history as the best-remembered Sherlock Holmes."[16]

A well-known stage performer with a chiseled face and tall, lean build, Brett bore a striking resemblance to the original Sidney Paget illustrations of

Holmes in the *Strand* magazine. He also had the elegance, grace, and aristocratic air that the legendary detective possesses. And as the rest of the cast and crew soon discovered, Brett was a resolute perfectionist. It was he who became the official defender of Doyle's words, forbidding any change that somehow contradicted the original characterization. History has it that Brett carried a copy of Doyle's complete works around with him wherever he went, and even wrote his own handbook on Holmes (one wonders what Cox's handbook could have missed). If Brett saw something in the scripts that didn't seem right, he immediately went to the original story to see how Doyle handled it.

This is not to say that Brett didn't add his own distinctive touches. One was sex appeal. Long before Benedict Cumberbatch's aqua-eyed, lithesome incarnation inspired a legion of female fans to pronounce themselves "Cumberbitches," Brett's Sherlock Holmes mesmerized millions of women, turned on by the combination of the actor's ravishing good looks and his character's aloofness. "They get obsessive, ringing me up, grabbing me, sending me all sorts of presents," said Brett. One resourceful American fan tracked down the actor's London apartment, proposing marriage to him dressed as Watson.[17]

Brett was also the first major actor to give a dark-hued portrayal of Holmes, seen right from the opening episode, *A Scandal in Bohemia*. Entering Holmes's rooms, Watson finds his friend sitting alone and morose in front of the fire. On a nearby table, Watson spies a hypodermic needle and asks disapprovingly, "What is it tonight—morphine or cocaine?" "I can strongly recommend a seven percent solution of cocaine," says Holmes. "Would you care to try it?" Watson berates him, but it's of no use. "I abhor the dull routine of existence," Holmes replies. For all his talents, Holmes is a lonely, unfulfilled man who suffers from perpetual restlessness. Brett therefore inflected each performance with nervous energy. It's there in all his actions, from his finger drumming to his sudden exclamations to the way he shifts in his chair, hunching his legs one moment, splaying them the next. Even in those episodes that adopt a lighthearted tone, Brett's Sherlock always seems tortured by his own psyche.

In real life, Jeremy Brett was witty and garrulous, a real charmer who could walk into a roomful of strangers and make friends immediately. But he suffered from bipolar disorder, exacerbated by the untimely death of his wife, *Masterpiece*'s Joan Wilson. She died of cancer the same year that *Sherlock Holmes* debuted on *Mystery!* Grieving and lonely, Brett experienced recurring nightmares about Holmes, whom he referred to as "my deranged penguin" and "the man without a heart." "Holmes is a very difficult man to live inside of," Brett confessed to a journalist. "He's obsessive, and he's dazzling, and I became very weary in my psyche, in my head."[18] The stress of playing Holmes even landed Brett in a mental hospital for several weeks (and as Brett lovingly recalled, it was Edward Hardwicke—his best friend onscreen and off—who picked him up from the hospital and took him out for wine and pasta).

As any fan of the series will admit, the quality of the *Sherlock Holmes* series took a visible downturn in its last few years. One reason was Brett's health. The drugs he took to combat his depression gradually weakened his heart, making him seem tired and frail onscreen, his face and body bloated. He valiantly struggled through the last six episodes, almost unable to move.

Also contributing to the show's decline was Granada's decision to curtail the series' budget. Although *Sherlock Holmes* was doing consistently well in the ratings, executives ordered its new producer, Joan Wyndham Davies, to limit rehearsals, film scenes more quickly, and cut spending on props in order to create bigger profits for the studio. As a consequence, the late episodes are noticeably sloppy, with slapdash editing and incoherent plotlines.

Big changes in the television industry also impacted the show. By the early 1990s, television had become a global market aimed at capturing an international audience. Within this new landscape, Cox's original mission to offer the "definitive version" of Sherlock Holmes, assuming as it did a body of viewers who knew the stories intimately and had an eye for historical detail, no longer made the same sense. *Sherlock Holmes* needed adjusting. Wyndham Davies therefore advised writers to add new content to the stories, punching them up with more action and melodrama. But by this point, the show's writers had lost their direction. They were also frustrated that the best stories in the Holmes canon had already been adapted, leaving them with the clunkers. The series ended a mess—but it had achieved such excellence in its first six years that fans and critics alike now tend to remember the show only in glowing terms. As they should.

"KING OF THE NERDS"

Sometime in 2002, while riding the train from London to their scriptwriting jobs at BBC Wales in Cardiff, Mark Gatiss and Steven Moffat lit on the idea of modernizing Sherlock Holmes. The Granada series, they thought, was "too reverential and too slow" for the current generation of TV viewers. Their idea was to "remove the filter of a misty London, full of hansom cabs and gas-lamps" and place Holmes squarely in the contemporary, high-tech world of the city. At first, the idea seemed like heresy, bound to infuriate fans. But the more they discussed it, the stronger its hold became.[19]

They decided to float the idea past the Sherlock Holmes Society in London, where Gatiss had been invited to speak. After assuring the audience of his and Moffat's "lifelong interest" in Holmes, Gatiss explained that their detective would be a "geeky, nervous young man rather too fond of drugs, who's amassed a lot of out-of-the-way knowledge on his laptop."[20] Watson, he added, would be a young army doctor just out of Afghanistan, alone and friendless in London—waiting, like Doyle's character, for someone to add zest to his life.

Gatiss breathed deeply and then sat back to hear his audience's reaction. Sherlockians are a mistrustful bunch, used to seeing one adaptation after another misfire and bomb. But the response among those present that night was encouraging. Everyone agreed that the idea was dicey, but it was also smart, funny, and very original. Gatiss and Moffat exchanged looks. The game was afoot.

Sherlock premiered on *Masterpiece* in October 2010. Starring Benedict Cumberbatch and Martin Freeman, it was an instant hit in the United States and a huge boost to *Masterpiece*'s ratings. "The appeal is elementary," said the *New York Times*. "It is good, unpretentious fun, something that's in short supply around here." *Slant* magazine observed, "It may be a contemporary update, but they [Moffat and Gatiss] have simply, and very successfully, lifted Doyle's characters out of the Victorian era and dropped them unchanged into present-day London." And the *Atlantic* praised the series for "staying ahead of its contemporary peers in its nods at the war in Afghanistan and British surveillance policy, its social comedy of friendship and attraction, its progress from the city's galleries to its underpasses. It is a brilliant series from first shot to last."[21]

Americans had been primed for *Sherlock*'s arrival. Several adaptations had just come out boldly recasting Holmes. In 2009, novelist Lyndsay Faye published a runaway bestseller called *Dust and Shadow*, which pitted the detective against Jack the Ripper. That same year, director Guy Ritchie released his film *Sherlock Holmes* (2009), starring Robert Downey Jr. and Jude Law as scrappy, action-hero versions of the duo. *Sherlock* slipped right into this milieu, the latest and best of these brazen rewritings. Drawing on Gatiss's and Moffat's experience writing for *Dr. Who*, the series brought a can-do, boys' adventure spirit to the stories, making Holmes and his sidekick younger than most earlier versions. In vivid contrast to the "let's-get-this-absolutely-right" approach of the Granada series, *Sherlock* also displayed a kind of offhand virtuosity, as if all its clever elements were simply the result of trying to keep up with its brilliant detective. And it turned Holmes into a digital junkie who used GPS, texting, and Google to solve crimes. As one critic puts it, "BBC's Holmes profits from the free availability of information to find new ways to be bored and more time to be bored in."[22]

All these changes were designed to capture a young audience—and sure enough, teenagers and twenty-somethings turned out to be *Sherlock*'s most important demographic.

These young fans studied the show with fanatical attention, tweeted and hashtagged and Instagrammed about it, penned their own fan fiction based on its plotlines and characters, and wore t-shirts that proclaimed "Smart Is the New Sexy." Some fans in America followed a Twitter hashtag—#setlock—that crowd-sourced information about filming locations. Others would patiently wait for an American tour of the *Sherlock* cast, standing in line for 24, 30, 36 hours just to catch a glimpse of Freeman or Cumberbatch. And when one of them arrived: Beatlemania.

After the finale of Season 2, where Holmes falls off a building to his apparent death, *Sherlock* buffs teamed up on the Internet to solve the mystery of how the series would bring its detective back—even creating a Google street map that allowed them to test their various hypotheses. In a meta-ish twist, *Sherlock* pays homage to these fans by making them characters in the first episode of Season 3. They meet in a support group, using hashtags like #sherlocklives and exchanging theories about how Holmes could have survived the fall. The episode's opening is a classic piece of narrative trickery: we watch Holmes escape, with Bond-like bravura and a long, deep kiss for the woman who's been pining for him for two seasons, only to discover that the whole thing is one of the club members' theories. The device is an affectionate hat tip, an acknowledgment of how much the series owes to its fans. It's also an admission that the series itself is fan fiction, written by two men who, in their late forties at the time, still possessed the goofy exuberance of their youthful audience.[23]

Despite its very twenty-first-century sensibility, *Sherlock* somehow managed to capture the heart of the original stories. That was its genius, to be sure. Gleefully fannish, Gatiss and Moffat knew the Holmes canon inside and out, both of them drawn in as kids by the Basil Rathbone series. Only screenwriters like these two could have pulled off their particular type of adaptation, where each episode weaves in bits and bobs from as many as twenty different stories. They also played up the post-2001 relevance of original elements, like Moriarty's vast criminal network. And in stark contrast to the Granada *Sherlock Holmes*, they returned Holmes to the city. Granada had made it a point to shoot many of its episodes within England's grand estates and rural landscapes, but nearly every episode of *Sherlock* was set in London. "It's a hobby of mine," the original Sherlock says in "The Red-Headed League," "to have an exact knowledge of London." It was a hobby of Doyle's, too. He packed the stories with vivid details about the metropolis, so much so that readers might easily have imagined Holmes being just around the corner, riding in the next hansom cab. Similarly, *Sherlock* entwined its principal characters with London, rendering it a city of speed, gadgetry, and bright lights. In *Sherlock*, London is the city of the future, just as it must have seemed in Doyle's day, too.

Though *Sherlock*'s Holmes and Watson seem worlds away from the top-hat and tweed duo of Doyle's and Paget's imagination, they're the same under the skin. *Sherlock* casts Watson as a returning veteran, wounded in the leg and bored with civilian life, just as Doyle did. Martin Freeman plays Watson with the same kind of practical, questioning intelligence as Doyle's creation, though he gives him a wonderful puckishness that the original lacked. And like the original Watson, Freeman shows empathy for a man who really does act, sometimes, like a sociopath. By modernizing Holmes as a tech geek, *Sherlock* gets right to the heart of the original detective. The Holmes of Doyle's imagination possesses both a devotion to scientific knowledge and a mastery of trivia; what could be more suitable, then, than placing him squarely in the digital age?—an era when specialized, obsessive knowledge can make someone "King of the Nerds," as one fan calls Sherlock. Most importantly, *Sherlock* renders the friendship between Watson and Holmes with the same measure of affection, loyalty, and respect Doyle gave it.

Benedict Cumberbatch was indelible as Sherlock Holmes. Like Brett, Cumberbatch physically resembles the tall, lean Holmes of Paget's illustrations. "He does have the look," said Moffat of him, "that imperious style."[24] But while Brett gave Holmes psychological depth and intensity, slowly transforming him into a darker, more haunted character, Cumberbatch stays on the surface; his Holmes is more comic, almost cartoonish at times. He's also a bit of an action hero. Perhaps that's why Cumberbatch has been recruited for films like *Star Trek Into Darkness* (2013), and *Doctor Strange* (2016) since *Sherlock*'s debut. These days, Cumberbatch is his own phenomenon, inspiring adoring memes and selling out *Hamlet* a year in advance.

Sherlock faltered spectacularly in Season 4, as even its most devoted fans will admit. No doubt, one reason was the enormous pressure on Moffat and Gattis. The show had achieved such a staggering level of popularity that it became harder to sustain its genius. During Season 3, fans were also complaining loudly about its confusing plotlines, prompting Gatiss to nastily remark, "Go and read a children's book with hard pages if you don't want to be challenged. We're making the show we want to make. We don't make it a certain way because fans are pressuring us." Meanwhile, Cumberbatch and Freeman had shot into the stratosphere, in constant demand for television, film, and theatrical roles. The clogged schedules of each actor meant tight shooting schedules and rushed rehearsals, no doubt also affecting the show's quality.

Whatever the reasons, *Sherlock* spun out of control, its final episodes resisting all attempts to make sense of them. What had been a clever detective drama ultimately turned into a comic book fiasco, complete with improbable antagonists and a cringe-worthy, final showdown. But for three spectacular seasons, *Sherlock* was a celebration of the wit and intelligence that define *Masterpiece*—and a pure-gold standard for classic adaptation.

ANIMATING AUSTEN

"Every time I read *Pride and Prejudice*, I want to dig her up and hit her over the skull with her own shin-bone." This line is from that great American man of letters, Mark Twain, who trumpeted his hatred of Jane Austen every chance he got. Perhaps he was jealous. By the time Twain wrote that comment in 1898, Austen had already attracted a wildly devotional fan base in the States. Today, she's an American institution, thanks largely to Andrew Davies, the "King of Classic Adapters."

It is a truth universally acknowledged that Davies's 1995 version of *Pride and Prejudice* is the best dramatization of Austen's work ever to grace the screen, large or small. It perfectly captured the author's wit and irony, targeting her most despicable characters—shrill Mrs. Bennett, the odious Mr. Collins—with wicked glee. It captured Austen's delicate attention to social interactions while portraying Darcy and Elizabeth's relationship with just the right measure of sexual tension. And let's not forget the shirt. Davies's *Pride and Prejudice* also sent millions of women into a swoon by showing Mr. Darcy (Colin Firth) emerge from a lake in a clinging wet shirt (Firth later confessed he was too "prudish" to comply with Davies's original idea: to come out of that pond *au naturel*). *Pride and Prejudice* was Davies's first Austen adaptation, and along with Ang Lee's *Sense and Sensibility*, it launched an "Austenmania" here in the United States that lasted nearly twenty years. Since its release, Davies has adapted *Emma* with Kate Beckinsale (1996); *Bridget Jones's Diary* (a modern-day retelling of *Pride and Prejudice*) with Renée Zellweger (2001); *Northanger Abbey* (2007) and *Sense and Sensibility* (2008) for *Masterpiece*; and Austen's last, unfinished novel, *Sanditon* (2019).

What makes Davies so good at adapting Austen? Perhaps one reason is that, like the author herself, Davies leads a provincially English life. He lives in the small, historic village of Kennilsworth, where Sir Walter Raleigh planted the first potato. He travels infrequently, choosing to remain home as much as possible so he can follow his beloved daily routine: write in the morning, walk downtown for lunch, write some more in the afternoon, and then settle in for a night of television watching with his wife of sixty years, Diana. He has frequently said that he writes adaptations because his own life is "too boring" to inspire original drama. But one senses that his lifestyle has been a calculated choice, the reflection of someone who, like Austen, values ordinary people and activities.

Davies also shares Austen's genius for comedy. Like her, he consistently develops a point of view that is witty, observational, and ironic. And he packs his adaptations with one-liners that linger in a viewer's mind long after the credits have rolled. To cite a few:

From *Bridget Jones's Diary*: Bridget's mother: "Oh, don't be silly, Bridget. You'll never get a boyfriend if you look like you've wandered out of Auschwitz."

From *Wives and Daughters*: Lord Cumnor: "I'm sorry I said anything about it now. I'll try to find a more agreeable piece of news." [pause] "Old Marjorie at the lodge is dead."

From *Middlemarch*: Sir James Chettam, upon finding out that the heroine of the novel, Dorothea, is about to marry a man thirty years older than she: "But he has one foot in the grave!" Mrs. Cadwallader, a neighborhood biddy: "He means to take it out again, I suppose."

Davies also knows how to play up the romantic comedy of Austen, using all the Hollywood conventions we love—verbal wrangling, comic misunderstandings, sex never far from the surface—to develop his plotlines and characters. To him, the connection between *Pride and Prejudice* and a movie like *When Harry Met Sally* is "as clear as day." No wonder, then, that his adaptation of Helen Fielding's *Bridget Jones's Diary*, a modern retelling of *Pride and Prejudice*, turned out to be one of the "best romantic comedies of its generation," according to the *New York Times*.

Even more important than these elements is Davies's uncanny gift for portraying young women, whether it's Lizzy Bennett in *Pride and Prejudice*, Dorothea Casaubon in *Middlemarch*, Gwendolen Harleth in *Daniel Deronda*, Lara Antipova in *Dr. Zhivago*, Esther Summerson in *Bleak House*, Dickens's Little Dorrit, or *Les Misérables'* Fantine. To look at him, you wouldn't be able to guess. "Here's this man of a certain age [currently eighty-three], happily married and a grandfather, able to channel eighteen-year-old girls from another century. It's preternatural," said Rebecca Eaton.[25] He finds their story amid the novels' multiple and often convoluted plotlines, sometimes when the books' writers failed to do so themselves. Often Davies gives minor female characters more attention than their original authors—like Jane Fairfax in Austen's *Emma*, whom he sees as the book's "disguised heroine. . . . Emma and Frank Churchill keep telling everyone what a cold fish Jane Fairfax is. But I saw her as a passionate woman who's probably already been seduced by Frank. She realizes he is not her equal, but she cannot help loving him anyway."[26]

However much Davies respects and follows Austen's genius, he also knows her weak spots. One of them is men. "Jane Austen would never write a scene with just one man or a group of men in it."[27] Davies is right; women dominate her novels, and it is their viewpoints, and only their viewpoints, we see. Meanwhile, her menfolk often come across as stuffed shirts. So Davies loosens them up and gives them airtime. All six of his Austen adaptations add scenes that feature men, alone or in the company of other men, doing "manly" activities like hunting, riding, and fencing. The physicality of these scenes nicely offsets the feminine, sedentary atmosphere of Austen novels, implying we could all use a break from it.

What else stamps a Davies adaptation of Austen? A full-on, gaminesque mixture of highbrow and low. He loads his adaptations with melodrama, a mode of writing Austen avoided like the plague. But Davies uses it to unleash her characters' pent-up emotions. He also delights in linking Austen with TV programs like *Love Island*, an ITV2 dating reality show that sent a host of sexy young singles to a Spanish island for a rollicking, frolicking week back in 2005 and 2006. Davies loved it so much he based his most recent Austen adaptation, *Sanditon*, on it. "It's the same idea," he explained, "a young, beautiful woman with her choice of suitors in a seaside resort. . . . After all, it's not as if *Love Island* can't teach us a thing or two about life as well."[28]

Davies's most publicized and controversial trait—by now, his own convention—is a tendency to "sex-up" Austen. He likes her novels, he says, because they focus on young people "raging with hormones" and "bursting with energy." For him, the driving engine in Austen, always, is sex. "Perhaps I see her this way because I took a seminar once with this storytelling guru in America," he said. The guru was American screenwriter Robert McKee, whom Davies described as a "frightful bully." But he admitted learning a lot from McKee, who advised him, "If there's sex in your story, put it on the SPINE." And so Davies does, every chance he gets. "It's all there, you know. There's quite a lot of seduction, teenage pregnancies, and the like in Austen."[29] For *Sanditon,* he inserted a scene in which Charlotte Heywood (Rose Williams), the innocent country girl who is visiting the loose-moraled resort of the title, spots the rakish Sir Edward Denham (Jack Fox) and wannabe aristocrat Clara Brereton (Lily Sacofsky) in a compromising clinch. And just for fun, Davies included a scene where the hero, Sidney Parker (Theo James), emerges from the ocean in the style of Daniel Craig's 007—*sans* swimsuit.

Davies explains that as soon as he agrees to adapt a novel, he checks out the audiobook from Kennilworth's public library, fills up his gas tank, and drives around the countryside for hours alone, listening. He calls this his "innocent reading" of the novel. "I ask myself, 'Do I like it? Which bits do I like best? Which characters do I love? What can be improved?'" Then he sits down to the "nitty-gritty" work. He rips up paperback copies of the novels so he can physically move parts of them around; he mercilessly slashes through scenes with a marker. For inspiration, he turns to a sculpture—made from a deconstructed book called *Mémoire*—that sits on his office coffee table, its form taken from the pages of another writer's words. But with Jane Austen, he says, he has far less ripping and rearranging to do. "It's all there already. She was brilliant at narrative structure, timing, and dialogue. . . . She's any adaptor's dream, really."[30]

ALL-AMERICAN APPEAL

What special attraction do these adaptations have for Americans? To begin, they reveal that our love of British literature, especially classic literature, may be the most salient expression of American Anglophilia. If literature does indeed inspire feelings of love, British literature doubles that love for Americans, winning our devotion not only because of its well-told stories and unforgettable characters but also because of its very Britishness. And as we view adaptations of this literature, the visual images they provide—whether of an eighteenth-century English countryside or a twenty-first-century London street—intensify our love, giving it a whole world, populated with actors, places, and things, to settle into.

Masterpiece's adaptations also show American audiences how adaptable the past can be. They offer a model for how to see and make use of what has come before, reminding us that tradition—far from being the oppressive, static concept we assume it to be—is always progressive, always developing.

Last, these adaptations, like many of those airing on *Masterpiece*, speak to American sensibilities. Holmes may be every stitch the English gentleman, but he also personifies the classic American figure of the lone individual triumphing over society's restraints. And the sexier, more physical versions of Holmes reflected in Brett's and Cumberbatch's performances heighten that American male vigor. Similarly, Davies's rewritings of Austen, with their promiscuous use of romantic-comedy conventions, strategically appeal to American tastes. They also play up the rebellious nature of Austen's heroines, making them seem just as American as Jo March.

These retellings are thus a fascinating blend of Anglophilic awe and American energy. We can make a similar observation about those *Masterpiece* dramas featuring real historic events and people. As we'll see now, they often turn out to have a special resonance for Americans, even as they pull us deeply into the world of Britain's past.

· 5 ·

History Lessons

$\mathcal{In}$ June of 1887, Queen Victoria posed for the photograph on this page. No queenly allure here; Victoria is a stout, jowly sourpuss garbed in widow's weeds. Unfortunately, it is images like this one that come to mind when we imagine the queen who, after her husband's death in 1861, insisted that the world see her as a grieving widow. And so we do, thinking of Victoria as the stern, sulky monarch who withdrew from public life and mourned her husband up to her last dying breath.

Roughly 120 years after this photo was taken, in a London townhouse full of nineteenth-century antiques, Daisy Goodwin was beginning her novel about Queen Victoria. Goodwin, a middle-aged woman with a ready laugh and easy confidence, held a very different view of the monarch from what the photo suggests. She had studied history at Cambridge and read the queen's diaries. The Victoria she knew was vivacious and modern minded, a monarch who fought for the values she believed in and worked until her sight gave out. She was also lusty, a full-blooded woman who loved her husband and let him know it. Writing such a version would present an entirely different image of the queen from what most people were used to. But where to start?

Goodwin thought about a row she had earlier that day with her fourteen-year-old daughter, Lydia, who was lying on the living room sofa, pouting. Staring at Ottilie, Goodwin wondered, "What if this girl were the boss of me?" At that moment, she decided to begin her novel with the mind-boggling story of how, at seventeen, Victoria inherited a monarchy ruled by a string of dissolute kings and surprised everyone by refusing to be molded or manipulated. Goodwin also decided to write the story as a miniseries for young female viewers, emphasizing how Victoria evolved from a sheltered princess into the world's most powerful queen.

Debuting on *Masterpiece* in January 2017, *Victoria* ran for three successful seasons. Several films have charted the queen's life, starring such formidable actresses as Bette Davis and Judi Dench, but *Victoria* is the first miniseries to do so. It stars Jenna Coleman, a diminutive actress with a button-bright face who, in her mid-thirties, readily passes for a teenage Victoria. Coleman performs the role with easy charm, rendering Victoria playful, impulsive, kind, stubborn, and passionate. For the first season, the miniseries paired her with two love interests, the dashing Lord Melbourne (Rufus Sewell) and brainy Prince Albert (Tom Hughes); remaining seasons focused on Victoria's turbulent marriage to Albert against such historical events as the Irish famine and Charter uprisings.

Victoria is a romance, punctuated with elements of fairy tale and young-adult fiction to please teenage and twenty-something viewers. It suffers from insularity (we never get a real sense of England's place in the world during this time) and tends to sensationalize historical events. But in Goodwin's defense, events like the uprisings are outside her purview. Her interest is in Victoria's private life, and in how Victoria grappled with many of the problems women do today, from placating resentful spouses to managing the egos of coworkers. Goodwin's particular theme—especially resonant in America these days as more and more women enter the political arena—is the contradiction between a female leader's power and the circumscribed gender roles that govern society.

Masterpiece specializes in series like *Victoria* that give Americans, so indifferent to history, an opportunity to learn about actual people and events from the past. A survey of this drama uncovers its dazzling array of tones, strategies, and approaches, from the camp of *I, Claudius* to the whirling melodrama of *Mr. Selfridge*. It shows how *Masterpiece*'s screenwriters strive to make history relevant to our contemporary landscape. And it also reveals how British historical drama sometimes has surprising things to say about America's present.

PAST IMPERFECT

It's a truism worth pondering: Americans are blasé about history, especially our own. One of our rock-bottom values as a country is innovation; we put a high premium on ingenuity, and we have a deep belief in the power of change. As Julian Fellowes, the creator of *Downton Abbey* diplomatically says, Americans are a "contemporary race." These beliefs make us a nation of forward, often fearless, thinkers, but the price is the past; we're so busy imagining our future, we have no time or inclination to study history. "American knowledge of civics and history is pitiful," says one writer. Another commentator concurs, sadly remarking, "We have forgotten so much of what Americans once knew about America." Yet another writer declares, "Our ignorance of history is becoming a national scandal."[1]

This ahistorical mindset may seem like a recent phenomenon, but it actually dates back to America's very beginnings. Freedom from the encumbering past was a virtual dogma of the American Revolution and new republic. The idea was to leave the Old World and its precepts and traditions behind: to start anew. The model American was "an individual emancipated from history, happily bereft of ancestry, untouched and undefiled by the usual inheritances of family and race; an individual standing alone, self-reliant and self-propelling," in the words of historian and literary critic R. W. B. Lewis.[2]

Three interrelated notions underlay this dismissal of the past: the image of America as a youthful country, possessed of a purity that contrasted with Old World degeneracy; a deep belief, articulated by writers like Thomas Paine, that autonomy is a birthright of every successive generation; and a faith that America, somehow lying outside the historical process, was divinely exempt from decline.[3] These assumptions inform the writings of essayists, novelists, philosophers, and politicians alike during the eighteenth and nineteenth centuries. Editor and columnist John O'Sullivan, who all but invented Manifest Destiny, proudly declared of Americans, "We have no interest in scenes of antiquity. . . . The expansive future is our arena." In a similar vein, writer Ralph Waldo Emerson said, "Whatever is old is corrupt, and the past turns to snakes. The reverence for the deeds of our ancestors is a treacherous sentiment." And American diplomat George Perkins Marsh pronounced in 1843, "It belongs to the character of youthful and vigorous nations to concern themselves with the present and the future rather than the past . . . not until the sun of their greatness . . . is beginning to decline [should] a spirit of antiquarian research be aroused."[4]

However far back we trace America's willful ignorance of history, there is no denying that it has become a matter of serious concern in recent years. Consider the current state of America's heritage sites. Colonial Williamsburg, one of our country's most well-known tributes to the Revolutionary era, is now on the brink of financial ruin. In 2016, it reported losing an average of $148,000 every day. History museums across the country face similar problems. In 2012, one research center reported that only 24 percent of Americans visited a historic site of any kind that year. Compare this with the nearly 75 percent of British adults who traveled to a heritage site in their country last year, and the statistic becomes especially woeful.

Far more alarming is the disappearance of history in our school curriculums. "There is little reason to believe that there ever was a golden age when students were well-versed in American history," says one writer.[5] Perhaps. But student ignorance of America's past seems far greater than it was, say, even twenty years ago. One high school teacher in New York City flatly lamented in a recent interview, "Our students don't see the relevance to their own lives of what dead people did."[6] And because educators can't seem to agree on what should be taught, textbooks aim to include everything so as not to offend. Not surprisingly, the number of college students majoring in history has also plummeted, especially since the 2008 financial crisis. And with the new drumbeat of STEM, fewer college students are required to take even a single course in history.

Yet whatever Americans may think about the past's irrelevance, we want some connection to it. Novelist James Fenimore Cooper scorned European ruins and praised the open spaces of the American landscape, but he also Gothicized his family home. Nathaniel Hawthorne moaned the absence of a "pictured, illuminated Past" in his fiction. The liege lord of this ambivalence was Henry James, who fled America to find the historical depth he missed here and yet portrayed Europe as corrupt and decayed. And so it goes with Americans up through the present. We discount the past but find ourselves aching for it, falling in love with the age-old rituals of *Downton Abbey* even as we relentlessly invent new habits for ourselves and demolish our buildings. It's an essentially American contradiction, this vacillation toward the past—and one of the underlying reasons why *Masterpiece* still exists today.

For beneath our indifference, we understand that historical-mindedness is vital to human fulfillment. We realize, however vaguely, that history is a vehicle for promoting *amor patriae*; by knowing something of our shared past, we feel a deeper sense of citizenship. An understanding of historical events also helps us avoid the pitfall of *presentism*, a clunky word that describes the tendency to exaggerate our current problems relative to those that have previously existed. Most importantly, maintaining continuity with the past is vital to our sense of self. It provides a way of comprehending our place in the stream of time, of recognizing that we are all historical creatures.

One great paradox of our present moment is that while we seem to be demonstrating our indifference to history more than ever, interest in historical fiction of all kinds—novels, films, plays, television series—is currently at an all-time high. Students may be ignoring textbooks, history museums may be languishing—but popular stories about the past, from *Hamilton* to *The Favourite*, flood our current landscape. Remarking on the "deplorable state of history education," a commentator suggested ten years ago that "Americans might take a cue from historical novelists like Thomas Mallon, Gore Vidal, and Howard Zinn and use the immense pool of human narratives in history to present a more inviting face. . . . After all, who doesn't like a good story?"[7] It seems popular culture is finally taking that cue. *Masterpiece* is the granddaddy of this trend. It's a program built on the hope that the transporting power of narrative might spark historical-mindedness.

As for the issue of dramatizing American history: *Masterpiece*'s distinctive brand as a purveyor of British culture coupled with its financial limitations, prohibits it from doing so. But if *Masterpiece* can't provide Americans with stories of their own history, it does encourage them to appreciate the past as vital to the present. This may be its single most important contribution to American culture.

HISTORY THROUGH THE CAMERA LENS

Historical drama is a baggy term, but it generally specifies films or TV series that focus on actual people and events from the past. The genre has a rich tradition in Britain, stemming back to films of the 1930s like *The Barretts of Wimpole Street* (1934) and *The Private Lives of Elizabeth and Essex* (1939), either produced in England or employing a British cast and crew. Taking illustrious figures or monumental events as their subjects, these movies were designed to lend prestige to the film industry while instilling admiration for England during its grim, interwar years.

Historical miniseries, first appearing in the 1960s, had a similar aura of quality, though their nationalist purpose was trickier. Many of these series were penned by left-leaning screenwriters who used historical drama to interrogate the myths of Englishness or to comment indirectly on the social tensions that faced England in the 1970s. Like those produced now, these series are notable for their variety of tones, approaches, and subjects. Those that aired on *Masterpiece* include *The Six Wives of Henry VIII* (1972), *Elizabeth R* (1972), *The Edwardians* (1974), *Vienna 1900* (1975), *Shoulder to Shoulder*

(1975), *Edward the King* (1975), *Edward & Mrs. Simpson* (1981), *I, Claudius* (1977–1978), *The Duchess of Duke Street* (1978–1979), and *Lillie* (1979). The titles indicate their wide range of subjects, from King Edward to Lillie Langtry. Some series (*Elizabeth R*) are relentlessly intense; others (*The First Churchills*) are playful and bawdy. Some (*I, Claudius*) wallow in irony; others (*Lillie*) rely on the familiar appeal of nostalgia. Just as striking is their palpable effort to use the new form of the miniseries to deepen our understanding of history, not only by providing epic accounts of people's lives but also intimate portrayals of their thoughts and emotions.

Historical dramas declined in the 1980s and 1990s as literary adaptations and more contemporary fare came to dominate BBC productions and therefore *Masterpiece* programming. Within the past ten years, however, they have returned with a vengeance. Those on *Masterpiece* include *Wolf Hall* (2015), *Churchill's Secret* (2016), *To Walk Invisible* (2016), *Victoria* (2017–), and *Mrs. Wilson* (2019). So popular has the genre become that there is now an unprecedented demand for historical consultants in television. In the UK, for example, a consultancy firm called "Past Preservers" employs roughly twelve hundred academics and TV contributors to advise producers and writers on everything from Victorian dog breeding to the London Peace Conference of 1912.

One essential difference between our current explosion of historical drama and the one of the 1970s is that while the BBC and *Masterpiece* monopolized the genre then, they now compete with a wide variety of venues offering edgier, grittier, or more radical versions of history. Take Cinemax's *The Knick*, a historical drama about a turn-of-the-twentieth-century Manhattan hospital, which is horror filled and gallows humored and legitimately nihilistic about the conditions of scientific and medical progress.

To follow this path would violate *Masterpiece*'s ethos. Even so, *Masterpiece* needs to demonstrate a greater willingness to include dramas that unsettle our view of history rather than affirm it. Early *Masterpiece* series frequently offered a harsh look at Britain's past, it's true. But they also tended to focus on iconic figures and well-traveled events. That was the 1970s; such an approach will no longer work, as *Masterpiece* producers are well aware. More stories about underrepresented people, forgotten moments, and silenced viewpoints also need to fill its programming.

What, from an artistic viewpoint, makes historical drama so compelling? One fundamental answer to this question is that it provides an uncanny illusion of presence; historical drama animates the dead, making them breathe and move and speak. In these stories, figures like Henry VIII in *Wolf Hall* or Jane Austen in *Miss Austen Regrets* (2008) are the central characters, vividly reimagined. They command our rapt attention—and their actions, no matter how small or trivial, seem to carry the weight of a vast history unfolding before us. When Claire Foy, who plays Queen Elizabeth II in Netflix's *The Crown*, prepares to greet the press for the first time as queen, we watch her smooth the skirt of her mourning dress, tighten her jaw, and brush past her husband without so much as glancing at him—and we know, through these gestures, that she is transforming from married woman to monarch. Similarly, when Charlotte Brontë enters the office of a publishing company in *Masterpiece's To Walk Invisible*, we watch her pause and stammer as she reveals her identity. Viscerally, we feel how difficult it would have been for Brontë to acknowledge that she—reclusive, reserved, and a little ghoulish—was the author of London's bestselling novel *Jane Eyre*. Such gestures rarely make their way into official chronicles, but they are the special province of the historical dramatist.[8]

Dramas about the past also deliver two stories: the series' own plot and history's plot. One is about the private concerns of characters, the other about the public events of social existence. Within these series, a delicious tension exists between history's portrayal of the past as finished and the drama's narrative uncertainty. "The triumph of historical fiction is to reach the point of ignorance," says Hilary Mantel. And sure enough, when we watch the final episode of *Wolf Hall*, where Ann Boleyn faces her imminent execution, an ages-old story is suddenly full of suspense.[9]

One of *Masterpiece's* best historical dramas in recent years, *Churchill's Secret*, makes this division between private and public the stuff of its narrative. It recounts the story of how Winston Churchill suffered a severe stroke during the summer of 1953 without the public ever knowing about it. Among the recent biopics of Churchill, this drama may offer the most intimate look at the British Bulldog yet. Most of it is shot in the domestic spaces of Chartwell, Churchill's country home, as he learns to speak, walk, and regain use of his left hand under the affectionate, competent care of his nurse.

A central theme of *Churchill's Secret* is the struggle of growing old and of coming to terms with past mistakes. We learn in this series that the Churchills lost a daughter, Marigold, at the age of three, and that her death haunted their marriage. We also discover that Churchill's surviving children, all but the youngest, grew up emotionally damaged by their parents' neglect. And we get an intimate portrait of Clementine Churchill, the woman behind the bulletproof man. Played by Lindsay Duncan (*Oliver Twist*), Clementine is a masterpiece of devotion, resentment, and surrender. "We would not be here without him, and he would not be here without you," Lord Moran says to her, and we believe him. But Duncan also lets us see how little comfort that knowledge brings.

An anthropological lure also lies at the heart of historical drama. While the human heart and body remain the same, the societies humans live in vary dramatically over time and across cultures. To see a past world fully captured, watching how people lived under a different set of rules and expectations from our own, is fascinating just for its own sake. Related to this pleasure is the dream of full access offered by historical drama. *To Walk Invisible* gives us an inside look at Bramwell Brontë, the no-account brother whose alcoholism tortured his family and stifled his sisters' ambitions until they finally rebelled. In *Edward and Mrs. Simpson*, a riveting portrait of the marriage that rocked England, the camera closes in on Wallis Simpson, crying, as she listens to Edward give his renunciation speech on the radio. The camera lingers on her face, making us feel we are privy to her innermost thoughts. Yet we wonder whether she is overcome by the sheer romance of it all or is mourning the end of her regal ambitions.

Historical fiction is always about contemporary life. It brings the past into the present and shapes it for present purposes. *Masterpiece*'s *Mr. Selfridge* (2013–2016), a sumptuous drama about the Chicago businessman who founded England's luxurious department store, casts a dark, deliberate light on our own era of soulless, online shopping. *Shoulder to Shoulder*, a 1974 miniseries focusing on the activities of the Women's Social and Political Union (WSPU), pointedly spoke to the feminist movement of the early 1970s. And *Churchill's Secret* consciously invites comparison between a past media landscape and our own hyper-invasive one.

Over the years, *Masterpiece*'s historical dramas, like most in the genre, have sparked criticism for their inaccuracies or inventions. But we should keep in mind that the primary obligation of these series is to drama, not history. To quote Mallon: "Nouns always trump adjectives, and in the phrase 'historical fiction,' it is important to remember which of the two words is which."[10] To make a compelling story, characters have to be invented, their behavior and actions cooked up. Accuracy doesn't always matter. What matters is that the story takes imaginative hold on its audience, pulling viewers in through the intensity of attention it bestows on the past.

Since 1971, *Masterpiece*'s historical dramas have often achieved such intensity. Some of them have even reflected our history back to us, weaving American characters and stories into their plotlines. And every once in a while, history has Americanized *Masterpiece* drama for us. In December 2016, when *Victoria* premiered in select theaters across the country, many of those attending were young women eager to see a female leader onscreen after Hillary Clinton's defeat the month before. In the lobby of one Missouri theater, the conversation after the film was full of the election, with several girls expressing indignant wonder that Victoria could have ruled England in the nineteenth century but Clinton couldn't lead America in the twenty-first. There was no way Daisy Goodwin could have planned this timing. But there is also no question that the presidential election and its fallout shaped American responses to *Victoria*.

When we survey the dozens of historical dramas produced by *Masterpiece* during its fifty years, four miniseries stand out as having had particular resonance with American viewers. They're also master classes, every one, in how to dramatize history with intelligence, verve, and some daredevilry.

I, CLAUDIUS

When *Masterpiece* celebrated its twentieth anniversary in 1991, PBS viewers voted on which of the show's hundred-plus series they would most like to see rebroadcast. The hands-down winner was *I, Claudius*, starring John Hurt, Siân Phillips, and Derek Jacobi in a career-defining role. Debuting on November 6, 1977, and running for thirteen spectacular weeks, the series earned four Emmys and a clutch of other awards. It also left American viewers gobsmacked; no other show on American television had ever been this blithe about evil, this graphic about sex, this insistent about human depravity, or this smart about examining the past through the lens of modern psychology. And no *Masterpiece* series then, or since, had spoken as directly as *I, Claudius* to American culture and politics.

The basis of *I, Claudius* is a duo of novels: *I, Claudius* (1934) and *Claudius the God* (1935), by Robert Graves, the oddball classicist who boasted that he conversed with Roman gods on a regular basis. Written in the form of autobiography, the novels are based on the audacious conceit that Claudius, the stuttering, maladroit cripple who became one of Rome's most revered emperors, wrote a searing history of his family and, fearing its discovery and certain destruction, buried it for "posterity"—until Graves found and published it nearly two thousand years later. Although Graves intended them as potboilers, both novels are widely regarded as pioneering masterpieces of historical fiction. They take cheeky liberties with Roman history, but they're also scrupulously researched, epic in scope, and populated by hundreds of characters. Their tone is almost flip—as though the sinister events in Rome following the death of Caesar Augustus were as contemporary as lobby reports today.

Before the BBC got its hands on it, *I, Claudius* had been a graveyard for adaptation. Seven illustrious directors tried to adapt it, and all seven failed. One of them was Alexander Korda, Hollywood's High Priest of Period Drama. He undertook an adaptation of *I, Claudius* in 1937, with hammy Charles Laughton as Claudius, but had to cancel the project when Merle Oberon, Laughton's costar, was seriously injured in a car accident. Another director was John Mortimer, who produced a disastrous stage play in 1972 (not helped by the looming presence, every night, of Graves himself in the audience). By the time BBC2 turned its attention to them in 1975, the novels had acquired a reputation as unadaptable, especially for television's limited resources and technology. But the station forged ahead, hiring Jack Pulman— "adaptor-extraordinaire," as industry insiders called him—to write the screenplay. Authoring all thirteen episodes himself, Pulman made *I, Claudius* into a historical drama that, in the words of TV critic Mary McNamara, "completely changed television."[11]

Playing to the medium's strengths, Pulman reconfigured the story as a family drama, thereby minimalizing its battle scenes and constricting its scope. He used colloquial language rather than the highfalutin English of most historical dramas to give the series contemporary inflection. And he made sure *I, Claudius* brimmed with sharp, witty dialogue. In fact, if we compare Graves's novels with the television version, the best bits of dialogue turn out to be pure Pulman. That's the case with Caesar Augustus's memorable line, roared out by actor Brian Blessed, "Is there anyone in Rome who hasn't slept with my daughter?" In fact, the whole scene of the emperor grilling the guilty senators ("Have YOU slept with my daughter?" "Not slept, Caesar . . ." "So you did it standing up?") was a masterstroke of Pulman's.

It was also Pulman's idea to camp-up *I, Claudius*. "The essence of Camp," Susan Sontag tells us, "is its love of artifice and exaggeration."[12] And *I, Claudius* is nothing if not exaggerated. "The overacting is splendid," wrote the *New York Times*, adding, "*I, Claudius* is full of broad, impassioned, 'this-is-the-only-chance I'll-ever-get-to-do-this-kind of thing' performances."[12] Camp also converts the serious, even the deadly serious, into an object of comedy. With all these traits, *I, Claudius* not only lightened up the topic of political corruption—on everyone's mind in 1977 America—but, like *Upstairs, Downstairs* a few years earlier, allowed *Masterpiece* to unstuff itself.

And Pulman was also the gutsy genius who loaded *I, Claudius* with sexual couplings, rape, bloody beheadings, incest, adultery, and nudity of every imaginable extreme. "No other *Masterpiece Theatre* presentation in years has been as eagerly awaited as 'I, Claudius.' And no other *Masterpiece Theatre* presentation has been such a departure from the genteel, civilized world populated by the likes of the Bellamys of *Upstairs Downstairs*," publicity proudly stated. Yet producers at WGBH and PBS were more than a little nervous about viewer reactions, especially in the South and Midwest. As a consequence, *Masterpiece*'s executive producer, Joan Wilson, cut several scenes from the series, including one where Caligula eats the fetus of his unborn child. "I don't believe in censorship but I do believe in good taste," she later remarked of her handiwork.[13] Still, even the cleaned-up version caused grumbling. One public station in Utah refused to show it; some viewers even cut up their Mobil credit cards.

But many more expressed gratitude that PBS "trusted them" to watch adult entertainment. "This seems to be a year for stretching the boundaries of what is acceptable for television," wrote one critic for the *New York Times* who praised both *I, Claudius* and the controversial TV series *Soap* for pushing the limits of "acceptable television."[14]

Critics and viewers alike commented on the correspondence between Pulman's adaptation and Francis Ford Coppola's *The Godfather* (1972) and *The Godfather Part II* (1974). It was a purposed parallel. Knowing how popular the films had been here in the States, Pulman based many parts of *I, Claudius* on them. In fact, as Brian Blessed recalled years later for *Masterpiece*'s twenty-fifth anniversary, it was Pulman's explanation that *I, Claudius* was really a story of the American Mafia that made the actors finally relax into their roles. "We none of us knew for the first fortnight how to play the parts," Blessed explained. "But as soon as Pulman said 'Mafia,' we got into our parts immediately. I suddenly started to touch people, smile at people. And then when their backs were turned, say 'I can't stand him.' Suddenly, the 'Godfather' note was the key."[15]

Viewers here also recognized in *I, Claudius* a wealth of contemporary American issues, including the recent wake of celebrity sex scandals, the emergence of a new "generation gap," the rise of sexual promiscuity, racial unrest, the breakdown of male authority due to women's lib, and increased divorce rates. Most importantly, they saw in *I, Claudius* a chilling reflection on their own government. "*Masterpiece Theatre* is bringing the Graves story into the atmosphere of post-Watergate America," observed one critic for the *New York Times*, "and it's making our Yankee blood run cold." Another reviewer said, "If you look beyond the togas and the Roman Legion, you can begin to see a startling resemblance to our country's present condition: corruption in the highest places, sexual excess masquerading under the banner of freedom, power politics that doesn't hesitate at assassination to serve its purpose—*I, Claudius* is almost as fresh as today's headlines."[16] Brian Blessed confirmed that all the connections Americans had spotted between ancient Rome and their country were deliberate: "The material wealth portrayed in *I, Claudius* is hard for British citizens to understand because we're a poor country now. The director [Herbert Wise] told us that to play *I, Claudius* we must understand American society. Of course, there are great differences, but America is the only place now that you could relate ancient Rome to."[17]

I, Claudius remains as smart, shocking, and plangent a television drama today as it was in the late 1970s. It may have a dated theatricality to its look—all interior sets, cakey makeup, the occasional echo of a microphone. But its storyline, dialogue, and glittering performances have never been surpassed in television. And as for its status as historical drama: no other TV series has managed to take an era so remote in time, ironize and stylize the hell out of it, and still make it seem so utterly believable, so very much here and now. For proof, just Google "I, Claudius" and "Donald Trump."

ELIZABETH R

During its first year, *Masterpiece* ran through several shows before striking gold: first with *The Six Wives of Henry VIII* and then with *Elizabeth R*, produced by BBC as companion pieces. Airing back-to-back in the early months of 1972, these series still figure among the most beloved and respected ones in the *Masterpiece* canon. That the BBC devoted two dramas to this historical era is no surprise. Tudor history blends the dramas we associate with monarchy (war, court intrigue) with storylines of family sagas (courtship, marriage). It also features powerful women—Katherine of Aragon, Anne Boleyn, Queen Mary I, and Queen Elizabeth I—who took on the challenges usually reserved for men. The creators of *Elizabeth R* ran with this last theme—and turned *Elizabeth R* into a feminist touchstone for 1970s America.

The daughter of Henry VIII and Anne Boleyn, Elizabeth I came to the throne as a young woman who had already survived torments and calamities that would have shattered a weaker person. Her mother was beheaded under her father's instructions, and so was her stepmother, Catherine Howard. She had been declared illegitimate, accused of treason, and imprisoned in the Tower to await execution. Henry's will stated that the crown should pass to his other children, Edward and Mary, but when both of them died—Mary with the blood of thousands of Protestants on her hands—England welcomed Elizabeth to the throne with tremendous relief. She was ready for the challenge, and the BBC scriptwriters gave her one hell of a line to mark her ascendancy: "I will survive because I have the heart of a lion—and I am a lion's cub!" And survive she did.

When producer Roderick Graham decided to adapt the queen's story for television, he was determined to make full use of the miniseries' length and capacity for detail. He immediately envisioned a nine-hour series that would span Elizabeth's long, adult life, and he would make sure its five directors—among them *I, Claudius*'s Herbert Wise—focused on her in virtually every scene, using "an obscene number of close-ups" to give the drama an "intimacy and "intensity" never before seen in a historical drama.[18] Graham's series would humanize Queen Elizabeth, showing her as a woman of many different temperaments, desires, strengths, and weaknesses.

Six different authors wrote the script for *Elizabeth R*, each of them assigned a specific episode designed to cast the queen in a different light. It was the same principle operating behind *Upstairs, Downstairs*: multiple writers deepen and widen characterization. "The series is like a repertory season," claimed publicity for *Elizabeth R*, "with each play creating a different atmosphere and being in a different style."[19] Rosemary Ann Sisson, one of England's best TV writers in the 1970s, wrote "The Marriage Game," portraying the complex relationship between twenty-five-year-old Elizabeth and the Earl of Leicester, the one man she may truly have loved. Hugh Whitemore, a specialist in contemporary thrillers, wrote "Horrible Conspiracies," which explores Mary Queen of Scot's plans to assassinate Elizabeth—and Elizabeth's calculated retaliation. In an interview, Whitemore explained that he wanted to portray Elizabeth in this episode as "a hard, realistic, sovereign with a secret service system as efficient as the CIA or KGB."[20] And so he did; the episode ends with Mary's bloody head lying on the floor, in unflinching close-up. Other episodes show a valiant Elizabeth leading the Battle of the Spanish Armada; a coquettish Elizabeth flirting with the Duke of Alencon; and an old, ugly Elizabeth forgotten by her people and abandoned by her counselors.

Glenda Jackson's performance as Elizabeth I is no doubt what insured that this historical drama would play like a modern, feminist tale. By 1972, Jackson had already earned a reputation as an uncompromising and whip-smart actress, though she was relatively unknown in the States. Her role in *Elizabeth R* exhibited a quality of performance—edgy, erotic, raw, spontaneous, ball busting—that hadn't been seen before, certainly not on television. She soaked herself in Tudor history, reading everything she could find. She refused to wear a bald wig because she believed they never look real—so she shaved her head four inches back. She blackened her teeth, suffered under tightly cinched and padded corsets. Thanks to the series, Jackson quickly became an image of defiance in America and, along with Jane Fonda and Ellen Burstyn, emerged as a new breed of female star, committed to using her roles as vehicles for social change. When asked by an American interviewer in 1976 if she was "waving the flag for women's lib" in her performances, Jackson replied, "Waving it? I'll poke it in your eye if I have to."[21]

Regardless of whether they had seen the series or not, millions of American women were fascinated by the image of Jackson and her fearsome queen. This was, after all, the era of Gloria Steinem, the founding of the National Organization for Women, and Kate Millett's *Sexual Politics*, published in 1970, about which one Columbia professor observed, "Reading the book is like sitting with your testicles in a nutcracker." (He should have known; the book was Millett's PhD thesis, and he was one of her advisers.) Thanks to cultural forces like these, American women were now demanding equal pay for equal work and a chance at jobs traditionally reserved for men. The most radical feminists wanted far more. Their eschatological aim was to topple the patriarchal system altogether. Against this cultural backdrop, *Elizabeth R* became a feminist extravaganza, its influence extending well beyond the limits of the TV screen. It boasted lines like these, all quoted on American t-shirts, bumper stickers, and coffee mugs:

> If I follow the inclination of my nature, it is this: beggar-woman and single, far rather than queen and married.

> I will have but one mistress and no master.

> Men fight wars. Women win them.

In 2019, Glenda Jackson performed on Broadway as the title character in Shakespeare's *King Lear*. She was eighty-two, an object of much wonder for having renounced her career in the 1990s to take a seat in Parliament. Her performance earned bad reviews, but it did unleash a torrent of reflections on *Elizabeth R*. John Leonard, writing for *New York* magazine, remarked, "Jackson's performance remains not only the pure-gold standard by which all other virgin queens will be measured—an embodiment *and* an exorcism—but also one of the greatest theatrical experiences available to us on DVD command."[22] He neglected to say that *Elizabeth R* still has bad-ass appeal. At a time when American feminism is so bound up in stories of victimhood, it's exhilarating to hear Jackson deliver some of the fiercest lines ever written for a woman on *Masterpiece*, spitting them out with lethal relish. When a foreign ambassador begins to threaten her by saying, "Madam, I must warn you," she interrupts immediately: "No, sir, you must not! You must guard your rattling tongue lest I have my hangman pluck it out." Now *that's* a line fit for a queen of any era.

MR. SELFRIDGE

Airing on *Masterpiece* from January 2013 to May 2017, *Mr. Selfridge* springs from Lindy Woodhead's biography of American retail pioneer, Henry Gordon Selfridge, and the fashionable London store he founded in 1909. Woodhead's book is a lively account chockablock with historical detail, revealing how the Chicago native brought Yankee ingenuity and unabashed salesmanship to the art of retail. It recounts a pivotal moment in British and American cultural history—and when Rebecca Eaton first heard about the idea, she jumped on it for *Masterpiece*.

Like *Downton Abbey, Mr. Selfridge* is epic drama, spanning from 1908 to the late 1920s over four seasons and thirty-two episodes. It charts Selfridge's founding of the store and other capitalist ventures; his fraught relationships with family and employees; his addictions and vices; and his eventual undoing. It juggles multiple plotlines and a huge ensemble cast, but its focus is always on the man himself—who, as PBS put it, "combined guile, taste, boldness, the poise of a swindler and the seductive charm of a Casanova." As crafted by screenwriter Andrew Davies working with a team of directors and script-writers, the series careens along briskly. *Variety* praised it for bringing "an American energy to the *Masterpiece* franchise." The *Chicago Tribune* agreed, saying, "*Mr. Selfridge* is a refreshing change from the languid pace of most period drama."[23]

The series offers a fascinating look into the psychology and evolution of early twentieth-century shopping. Watching it, we discover that the prominent display of perfume was considered just as shocking in 1909 as carrying all dress sizes to accommodate women's varying shapes. We learn it was Self-ridge who came up with marketing maxims like "Only X shopping days until Christmas," created the concept of window-shopping after dark, and invented the "bargain basement." His most significant change was to alter the way customers saw department store goods. As Woodhead writes, "Shopping, he reasoned, should be both a visual and tactile experience, one best enjoyed in a moment of self-indulgence and not requiring a salesclerk to unlock a cabinet."[24] For the first time in the history of high-end retailing, thanks to Harry Selfridge, products were displayed on tables, allowing the discerning shopper to examine and feel the gloves, cashmere shawls, and lace handkerchiefs she might purchase.

Mr. Selfridge gives us all this history plus the pure romance of department store shopping. In an era when more and more of us do our shopping online, it reminds us of how sensuous an experience shopping could be. Visiting a place like Selfridge's or Marshall Field's felt like entering another world. And *Mr. Selfridge* captures all of it, from the perfectly reproduced mascara and rouge boxes to the Palm Court restaurant that served a three-course luncheon on the store's eighth floor. Its look is pure nostalgia, meant to make us feel the loss not just of stores like Selfridge's but of a world where consumption still held allure and promise.

In scripting *Mr. Selfridge*, Davies and his team of writers drew on a wealth of American TV shows, aiming to give the series a "conspicuously transatlantic vibe." One of these shows was the HBO sitcom, *Entourage*. No doubt, part of the pleasure of watching *Selfridge* for many viewers was noting the close resemblance between its American protagonist and Ari Gold, the fast-talking, hucksterish Hollywood agent in *Entourage* (Jeremy Piven, who played Gold, also played Selfridge). But the deepest influence from American television was *The Sopranos*, Davies's "favorite television show of all time." "*The Sopranos* is a richly satisfying blend of family story and workplace drama," he said. "I wanted *Mr. Selfridge* to be that too, without the garrotings." More to the point for Davies is that both series are "American dreams gone wrong." In Selfridge's life, as Davies tells it, we find a story much like Tony Soprano's; each man is a tragic hero, possessed of tremendous charisma and haunted by demons, done in by the very things that make him so compelling.[25]

Yet for all the attention *Mr. Selfridge* gives to its protagonist, he is its major failing. His character lacks nuance, and Piven seems conspicuously uncomfortable in the role, as if intimidated by the whole business of British period drama. It's regretful, for the figure of Harry Selfridge is psychologically compelling and historically important. Selfridge was the consummate entrepreneur and showman, a figure every bit as vital to America's past as P. T. Barnum.

Regardless of its shortcomings, *Mr. Selfridge* demonstrated how easily American culture—its myths, values, and even its TV shows—could be interlaced with British historical drama. The series embraced the American rags-to-riches story and celebrated the pioneering spirit that underlies it. What's more, it showed how that success story hinged on breaking down England's rigid social mores by marketing "Selfridge's" to wealthy and poor alike. Davies said that he wrote the series as an answer to *Downton Abbey*, with its "old English interest in tradition, continuity, privilege, class."[26] In *Selfridge*, full round, we see and feel the energy of historical drama now buttressing Anglophilia with its reverse: Amerophilia.

WOLF HALL

Premiering on *Masterpiece* in April of 2015, BBC's *Wolf Hall* astounded American critics. It had been nearly twenty-five years since the program aired a drama set during the Tudor age. And this one was unapologetically esoteric, weighty with historical references and unrelenting in its demand on audience concentration. While a few reviewers found *Wolf Hall* too "serious" and "slow," almost all of them agreed that it was a bona fide masterpiece. Critics praised the performances of the three principal leads: Damian Lewis as Henry VIII, Claire Foy as Anne Boleyn, and the acutely intelligent Mark Rylance as Thomas Cromwell. They commended the series' "dark and evocative" cinematography, with its hypnotic close-ups and strangely formal frames. Most of all, they extolled the script, written by Peter Straughan, who somehow managed to compress Hilary Mantel's two Booker-winning, concrete slabs of a novel into a six-part miniseries.

Wolf Hall opens with the night that begins the fall of Cardinal Wolsey in 1529. Henry VIII, after twenty years of marriage to Catherine of Aragon, has no son. His heart is set on the winsome wench, Anne Boleyn, but Wolsey has been unable to convince the pope to annul the king's marriage, his power a casualty of Rome's plot to thwart the king. Wolsey remains safe for one final night thanks to his quick-thinking lawyer, Thomas Cromwell. From that dark night, the twisted terrain of the miniseries unfolds: the legal havoc wrought by Henry's pursuit of Anne, the political fallout stemming from their relationship, Cromwell's rise from Wolsey's aide to Henry's right-hand man, and a desire for revenge that won't be quenched. It turns out Wolsey's fall presages many others.

A notably quiet miniseries, *Wolf Hall* avoids testosterone-charged scenes of action, choosing instead to locate its drama within conversation and silence. Following Mantel, the series is intensely psychological, portraying Henry VIII as a somewhat attractive figure—lusty, strutting, and athletic—who quickly devolves into his own worst self, and Anne Boleyn as a calculating, seductive, and witty woman who knows all that matters are the illusion of her virginity and the production of a male heir. Two of English history's most famous figures are thus made eerily intimate, their darkest thoughts revealed to us.

Wolf Hall takes a story we all know—Henry VIII's pursuit of Anne Boleyn and his break from the Church—and makes it feel strangely new. And strangely American. Straughan patterned his entire script, he said, on *The Godfather*. "I thought of *The Godfather* a lot while I was writing," he explained. "And that's because mob dramas are based on Machiavellian Italian politics in the Renaissance era, where families and politics mix. That's exactly what the Tudors were. You can view Cromwell as a Michael Corleone, moving from a place of loyalty and some sense of virtue, and [with both] wonder: At what point is he going to lose his soul?"[27] Straughan also slanted his story on a revenge plot, just as Francis Ford Coppola and Mario Puzo had done with *The Godfather*. To avenge the murder of Wolsey, Cromwell has to survive. And just like Michael Corleone, he has to demean everything that is tender and noble in himself to do so.

Thomas Cromwell is also a Tudor version of the American self-made man. Born as a blacksmith's son, he rose from the gutter to become the second most powerful man in England. In fact, much of *Wolf Hall*'s appeal is the American theme of low birth triumphing against the odds. And as critics noted, Cromwell deliberately recalls other strategic geniuses in American television, including Francis Underwood in *House of Cards*, Don Draper in *Mad Men*, and Mike Ehrmantraut in *Breaking Bad*. Cromwell's most interesting relationship is with Anne, the woman who, in Mafia speak, gets whacked. Like Cromwell, she is also on the outside—and while she repels us in many ways, her intelligence and shrewdness is just as captivating as Cromwell's. Straughan's sympathies, it's clear, are with those on the margins of monarchy. Specialists in deceit they may have been, but in their own self-serving ways, Cromwell and Anne were also laying the foundation for American democracy.

★ ★ ★

"History is always changing behind us," says Hilary Mantel, "and the past changes a little each time we tell it."[28] The historical dramas on *Masterpiece* vivify Mantel's observation, showing us how fiction can revamp the past. They also feed our anglophilia by capturing Britain's anterior worlds so sumptuously. *And* they provide a means for us to think about contemporary issues, sometimes even American ones. Far from evoking a simple, one-note nostalgia for the past, as critics sometimes charge, these dramas rework history even as they call attention to England's lost beauties and values.

Let's turn now to a different kind of drama altogether, one also accused of being simpler than it is: the British detective mystery. This "cozy" and conventional genre, as we'll see, often contains surprising ironies and innovations, made all the richer by *Masterpiece* and the sister show that, for twenty-six years, charmed and spooked American audiences: PBS's *Mystery!*

· 6 ·

Masterly Mysteries

$\mathcal{I}$n December 1944, detective writer Raymond Chandler wrote an essay for the *Atlantic Monthly* called "The Simple Art of Murder." He was fifty-six at the time, having recently become famous after twelve years of penning fiction for the pulps. Coming out of that experience, the essay was at once a meditation on the genre, an artistic manifesto, and a nice piece of self-promotion.

Chandler had a lot of fun eviscerating British mysteries in "The Simple Art of Murder," describing them as "dull, pooped out pieces of utterly unreal and mechanical fiction." His particular target was mystery writers of the 1920s and 1930s (the so-called Golden Age of detective fiction), who set their stories within upper-class milieus that were "stuffed with dukes and venetian vases." Even worse for Chandler was how these writers demonstrated more interest in plot, in the cool mechanics of crafting an ingenious puzzle, than in human psychology or emotion. In short, their work was "too contrived," "too detached," and "too little aware of what goes on in the world."[1]

"The Simple Art of Murder," like the writer himself, is petulant, dead-on, smart, and ungenerous. Chandler was right about how Golden Age mysteries, such as those of Agatha Christie and Dorothy L. Sayers, tend to gentrify crime and contort their plots. But bent on valorizing American fiction, he refused to acknowledge that the very things he criticized about these novels were precisely what made up their appeal: then *and* now. The arithmetic of Christie's accomplishments alone, a woman outsold only by the Bible and Shakespeare, tells us that. What Chandler called "dull" and "contrived," millions of readers have found comfortable and reassuring. Fans of these mysteries enjoy the decorous settings, the intricate plots, the unapologetic use of conventions, and the feminine slant. Even more, they are gratified by the restoration of peace at the end and the underlying assumption that we live in an essentially moral, ordered world.

Satisfying America's appetite for British murder and mayhem, *Masterpiece* and its sister show *Mystery!* have dramatized a wide range of British mysteries over the years. What special appeal do these shows hold for American viewers? To begin, they illustrate how conventionality—a vital part of the *Masterpiece* (and *Mystery!*) ethos—provides its own forms of pleasure; we love these dramas because they bring a pleasing sense of familiarity coupled with a strong spirit of innovation. They also feature super-smart protagonists whose quirks and eccentricities—Hercule Poirot's waddle of a walk, Christopher Foyle's inability to drive a car—charm us. In contrast to their American counterparts, these detectives think things through rather than rely on flashy forensics.

Masterpiece mysteries also lure us into believing that they offer a more penetrating look into British life and character than what we normally see on the program. The cozier ones, such as *Miss Marple* and *Grantchester*, are set in English villages where psychopaths lurk amid small, intimate communities. They present crime as a titillating adventure, a delicious but not destructive subversion of what the Brits call "chocolate-box England." Packed with irony, they indulge our Anglophilia and undermine it, too. The darker shows, such as *Inspector Morse* and *Prime Suspect*, showcase a variety of modern social issues, including homophobia, racism, and sexual assault: a Britain, in short, that feels a lot like contemporary America.

THE SCENE OF THE CRIME

One summer day in 1979, WGBH manager Henry Becton received a phone call that would make any station head's heart race. It was from Herb Schmertz at Mobil Oil, who informed Becton that Mobil wanted to sponsor another British anthology program devoted just to mysteries. Granada and London Television had recently started producing scores of them for ITV, including *Father Brown*, *Raffles*, and *The New Scotland Yard*, and American audiences had loved Ian Carmichael as Lord Peter Wimsey in the Dorothy L. Sayers mysteries that had run on *Masterpiece* a few years earlier. "If you'd be interested in putting together a second series," Schmertz said, "we'd be interested in funding it."[2] A soft-spoken man who wears wire-rimmed glasses and, at seventy-six, still boasts the disciplined physique of an army captain, Becton exudes self-composure. But even he must have let out a whoop when he got off the phone. He rushed to tell *Masterpiece*'s executive producer Joan Wilson, who loved the idea.

A program specializing in British mysteries would be a singular contribution to American television. In the 1980s, commercial networks were bursting with crime shows like *Magnum, P.I.*; *Hart to Hart*; *CHiPS*; *T.J. Hooker*; and *The Fall Guy*. But most of these were indisputably crappy, with shoddy scripts and low-grade actors. And those that were good, such as the award-winning *Hill Street Blues*, tended to be urban, gritty, and action packed. *Mystery!* would specialize in less hard-hitting dramas where detectives reasoned their way through a case. British mysteries nourish our love of deduction. This smarty-pants quality makes them ideal for PBS, given its aspirational promise to offer intelligent television. Bearing this out are the scores of reviews over the years that have expressed gratitude to the station for the "brainy pleasures" of *Masterpiece* and *Mystery!*'s crime dramas. As Sophie Gilbert of the *Atlantic* noted about BBC's *Sherlock*, "At its best, it was unlike anything else on the air: a celebration of a hero whose primary motivation was simply thinking things through."[3]

Mystery! debuted on Tuesday, February 5, 1980, at 9:00 p.m. EST. Publicity stressed that while it would maintain *Masterpiece*'s air of "high quality," it would be more "whimsical" and "tongue-in-cheek." *Mystery!* would prove, if *Masterpiece* hadn't, that watching British drama didn't have to feel like homework. And to make sure this point came across, Joan Wilson, who had a touch of whimsy herself, created a special set for *Mystery!* that felt like a Gothic parody of *Masterpiece*'s. It was an eerie room in some imagined Victorian mansion, stuffed to the gills with books and antique furniture. But it also had crystal balls, rusted birdcages, dusty baubles, and ratty taxidermy. Presiding over it all would be a host dressed in an elegant black tuxedo, inviting viewers in.

The original emcee was the afro-haired, pun-loving Gene Shalit, resident film critic of NBC's *Today Show*, and as far afield from Cooke as Velveeta is to Le Chevrot. He was gone within the year, replaced by the perfect Vincent Price. Familiar to PBS audiences from classic horror films, Price was American (he grew up in St. Louis and studied at Yale) but had the indisputable air of a British gentleman. (He received a master's degree from Oxford and spent close to a decade acting on the London stage.) Audiences loved Price, who brought sophistication and just the right touch of camp to *Mystery!* He left the show in 1989 when his health started to fail. Dame Diana Rigg, known to many Americans as leather-clad Emma Peel from *The Avengers*, then took over. She presided over *Mystery!* for fourteen years, using her cool, measured, theatrical voice to full effect as she introduced each episode. She seemed less to speak her remarks than exhale them.

Anyone familiar with *Mystery!* will remember the show's legendary titles. They were the brainchild of Edward Gorey, the Boston-based illustrator known for his semi-ghoulish drawings and books who paraded around in a full-length raccoon coat and high-top Converse sneakers. Over the course of nearly twenty years, Gorey sketched a series of marvelous cartoons for *Mystery!*: swooning heroines in long gowns, sinister men in bowler hats and handlebar mustaches, dark figures playing croquet in a rainstorm. Tracked by tango music, they were worked up by the animator Derek Lamb and his team, who brilliantly replicated Gorey's sensibilities: the humor that offsets the danger, the camp that winks at the macabre. Almost overnight, the titles became the show's trademark (even today, they draw thousands of visitors on YouTube).

In 1980, Gorey had a circle of devoted followers, but he was far from famous. *Mystery!* catapulted him into the mainstream. Today, the seep of Gorey's sensibility is all over. In America, graphic-novel author Neil Gaiman and cartoonist Alison Bechdel, along with many other American fantasists who dwell in the haunted landscapes of childhood, credit Gorey with inspiring them. "When I was first writing *A Series of Unfortunate Events*," remembers Daniel Handler, the American author of the Lemony Snicket series, "I was wandering around everywhere saying, 'I am a complete rip-off of Edward Gorey.'" How did Handler first come upon Gorey's work? By watching *Mystery!*[4]

Airing from 1980 to 2006, *Mystery!* turned out to be a runaway success, often surpassing *Masterpiece* in the ratings. It offered a robust selection of drama, from adaptations of Gothic novels like *Rebecca* (1980) and *Dr. Jekyll and Mr. Hyde* (1981) to courtroom dramas like *Rumpole of the Bailey* (a viewer favorite, 1980) to psychological thrillers like *A Dark-Adapted Eye* (1995). "We've always had the philosophy," explains Henry Becton, "that we'd take what was well done and had superior characterizations rather than worry about whether or not it would fit the format."[5] But hands down, the most popular shows on the program were detective mysteries. As Rebecca Eaton explains, "Mystery novels and television drama series are a match made in production heaven. They're both about repetition: the murders and crimes in each book or each episode might be different, but the pattern of chaos and the orderly resolution is identical. . . . In storytelling, especially on television, there's great audience satisfaction in repetition."[6] *Mystery!* viewers loved watching classic detective stories get revamped for television, and they enjoyed seeing how contemporary novels, like those of P. D. James and Colin Dexter, borrowed from the classics and hard-edged them. In short, they delighted in all the pleasures of conventionality.

The dramas on *Mystery!* and *Masterpiece* did far more than offer viewers the "satisfaction of repetition." They *improved* the mystery genre. These series gave the figure of the British detective—even comic ones like Poirot and Miss Marple—psychological and emotional depth, providing them with backstories, inner conflicts, and occasional dark moments of the soul. The sheer ongoingness of television, coupled with its love of detail, enabled their enrichment.

So did the skills of talented screenwriters—and superb performances by actors like Jeremy Brett, Joan Hickson, Helen Mirren, and David Suchet. In addition to deepening characterization, the dramas on *Mystery!* refined and widened the genre's conventions. They made the British mystery a far more varied, self-reflective, and dynamic genre than Chandler, the old grump, would have ever thought possible.

Among *Mystery!* and *Masterpiece Mystery!* favorites, four shows stand out for their consistent excellence and sheer longevity. Together they illustrate the particular blend of conventionality, nostalgic appeal, innovation, and irony that form the heart of the programming.

MISS MARPLE

A female octogenarian who wears tweed suits, possesses a temperament as sensible as her shoes, and beats male professionals at their own game of solving murder: how can you not love the conceit of Miss Marple? She made her first appearance in 1930 as a peripheral character in Agatha Christie's *The Murder at the Vicarage*. Christie's readers warmed to her immediately, prompting the author to give her top billing in twelve more novels and a dozen short stories. It's not hard to see why readers love Miss Marple. She represents every one of us who has ever felt overlooked or excluded. The very essence of Miss Marple is her unassuming manner, which masks her sharp eye and shrewdly analytical mind so thoroughly that the police shoo her out of the way when they should be begging her for help.

One of the foremost criminologists in England, Miss Marple introduced the notion that solving murders is more about understanding human behavior than knowing every possible variety of bicycle tire. This is her unique, essentially feminine contribution to detection. Her method is to mine idle conversation—at tea parties, over her garden fence, in church pews—for nuggets of information. She understands the world solely through the prism of her village, drawing conclusions about what makes people commit violent crimes based on what she observes of her neighbors: she's the Jane Austen of Murder.

Miss Marple couldn't have been a better fit for *Mystery!* and *Masterpiece*, participating in all the delights of a cozy English village while using her five-star brain to solve the problem before her. Her character has a surprisingly feminist appeal. Far more clever than everyone around her, she bides her time, waiting for the male blowhards in the stories to let up for a moment so she can slip in a few dead-on observations. She thus holds a special attraction for the largely female audience of *Mystery!* and *Masterpiece*—especially those of a certain age.

Drawing on these various appeals, WGBH aired two series featuring Christie's legendary character: the BBC's *Miss Marple*, starring Joan Hickson, which ran from 1986 to 1989, and ITV's *Agatha Christie's Marple*, running from 2002 to 2013 and starring both Geraldine McEwan (2002–2009) and Julia McKenzie (2009–2013). These series present contrasting aims and intentions. The BBC version took a scrupulously faithful tack, capturing Christie's light, breezy tone and faithfully re-creating the settings and characters of her fiction. Very much a product of the 1980s, this version, like Granada's *Sherlock Holmes* series, evokes viewer nostalgia for classic detective fiction and a simpler, more stable England. The opening title sequence sets the stage with its charming montage of illustrations that depict an English village. Like those for *Sherlock Holmes* or *Poirot*, it's one of those sequences you can watch over and over again just to make yourself feel good.

ITV's *Marple* adopted a more experimental and ironic approach. In keeping with recent adaptational trends, it designed most of its episodes as pastiches. The underlying aim of pastiche is to imitate an author's style, not to re-create content. Watching ITV's *Marple*, we are drawn far more to how it mimics what we all know of Christie's style—her taste for isolated settings, knotty plots, closed groups of suspects—than to the stories themselves. The ITV series also plays up the inherent absurdity of the Marple conceit by merrily employing loads of camp. It exaggerates her little-old-ladyness, costuming her in dresses that look more like doilies. It populates each episode with a coterie of kooky old women. And it heightens the sinister plots lurking amid her ultra-genteel surroundings. The camp mocks Christie's conventions while reminding us of just how much fun they are.

Grand debates have been staged on which of the three actresses—Hickson, McEwan, or McKenzie—is the best Miss Marple. Most British fans give the award to Hickson, who, in keeping with the overall spirit of the BBC production, played Marple with scrupulous authenticity. The oldest actress ever to take the lead in a TV series, Hickson was seventy-eight when she started performing the role. Sadly, Agatha Christie, who once wrote Hickson a note saying, "I hope one day you will play my dear Miss Marple," never got to see her do it. Christie wrote that note in 1946, just after seeing Hickson play a minor role in a London production of *Appointment with Death*. Hickson was thirty-nine at the time, and none too pleased. But it turns out the actress was almost eerily well suited for the role: a perfect alloy of sweetness and steel.

While British viewers tend to prefer Hickson, American viewers have varying opinions on the matter. Some, like Sarah Lyall of the *New York Times*, like how Hickson "played the part just as Christie had written it: as a "seemingly fluffy and disorganized spinster." But others, like the TV critic for the

Huffington Post, enjoy how Geraldine McEwan portrays her with such campy zest. And others, like Mary McNamara of the *Los Angeles Times,* commend Julia McKenzie for giving us a "more solidly tweedy Miss Marple" and a "much more intentional detective" than the other two.[7]

One delicious element to both McEwan's and McKenzie's performances is their easy interactions with the young, handsome inspectors assigned to a case. The exchanges play a minor role in the fiction, but the ITV series foregrounds them to titillating effect. Played by a string of British heartthrobs like Matthew MacFadyen and John Hannah, inspectors come to like and respect Miss Marple over the course of solving a case. We see their admiration develop in loving detail, with well-crafted, exquisite scenes that show the inspector and the old lady engaged in serious analysis, or playful banter, or heartfelt confidences. The result is a form of onscreen chemistry we won't find anywhere else on television.

AGATHA CHRISTIE'S POIROT

Agatha Christie's Poirot premiered on *Mystery!* on January 8, 1989. Although everyone at WGBH had high hopes for it, no one could have predicted it would air for twenty-five years, making it the longest-running series on *Mystery!* or *Masterpiece.* During that time, it gave us seventy episodes, divided into thirteen seasons. And in an increasingly multi-channel environment, it also managed to capture consistently high ratings—roughly five million viewers per week—here in the States.

Why? Because *Poirot,* like *Sherlock Holmes* and *Miss Marple,* is comfort viewing. Following the cardinal convention of Golden Age mysteries, it invites us into a world where threats to social stability seem easily identifiable and foiled. As the series' star, David Suchet, says, "It's a world where manners and morals are quite different from today. There are no overt and unnecessary sex scenes, no alcoholic haunted detectives in Poirot's world. He lives in a simpler, some would say more human, era."[8] Boasting the biggest budget of any British crime drama up to that time, the series also feeds our Anglophilia with lavish settings, gorgeous period costumes, and spectacular landscapes. Most importantly, *Agatha Christie's Poirot* gives us the most charming detective ever to appear on British television. And as the show progressed, he developed into a far more complex figure than Christie could have ever imagined.

The only fictional character to get an obituary in the *New York Times,* Hercule Poirot is a "little Belgian detective" with an "egg-shaped head and small waxed moustache." He clearly resembles Sherlock Holmes in his eccentricity, vanity, and improbable brilliance, boasting to nearly everyone he meets that he is the "world's greatest detective" (possessed of superior "little gray cells"). A neat freak who cuts his toast into four exact pieces and insists that his two hardboiled eggs measure exactly the same height each morning, Poirot approaches each case with a rigorously methodical mind. Christie herself grew tired of him, confessing in the *Daily Mail*, "There are moments when I have felt: Why, why, why did I ever invent this detestable, bombastic, tiresome little creature?"[9] She tried to force her detective into retirement, but the detective's legion of fans wouldn't have it.

And that's because there is so much to love about Hercule Poirot. Christie may have tired of his fussiness, but we find it endearing. We love Poirot's other eccentricities, too, such as his tendency to lapse into *Poirot-ese*, a combination of French idiom and English exclamation that produces phrases like "don't do the shilly-shally with me, *mon ami*." We also appreciate that Poirot is a foreigner, looking in on the world of English society as we do, criticizing the English for their terrible food, chilly behavior, and ridiculous pastimes. Amid all the drab tweed and knitted cardigans, we also admire Poirot's meticulous attention to clothing, and love even more how oblivious he is to the dandified figure he cuts. We delight in his sense of showmanship, played to full effect at the end of a case when he gathers all suspects together and recaps his brilliant reasoning (always timed in the TV series to occur somewhere between seventeen and twenty-two minutes from the end).

Most of all, we love Poirot because he loves people. Unlike Sherlock Holmes, Poirot shows a genuine interest in human beings rather than merely the crimes they commit. He is a warm and likeable man, charming to servants and waiters, loyal to his friends, always polite and respectful toward women. It is this amiability, coupled with his unparalleled skill, that made him such a *Mystery!* all-star.

Like *Sherlock Holmes* and the BBC version of *Miss Marple*, *Poirot* aimed to be faithful to the spirit of its original. But it also had an unapologetically extravagant air, indulging viewers in a fantasy lifestyle that included lush interiors, gorgeous clothes, five-star cuisine, and expensive vacations. Most of the stories are set in the striking Art Deco environment of England, circa 1936. Featuring a pantheon of modernist British buildings and interiors, the series evokes a world where people cared about style, good taste, and craftsmanship. *Poirot*'s set designers took special care with the detective's two apartments. They purchased English designer pottery and Art Deco figurines, ran wild with silk and velvet, filled porcelain vases with perfect bouquets, and made absolutely sure to use furniture with square shapes because, as every reader of Agatha Christie knows, Poirot hates curves.

By everyone's estimation, including that of Queen Elizabeth II and Agatha Christie's daughter, David Suchet is the definitive Poirot, eclipsing actors like Charles Laughton, Albert Finney, John Malkovich, and Kenneth Branagh. A method actor who claims to be a fusspot himself, Suchet studied his character with fanatical attention. He read every one of the thirty-three novels and fifty-five short stories in which the detective appears, taking detailed notes and assembling a "dossier" of "Poirotian traits" that he carried in his pocket whenever on set. "It was my business not only to know what he was like, but to gradually become him," Suchet explained in his 2014 memoir, *Poirot and Me*. By the time he finished preparing his file, Suchet knew that Poirot "would take three lumps of sugar in his coffee or five lumps in his tea; that he would always wax his moustache; and that he would always wear striped trousers to go to the bank."[10]

Suchet quickly assumed a proprietary stance toward his detective, ardently defending Christie's original choices just like Jeremy Brett did with Sherlock Holmes. But Suchet added some nice touches of his own. During the filming of an episode from Season 1, he insisted that before Poirot sat down on a public bench, he place a handkerchief there first. The director, Ed Bennett, thought the notion ridiculous. But Suchet refused to shoot the scene until Bennett gave in. It was also Suchet who perfected Poirot's penguiny walk. Christie vaguely described the detective as having a "rapid, mincing gait." That description flummoxed Suchet for weeks—until he remembered Laurence Olivier's account of how he learned to walk like a Restoration fop. "I put a penny between the cheeks of my bum, old boy, and tried my best to keep it there." Suchet followed Olivier's technique, although he boasts in his memoir that he used a smaller penny.[11]

Despite these comic touches, Suchet transformed his character into a figure of compassion, pride, loneliness, and implacable principles. "He was as real to me as he had been to Christie," Suchet writes in his memoir.[12] Thanks to Suchet and scriptwriters like Clive Exton, Poirot's emotions run far deeper in the series than they do in the books. Onscreen, he is a romantic figure touched easily by beauty, whether that of a young woman, a well-appointed home, or an exquisite meal. But he is also a lonely man, hampered by his own comic appearance and compulsions, aching for romantic love but knowing it will always elude him.

That last strain evolved over the course of the series, the detective growing grimmer with age. The early seasons, however, brim with affection and humor. Much of this has to do with Poirot's merry band of sidekicks: Captain Arthur Hastings, Poirot's loyal but dimwitted friend; Miss Lemon, Poirot's spit-curled, meticulous secretary; and Inspector Japp, the perpetually rumpled detective who turns to Poirot whenever a case baffles him. "I do think, for a television series, you need a basic family unit, whether it's a family or not," said Clive Exton, the creator and principal screenwriter for the series.[13] These three characters *are* Poirot's family, their own patient affection for him mirroring our own. But by 2004, the three of them had disappeared from the series, as had Exton, who left *Poirot* to write for the TV mystery *Rosemary and Thyme* in 2001.

These were a few of the changes that portended a new and darker *Poirot*. When Granada assumed production of the series from London Weekend Television in 2002, *Poirot*'s new producers, Michele Buck and Damien Timmer, made it clear they wanted the show to go darker and more cinematic. Beginning in 2003, most episodes were shot as two-hour films, with ITV spending more than two million pounds on each one. The series now featured recurrent motifs like abortion, drug abuse, and homosexuality, with the deeply religious detective alienated from the world he tries to safeguard. Crimes became more complex, criminals more elusive. Meanwhile, Suchet was instructed to bring an increased sense of loneliness, even existential despair, to the role. And so he did, with each season a harbinger of his sad, tragic end.

One of the most haunting episodes in the *Poirot* canon is *Murder on the Orient Express*, produced in 2010. In keeping with ITV's new cinematic approach, it boasted a cast that includes Jessica Chastain and Barbara Hershey, and its camerawork has all the sweep and dramatic intensity of a Hollywood film. *Murder on the Orient Express*, as in the novel, concludes with Poirot forced to decide the fate of twelve murderers, all decent people who turned vigilante for the sake of justice. The scene occurs outside in the piercing cold, with the culprits standing helplessly by as Poirot struggles to decide. Shot in the steely blue palette of American crime dramas like *CSI*, the sequence follows the detective's tormented face as he walks toward the police chief. He mutters a vague explanation that exonerates the murderers. Then leaving everyone behind, he walks toward us, holding his rosary beads and crying in anguish. We admire the scene's camerawork, its evocation of a bleak, inhospitable universe. We applaud Suchet's performance, worthy of an Emmy *and* an Oscar. Most of all, we marvel at the complexity *Agatha Christie's Poirot* has ultimately given its character, and his world, over twenty-five years.

Yet we miss the old Poirot, his twinkling grin, his irrepressible charm. We recognize that this new approach to Christie's detective challenges us far more than the light, nostalgic stories of earlier seasons. Still, we lament the world we have lost.

INSPECTOR MORSE

"If you think about it, it's unbelievable. A policeman driving a very nice old classic car, a red Jaguar, around Oxford, going into a pub and having a pint of beer when he feels like it. Oxford is having something like five murders a week. This is in the realm of Sherlock Holmes or Agatha Christie. It's certainly not in the realm of 'Prime Suspect' or 'N.Y.P.D. Blue.'"[14] That observation comes from John Thaw, the actor who played the titular detective in *Mystery!*'s beloved series *Inspector Morse*. But Thaw got it wrong. *Inspector Morse* does have a certain old-fashioned appeal, drawing on some of the mystery's cozy conventions while adding a few of its own. Yet its realism is so nuanced, so finely tuned to its protagonist's frustration and loneliness amid a bleak, contemporary landscape, that the show resonates as modern tragedy.

Based on the thirteen novels by Colin Dexter, a classics scholar who decided to try his hand at crime writing one rainy summer vacation, *Inspector Morse* ran on *Mystery!* from 1988 to 2000, killing off eighty-one people over thirty-three episodes. Its ratings reached a peak of eight million in the States and one billion across 210 countries. Winning twelve awards and nominated for nine others, *Morse* still generates swoony comments from critics and fans alike. Many viewers consider it the best television crime drama ever produced. And if this seems like exaggeration, check out the *Radio Times* website, which ranked *Morse* number one on its list of Britain's top twenty crime dramas in 2018. Or consider one critic's retrospective review, which says, "'Inspector Morse' is arguably the best character-driven detective series in the history of television."[15]

Setting a detective story in Oxford is a tried-and-true convention, dating back to J. C. Masterman's *An Oxford Tragedy* (1933), Mavis Doriel Hay's *Death on the Cherwell* (1935), and Dorothy L. Sayers's *Gaudy Night* (1935). It plays on the rich irony of murder within a tranquil setting, in this case one revered for its intellectual atmosphere and ages-old history. *Morse* makes full use of the convention, taking every chance it gets to show us a Gothic spire or stained-glass window. But the tales are wholly contemporary, covering subjects like heroin addiction, rape, and domestic abuse. And while crimes get solved, there is no sense of a social order restored. Oxford itself is exposed as a vicious place, populated by characters who think their intelligence or social position excuse them from human decency. In fact, one interesting feature of *Morse* is how it dissects the sense of privilege felt by older white men, focusing on lecherous dons (each one boasting an office outfitted with a liquor cabinet) and the young women who suffer at their hands.

At the center of it all is Morse. A former Oxford student who "could have made firsts" but left without a degree, he is defined by his cultured tastes and love of learning. He reads the poetry of A. E. Housman, quotes Tennyson at crime scenes, sings in a choir, plays opera, and drives a cherry-red Mark II Jaguar with a first-rate audio system. Possessed of a brilliantly idiosyncratic mind, he successfully theorizes about crime but sucks at routine police work. And while the combination of these traits gives him the eccentric charm we associate with British detectives, they also underscore a terrible poignancy: Morse inhabits a world to which he can never belong and from which he can never avert his gaze. Consciously or not, he tries, on his policeman's salary and policeman's beat, to live a life that resembles those of the Oxford dons he disdains.

Like most TV detectives, Morse is a single man with a roving eye. But the series' writers make him into a romantic ruin. Falling for one pretty woman after another as he searches vaguely for companionship, he has had more unrequited crushes than any other detective in the *Mystery!* or *Masterpiece* canon. And while his romantic relationships never work out, one of *Inspector Morse*'s true strengths is how delicately it portrays the detective's interactions with the female sex. A kind of modern-day knight errant, he is gentle with mistreated women and downright gallant with those he tries to woo. As one critic writes, "Millions of women are attracted to TV's number one detective, Inspector Morse. They are charmed by his sad, baffled sensitivity, his brooding melancholy. Intimate and remote, he is the thinking woman's idea of a good lay."[16]

But let's not paint too rosy a picture of Inspector Morse. Cranky and often morose, he can be a "real pain in the rectum area," as the murder suspect in "Driven to Distraction" says. And as his supervisor, Chief Inspector Strange, explains when turning him down for a promotion, "You're a clever sod, Morse, but you don't say the right things to the right people." Morse hates casual conversation and can be appallingly rude or insensitive. His lack of normal social graces is so pronounced, in fact, that his aide, Sergeant Lewis, looks positively flabbergasted when Morse asks him how the wife and kids are doing in the episode "Twilight of the Gods." It is the first time in seven seasons that Morse has shown any curiosity whatsoever about Lewis's personal life. And yet we *like* Morse. We respect his honesty, sympathize with him, and root for him. We forgive his moodiness and petulant behavior because he is so utterly vulnerable, a man who distracts himself from his loneliness by playing his stereo too loud or having one more beer than he should.

The one person who puts up with Morse is Lewis, and the series portrays their friendship with humor and pathos. In Dexter's novels, the two men are roughly the same age and have a solid but somewhat distant relationship. The

The Cast of *Downton Abbey*, Season Three

The Durrell Family In *The Durrells in Corfu*

Susan Hampshire and John Neville in *The First Churchills*

Damian Lewis and Gina McKee
in the 2002 remake of
The Forsyte Saga

Selected Cast Members of *Upstairs, Downstairs*

Gordon Jackson, Jenny Tomasin, and Angela Baddeley in *Upstairs, Downstairs*

Brendan Coyle and Joanne Froggatt in *Downton Abbey*

Alistair Cooke, *Masterpiece's*
Legendary Host

David Oyelowo in
Les Misérables

Jeremy Brett and
Edward Hardwicke
in Granada's
Sherlock Holmes

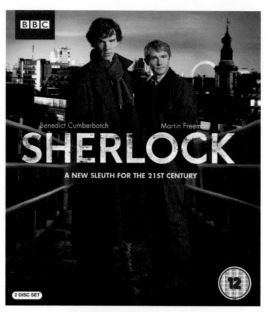

Benedict Cumberbatch and Martin Freeman
in *Sherlock*

Jennifer Ehle and Colin Firth in
Pride and Prejudice

Derek Jacobi, John Hurt, and Brian Blessed in *I, Claudius*

Glenda Jackson in *Elizabeth R*

Frances O'Connor
and Jeremy Piven in
Mr. Selfridge

Claire Foy and Damian Lewis in *Wolf Hall*

Vincent Price, *Mystery!'s* Inimitable Host

Joan Hickson in *Miss Marple*

The Principal Cast of *Agatha Christie's Poirot*

John Thaw and Kevin Whately in
Inspector Morse

Honeysuckle Weeks and Michael Kitchen in *Foyle's War*

Tom Brittney, Robson Green, and James Norton in *Grantchester*

Shaun Evans in *Endeavour*

Jenna Coleman
and Rufus Sewell
in *Victoria*

Bill Nighy in
Worricker

Hugh Laurie and Stephen Fry in
Jeeves and Wooster

Maggie Smith in
Downton Abbey

Art Malik, Susan Wooldridge, and Timothy Pigott-Smith in
The Jewel in the Crown

Helen Mirren in
Prime Suspect

Gillian Anderson in *Bleak House*

Kenneth Branagh in *Wallander*

Aidan Turner in *Poldark*

Highclere Castle, the Real-Life *Downton Abbey*

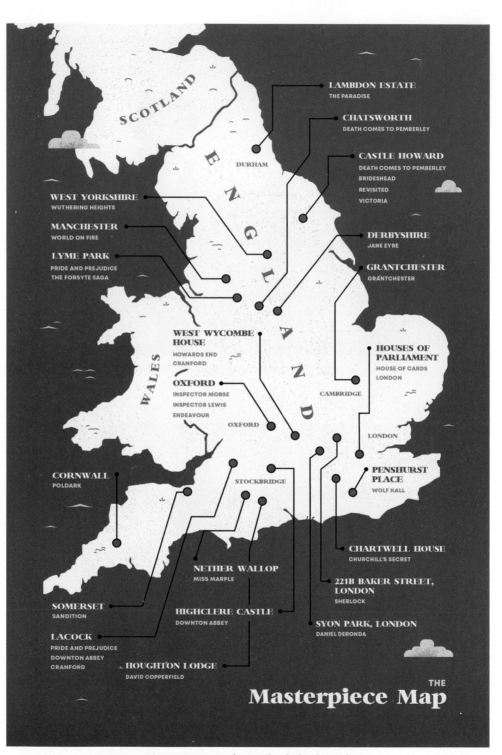

LAMBDON ESTATE
THE PARADISE

CHATSWORTH
DEATH COMES TO PEMBERLEY

CASTLE HOWARD
DEATH COMES TO PEMBERLEY
BRIDESHEAD
REVISITED
VICTORIA

WEST YORKSHIRE
WUTHERING HEIGHTS

MANCHESTER
WORLD ON FIRE

LYME PARK
PRIDE AND PREJUDICE
THE FORSYTE SAGA

DERBYSHIRE
JANE EYRE

GRANTCHESTER
GRANTCHESTER

WEST WYCOMBE HOUSE
HOWARDS END
CRANFORD

HOUSES OF PARLIAMENT
HOUSE OF CARDS
LONDON

OXFORD
INSPECTOR MORSE
INSPECTOR LEWIS
ENDEAVOUR

CORNWALL
POLDARK

PENSHURST PLACE
WOLF HALL

CHARTWELL HOUSE
CHURCHILL'S SECRET

NETHER WALLOP
MISS MARPLE

221B BAKER STREET, LONDON
SHERLOCK

SOMERSET
SANDITION

HIGHCLERE CASTLE
DOWNTON ABBEY

SYON PARK, LONDON
DANIEL DERONDA

LACOCK
PRIDE AND PREJUDICE
DOWNTON ABBEY
CRANFORD

HOUGHTON LODGE
DAVID COPPERFIELD

THE
Masterpiece Map

Masterpiece map by Michael Flinchpaugh

series deepens that relationship by making Morse into a kind of surrogate father for the much younger, less experienced Lewis. Yet as the show progresses, Lewis goes from being something of an awed flunky to a respected and even skeptical right-hand man, occasionally even solving the crime when Morse fails to do so. He also comes to care deeply for Morse, beaming when he learns his boss has a date, grimacing when he sees him order another drink.

Morse was played by John Thaw, who won nine best-acting awards for the role. Thaw hated Morse at first. After reading Dexter's novel *The Dead of Jericho*, he was put off by the detective's drinking habits and wolfish attitude toward women. He went to producer Kenny McBain and director Alastair Reid, determined to turn down the role. But they reassured him they would put a different Morse on the screen, inviting Thaw to help soften and enrich his character. For the actor, the answer lay in Morse's love of music: "You have to relate every character to yourself," he explained in an interview, "so I asked myself what it was about me—and therefore Morse, too—that finds solace in music. That became the key to his character for me."[17]

Thaw played Morse with quiet inscrutability, making him visibly sadder and more self-destructive as the series progresses. Gradually, Morse evolves into a tragic figure, pursuing a needlessly wanton, profligate lifestyle that he knows will undo him. In the show's last episode, Morse seems vague and vaguely defeated by years of alcohol, changing police procedures, and his own unmarried independence. He is determined to solve the case before him but cannot walk more than twenty steps without stopping to catch his breath. In a painfully slow scene, we witness him suffer a coronary on the grounds of Oxford's campus. He dies soon afterward in the hospital. The final shot is of Lewis, arriving too late to say goodbye, planting a tender kiss on Morse's forehead. In America, eleven million PBS viewers tuned in to watch the episode. Reviewing the show for its thirtieth anniversary in 2017, one critic claimed he found the scene so moving, he "couldn't bear to discuss it."[18]

Colin Dexter, who cameo-appeared on each episode of the show (usually as a patron in a pub), fell in love with the TV version of his detective. As a result, he deepened his character in later novels, even giving him Thaw's shock of white hair and "sad, blue eyes." Dexter also specified in his will that no other actor would play Morse again. And for eight years, no one did—until someone at ITV had the bright idea to do a prequel to the show, set in the 1960s, that would portray Morse as a young man. After many vigorous efforts, ITV finally persuaded Dexter to agree. That show turned out to be *Endeavour*, entering its seventh, triumphant season.

FOYLE'S WAR

As *Inspector Morse* drew to an end, ITV producers sent out a call, asking screenwriters to send in their bids for a new detective drama that might capture an equally wide audience. They received over three hundred entries. One of these entries described a story set during World War II, featuring a quiet, middle-aged detective named Christopher Foyle, his chipper young driver, Sam Stewart, and his stoic aide, Det. Sgt. Paul Milner. That story came to be *Foyle's War*, earning the number two spot in the *Radio Times* list of twenty best British crime dramas. Written by *Midsomer Murders* creator Anthony Horowitz, it launched on *Mystery!* in 2002 and enjoyed spectacular ratings until 2007, when the new director of programmes at ITV abruptly canceled it. Fans protested so strenuously, however, that the network quickly renewed it the next year—and replaced the lunkhead whose decision it was. *Foyle's War* then ran for four more glittering seasons. When ITV announced in 2015 that the eighth series would be the series' last, critic Mary McNamara of the *Los Angeles Times* declared, "The world I cover as a critic may be bursting at the seams with the exquisite and the innovative, the mind-blowing and the groundbreaking, but sustained excellence is still hard to come by. . . . Which is why I am not ashamed to beg. Piteously, publicly and for the record. Bring back Foyle."[19]

British mysteries love setting crime in self-enclosed worlds. *Foyle's War* flips that convention on its head, locating its drama in the picture-postcard coastal town of Hastings, but making World War II its ever-present, looming backdrop. In truth, *Foyle's War* ("Where history meets mystery," as its tagline describes) is a historical epic disguised as a detective series. It offers a penetrating glimpse into how the war shaped the lives of ordinary British citizens, with everyday violence and vice continuing unabated. Horowitz's much-publicized wish was to shed light on little-known corners of Britain's war experience, and to debunk the glory stories of wartime heroism and solidarity. This is not to say that *Foyle's War* is cynical—but Horowitz showed how, even under mortal threat from the Nazis, people in England weren't all pulling together. "I've found myself touching on stories that are often dark and disconcerting," Horowitz said, "all the more so because they are absolutely true."[20] Over its eight seasons, the series traveled from the disaster of Norway to Dunkirk, the Blitz, Pearl Harbor, Dresden, the D-Day landings, VE day, VJ day, and then into the Cold War with Soviet spies, traitors, war criminals, and the atomic bomb. Foyle took on foes of every type—Nazis, anthrax, looters, black-marketeers, spies, corrupt British officials, you name it—in tales that always seemed true to the era, while tackling a range of contemporary issues, including racism and domestic assault.

With all that going on, perhaps it's best that Christopher Foyle is something of a nondescript man. He is perpetually underestimated by colleagues and criminals alike. While most TV detectives display all the usual alpha-male tendencies, Foyle simply drops his head, quirks his mouth, and says nothing—until, having quietly amassed all the evidence everyone else missed, he brings his hammer down. One of the finest pleasures in television is to witness this happen, as when, in "War Games," he visits the home of Sir Reginald Walker, the arrogant head of a corporation sending food services to the Nazis. After having just exposed Walker to the police while ensuring he will lose his business, Foyle walks into his study and asks, "Where's your wife?" When Walker replies, "She just left me," Foyle coolly replies, "Not much of a day for you is it?"

The brilliance of Foyle's character, as every single critic on Planet Earth agrees, is largely due to Michael Kitchen. Reputed to ask scriptwriters for *less* dialogue, Kitchen relies almost entirely on the language of his body, especially his face: the cheek bitten from the inside, the head tilted backward in mock surprise, the eyes that remain averted in conversation until, boom! he confronts a suspect with knowledge he isn't presumed to have. Kitchen's acting is all about the art of mastering small movements and exploiting vocal syncopation. The result is a character who embodies a whole tradition of British moral rectitude without ever appearing a prig.

Like *Poirot* and *Inspector Morse*, *Foyle's War* shifted tone and mood over its long run. The first several seasons play up the affectionate relationship among Foyle, Stewart, and Milner. They also punctuate their stories of wartime crime with utterly charming elements: Foyle fly-fishing in his tweedy fedora and vest, Sam doing her first high-speed chase, and lines like "I don't know what the blue pencil is going on!"

Ironically, the series adopts a much darker tone once the war ends. The locale shifts from Hastings to bombed-out London, creating a very different atmosphere; gone are the cliffs, the rolling waves, the seagulls. While he's still solving crimes, Foyle's postwar mysteries now involve problems of the Cold War era—the special treatment given to certain "useful" Nazi war criminals, the presence of Russian spies in British intelligence, the West's attempt to secure Iranian oil. Foyle plays a much more passive role in these latter seasons; the world has become too complex for him. And while this narrative direction may be tonally and thematically, one can't help but miss the old Foyle, as we do the old Belgian and his little gray cells.

MASTERPIECE MYSTERIES NOW

Masterpiece currently features a sparkling array of mysteries. One of these dramas is ITV's *Grantchester*, launched in 2015 and entering its fifth season in 2020. Based on the collected short stories by James Runcie (whose father is the former archbishop of Canterbury), *Grantchester* has featured two vicars—first, the jazz-loving Sidney Chambers and now the motorcycling Will Davenport—who solve crimes alongside salty police officer, Geordie Keating. Set in a quaint 1950s village, *Granchester* has all the feel of a traditional British mystery. The setting is bonny, with lots of rose-covered cottages and picturesque pathways. And it follows the singularly weird tradition, dating back to G. K. Chesterton's *Father Brown* series, of making a vicar an amateur detective. But *Grantchester* also targets a young audience, giving us two hunky he-men of the cloth and tackling such subjects as homophobia, sexual harassment, and racism.

Endeavour is another of *Masterpiece*'s current mysteries. Launched in 2013 as a one-off to mark *Inspector Morse*'s twenty-fifth anniversary, it has evolved into a superior mystery that rivals its predecessor. The show's genius is in how it creates an inverse evolution of Morse. Starring Shaun Evans and Roger Allam as his senior partner, Detective Thursday, *Endeavour* jumps back to the 1960s, when the future chief inspector was a mere detective constable. *Endeavour*, like the original series from which it springs, is slow and quiet, haunted by a vague sense of doom. And Morse is played just as thoughtfully by Evans as he ever was by John Thaw. He yearns for love and fulfillment, unable to see that what he wants is actually within his grasp.

These two detective shows, along with *Masterpiece*'s *Unforgotten*, play within a new landscape of very good—and very grim—British crime drama. Recent non-*Masterpiece* examples include *Broadchurch*, *Luther*, *Happy Valley*, *The Fall*, and *Criminal*. Each series focuses on crime from the inside, portraying the twisted potential of human beings, whether serial rapists or PhD students specializing in nuclear physics. Sexual assault, murder, torture, kidnapping, missing children: they're all afoot. So, too, is the trauma of the victims' families, the dark psychoses of the perpetrators, and the neuroses of the detectives. This approach now makes Britain the undisputed leader in television crime drama, surpassing even the United States in grit and gore. Chandler must be turning over in his grave.

As critics agree, these hard-hitting dramas stem from a series that may be the darkest show ever to run on *Mystery!*: *Prime Suspect*. It redefined British crime drama, as we'll see in chapter 8. Even so, neither *Mystery!* nor *Masterpiece* ever went that dark again—and while this reticence may have its drawbacks, it also serves a purpose.

Judging by critical reviews and fan commentary, viewers appreciate crime dramas that add heart-warmth to darkness. "It's like a table perfectly set for afternoon tea," says the *Guardian* of *Grantchester*. "Familiar, elegant, and comforting."[21] The business of all detective dramas, it's true, is to explore the impulses that lurk in the shadows of human experience. But the detectives of *Mystery!* and *Masterpiece* cleanse the atmosphere by bringing those impulses into the light and defeating them, if only by exposing their perfidy. The series' affectionate portrayals of community, family, and friendship also underline that basic dynamic of reassurance. Mysteries like *Grantchester* and *Endeavour* may soft-pedal crime, but they also bestow hope and optimism. They occupy a definite place in the television landscape. That place is *Masterpiece*.

★ ★ ★

Miss Marple's grace. Poirot's impeccable manners. Morse's gallantry. Foyle's moral rectitude: we like to think human beings demonstrate such qualities in real life, or can summon them when called upon. But they seem to have all but vanished in America's politically divisive, digitally addicted, therapeutically minded culture. One of the best things about *Masterpiece* is how it tries to counter that influence. How? By giving us characters who model right behavior. In the chapter ahead, we'll meet the very best of them.

· 7 ·

Quality Assurance

Characters are the lifeblood of every story. We read, view, and binge on stories for their characters. Sometimes we attach ourselves to them, imagining they are our friends, lovers, or worst enemies. And in the case of exemplary characters, we may even call on their lives for wisdom. In fact, the publishing world is chock-full of memoirs—*A Jane Austen Education, My Life in Middlemarch, The Heroine's Bookshelf*—that chronicle how figures like Jane Eyre transformed an author's life or worldview, providing "life lessons" about the "things that really matter."

Looking over *Masterpiece*'s fifty years of programming, we find a treasury of characters who offer models for living. Take Molly Gibson, the young heroine in *Wives and Daughters* (1999). Devoted to her friends even when they don't deserve it, Molly can teach us about the value of constancy, that quality of sticking to something (or someone). The Victorians saw constancy as the foundation for all other virtues, and in our highly changeable, distractible society, we could all use more of it. Or consider James Hathaway in *Inspector Lewis* (who wields his erudition not to show off how smart he is but to solve real-world problems). Or Jean Valjean in *Les Misérables*, whom actor Dominic West described as "the best superhero ever written." Valjean is strong enough to climb the side of a building if need be. But what makes him a hero is that he tries to be the best man he can when all the odds, including his inner demons, are against him. As West says, "He makes goodness interesting."

And the list goes on. Ever since 1971, *Masterpiece* has featured characters who inspire and uplift us. Sure we enjoy watching the baddies, but the program's more admirable characters feed our souls. They are a vital part of *Masterpiece*'s aspirational pull: walking testaments that fiction, whether on-page or onscreen, can show us how to live with zest, integrity, kindness, and style.

These days, they also distinguish *Masterpiece* from a TV landscape tyrannized by the antihero.

With so many series, how do you choose which characters to spotlight? Hudson in *Upstairs, Downstairs* would make for a lovely meditation on loyalty. An essay on integrity and Holly Evans from *The Press* (2019) would practically write itself. Ditto, *Downton Abbey*'s Anna Bates and kindness. For American viewers, one approach is to look at characters who possess qualities we seem to lack, both on our television and in our lives. Below are six such qualities. Some are considered old-fashioned, others, very "British." And while none of them will solve the problem of climate change or lead our nation out of its staggering debt, each is a quality worth cultivating. Why? Because they enrich the color of life, brighten and intensify it. And in their own distinctive way, they remind us of why tradition, with its love of style and civility, is so vital to personal happiness.

CHARM: LORD MELBOURNE IN *VICTORIA* (2017–2019)

Charm: a word we use all the time yet barely understand. Even dictionaries stumble in defining it. *Merriam-Webster*, for example, describes charm as "a trait that fascinates, allures, or delights." OK, but how? And why?

One way to approach charm is to distinguish it from charisma. Charisma has to do with someone's presence, his aura. Those who possess charisma (Sherlock Holmes, Poldark, Harry Selfridge) have magnetic personalities, making it easy for them to influence others. Charm is about presence *and* connection. Charmers are rapport artists; they have a magical ability to make others feel attended to, even understood. In the presence of a charming person, we're enthralled by his manner, appearance, and words. But we also feel as if we're pretty special ourselves.

Who are *Masterpiece*'s great charmers? One of them is the current host of *Masterpiece Mystery!,* actor Alan Cumming, whose natural ease is among charm's requisite properties. He makes us smile the moment we see him. As for *Masterpiece* characters: Hercule Poirot has charm, especially when it comes to young women in trouble. So does Francis Urquhart in *House of Cards*, though his charm is all for nasty ends. Ditto, Willoughby in *Sense and Sensibility* (2008). Spiros in *The Durrells in Corfu* (2016–2019) has a kind of homespun charm. Mrs. Wilson's husband in *Mrs. Wilson* (2019) had so much charm he managed to juggle three unsuspecting wives for twenty years. And let's not forget Sidney Chambers and Will Davenport in *Grantchester*, whose superior listening skills, not to mention babelicious looks, qualify them both as master charmers. But *Masterpiece*'s 100-proof charmer is Lord Melbourne (Rufus

Sewell) from *Victoria*, the prime minister who shepherded the young queen through her early reign.

Judging by audience feedback, half of PBS's viewership was in love with Lord Melbourne, or "Lord M" as the Queen calls him, when *Victoria*'s Season 1 aired in the winter of 2017. And who could blame us? Like many charmers, Lord M is a hottie, with broad shoulders, smoldering eyes, and wavy dark hair. He also wears his britches very, very well. Tammy Hughes of the *Daily Mail* agreed, remarking, "Now Rufus Sewell is ready to assume the crown of Sunday night heartthrob currently taken by *Poldark*'s Aidan Turner."[1] Assume that crown he did, so much so that when Prince Albert arrived on the scene at the end of episode 3, viewers wished he'd go back to Germany. "Rufus Sewell stole the show as Lord M," tweeted one American fan. "Shame she [Victoria] fell for Albert." Another fan from Ohio wrote, "If anything, Rufus Sewell is *too* good in *Victoria*. Don't want Albert to swoop in and ruin things."[2]

It isn't just his bonny good looks that render Lord M a charmer. Unlike Albert, whose unremitting seriousness makes him a bore, Melbourne has wit. When he first meets Victoria, she immediately informs him that she won't marry the Prince of Orange because he has a "head the size of a pumpkin," to which he responds, "I see you have a keen eye for detail, mum." Melbourne also possesses the charmer's tact, helping ease Victoria out of her many faux pas by quietly slipping in and fixing a situation, as he does when he comes up behind her and discreetly whispers the names of the various personages she is meeting for the first time. All charmers have that kind of social acumen. And though he excels at conversation, Lord M is often quiet, suggesting the charmer's natural sense of self-restraint: his wish is to make others shine, not himself.

"There is something womanly about charm," observes writer Benjamin Schwarz.[3] Charming men *get* the opposite sex. They take obvious delight in female company, conveying the impression they'd just as soon spend the afternoon talking with a woman as they would taking her to bed. In fact, what gives the relationship between Victoria and Melbourne such chemistry is precisely the sense that sex would be one of many possibilities for their mutual entertainment. With Albert, contrarily, sex is right there from the start—primal, foursquare, and inevitable. Charming men also tend to possess an assortment of "feminine" traits, sensitivity among them. Upon meeting Victoria, Melbourne perceives her insecurity while everyone else sees only stubborn independence. More importantly, he recognizes her strengths. When she expresses worry early on in their relationship that she may be too "small" and inexperienced to pull off being a queen, he replies "You have a natural dignity that cannot be learnt," in his calm, dulcifying voice (another charm essential).

With a prime minister like that around, who'd want Robert Peel (aka Lord Anti-Charm)? When Victoria complains about having Peel as her new

PM, Melbourne diplomatically refrains from criticism, only saying, "I'm afraid Lord Peel doesn't understand the fair sex." Nope, not even close. But that's not the point. The line may be about Peel, but we know it's there to highlight Melbourne's own appreciation of women.

What other womanly traits make up the male charmer? Grace, elegance, subtlety, and poise, all of which bless Lord M from head to foot. He dances better than any man in the room, carries himself with deportment, and compared to the blunt and bigoted Prince Albert, is Lord Chancellor of the Subtle Remark. All Melbourne's criticisms of Victoria, for example, come gift wrapped in subtlety, making it impossible for her to take offense at them.

While charm is a form of magic, it's also a skill. That's why charm comes with age. It is also one reason why Albert, who's twenty-something to Melbourne's forty-something, lacks it (being German doesn't help). Masters of the social realm, charming people extend courtesy, defuse tension, bestow compliments, inject humor. And because they can't help themselves, they practice these skills every day, with everyone. That's why their charm seems utterly effortless.

Can the rest of us develop charm? These days, the quality seems nearly extinct, especially here in the States where our insane work schedules, therapeutic mindset, cell-phone addiction, and any number of other contemporary horrors make it impossible to give someone else the kind of singular attention charm bestows. What's more, we err in thinking about charm as beauty or magnetism, when deep down it is really about civility and kindness. We all can have a spritz or two of charm, Lord M would say. But we have some very uncharming habits to break first.

COOL: *WORRICKER* (2011, 2014)

Evoking classic film noir, *Worricker* opens with a jazz score and nighttime shots of London. A man glides through the city's streets, smoking a cigarette and wearing a well-tailored coat. That man is the series' hero, Johnny Worricker, a *Masterpiece* model of "cool." He illustrates how this enviable quality is really a blend of British and American traits.

Worricker is a three-part, BBC spy drama, written and directed by British playwright David Hare. It stars Bill Nighy, the actor who played the broken-down rock star Billy Mack in *Love Actually*, and stole the film. Here, Nighy is an aging intelligence officer with a passion for jazz, art collecting, and women. Recruited by MI5 to hunt communists for counterespionage service during the Vietnam War era, he now finds himself tracking Arabs and other terrorists. It's a bewildering job—and he longs for the days when, as one of his colleagues puts it, there was still such a thing as "pure intelligence."

Worricker's boss is Benedict Baron, head of MI5, and played by the sublime Michael Gambon (*Wives and Daughters, Churchill's Secret*). Shortly before he dies, Baron tells Worricker that the prime minister, Alec Beasley (Ralph Fiennes), has knowledge of secret overseas prisons where American authorities are torturing terror suspects. Worricker's mission, should he choose to accept it, is to gather evidence that will expose Beasley. The plot is complex, but as in film noir, plot doesn't matter; style does. And *Worricker* has plenty of style, from its sleek London locales to its moody photography to its protagonist, Mr. Cool himself.

As Worricker and Nighy both illustrate, cool is a signature style, so essential to the person possessing it as to exude an authentic way of being. In his onscreen-and-off personas, Nighy personifies cool. It's in his preference for well-cut clothes ("I've never worn a T-shirt"), his whispery way of talking, his feline movements, his sunglasses (a hallmark of cool because they keep people at a distance). It's also in Nighy's method of acting. Like Michael Kitchen (*Foyle's War*), Nighy is a quiet, measured actor. Resistant to big gestures and wild emotion, he relies on the calm, steady mastery of his craft to convey characters: very cool.

But cool is more than a style. It's an attitude with social import. In his richly textured history of the subject, Joel Dinerstein tells us that cool originated in mid-1940s African American jazz culture as a means of survival. The person to first invoke "cool" as a word meaning "relaxed" and "under control" was jazz musician Lester Young—and for Young, as well as scores of other African American jazz musicians like Miles Davis and Charlie Parker, cool was a way to assert their composure in the face of potential violence. Similarly, Worricker deploys his own style of cool to defuse the tense and treacherous world in which he operates. Cool is also a form of individual rebellion, especially against an unethical or immoral authority. That notion is played out in Worricker's ballsy defiance of the prime minister. Repulsed by the ministerial corruption he sees, Worricker openly challenges Beasley, thereby risking his life and dooming himself to political exile. And finally, cool is "the performance of calm in the face of ideological breakdown . . . it's what you adopt when the master narrative breaks down." *Worricker* is about a government teetering on the edge of a bottomless moral pit, no longer run by any identifiable values or beliefs. In such a world, staying cool may be the only viable option.[4]

America may have invented the concept of "cool" in the 1940s, but that doesn't mean we can't identify different manifestations of it elsewhere. Dinerstein draws a parallel between American cool and the mythic reserve of the British aristocracy—that grace under pressure once expected of those who topped the country's class system. In England, cool was formerly an indicator of social class; in America, it became a signifier of enviable self-mastery. Worricker embodies both notions. Oxford-trained and independently wealthy, his cool seems to be very much part of his social class. Yet his loner status and screw-you attitude toward British authority invest him with a particularly American style of cool, reinforced by his love of jazz and the series' studied invocation of film noir.

But what does all this have to do with the average American viewer? It suggests that far from being the self-absorbed, superficial behavior that now poses as cool, true cool is larger than image, and far more than a pose. If we're to adopt even a modicum of the quality, it has to be in service to something larger than ourselves. We also need to remember that even in its defiance, cool prizes the qualities of grace and restraint, displaying a kind of courteousness toward a fallen world. True cool thus has social significance *and* an element of civility. How cool is that? Watch *Worricker* and see.

ECCENTRICITY: *THE DURRELLS IN CORFU* (2016–2019)

In a contest of feel-good TV shows, *The Durrells in Corfu* would beat any contender. Critics call it an "island of charm," "blissful business," a "glimpse into a lost idyll," and as "warm and relaxing as a Corfu sunset." No wonder: the series takes place on the Greek island of Corfu, all blue sky and popsicle-colored houses. Its dialogue, scripted by Simon Nye, is also acidly funny. But what really gives the show its radiance is the collection of batty, dotty, squiffy characters who star in it. *The Durrells* is a parade of eccentricity: that bygone and very British quality.

Inspired by Gerald Durrell's memoir *My Family and Other Animals*, *The Durrells in Corfu* follows widow Louisa Durrell (Keeley Hawes) as she uproots her four children out of dank and grim England in 1935 to build a new life on the "cheap" island of Corfu. Nye first adapted the book in a ninety-minute film, *My Family and Other Animals*, starring Imelda Staunton and Matthew Goode, for the BBC in 2005. Nye had so much fun that he decided to adapt the story again, this time profiting from the resurgence of long-form drama.

The word *eccentric* derives from the Greek *ekkentros*, meaning "out of center." First gaining currency in the 1790s, eccentricity was quickly assumed to be an English quality—a byproduct of the liberty England gave its citizens. What seems more likely is that eccentricity developed as a harmless means of defying the British obsession with social decorum. Whatever the reason, the Brits swallowed the identity whole, proudly writing about their assorted weirdnesses in essays, poems, novels, and books, the most famous of which is Edith Sitwell's *English Eccentrics*, a veritable museum of fruitloopery published in 1933. What characterizes an eccentric? According to the editors of *Eccentropedia*, he or she is "nonconforming, creative, idealistic, and obsessed with at least one hobbyhorse."[5] Like each of the Durrells, an eccentric is determined to follow a private path irrespective of social expectations. A true eccentric also lacks self-consciousness. As one expert on the subject observes, the quality "has to be natural and unforced—people who try to be eccentric end up just being pillocks."[6]

To be labeled *eccentric* rather than *crazy* used to be a privilege only money could buy; being upper class gave one more license to stray from social norms. "The genius and the aristocrat are frequently regarded as eccentrics," says Sitwell, "because genius and aristocrat are entirely unafraid of and uninfluenced by the opinions and vagaries of the crowd."[7] If you were posh enough, in other words, you could get away with anything. Perhaps that's one reason why *My Family and Other Animals* has always been so beloved in Britain; it made eccentricity middle class. And indeed, each Durrell is a *rara avis*. Oldest son Larry (Josh O'Connor) is a pompous, self-absorbed writer who makes a point of typing in his bathrobe; middle son Leslie (Callum Woodhouse) is a gun-obsessed mama's boy; and Louisa's one daughter, Margo (Daisy Waterstone), is, as her mother puts it, "a sex-crazed twit." Gerry (Milo Parker), a budding zoologist, embodies the most common expression of British eccentricity: an unapologetic preference for animals over people. Even Louisa Durrell (Keeley Hawes) is always ready to try something once. "I'm thinking of learning the harp, or getting a cello between my legs," she writes to her Aunt Hermione.

It is Louisa, All-Time-Best-TV-Mother, who agrees to move the family to Corfu so her children can explore and experiment and find themselves. The house she presides over—pink!—is as ramshackle as can be, with peeling walls and rickety chairs. No matter: the house, like the island, feels utterly enchanted, there to help the Durrells find experiences that swell the heart and stretch the imagination. Gerry quickly discovers a companion and mentor, Dr. Theodore Stephanides, just as nutty about wildlife as he; Leslie gets to shoot off firearms to his heart's content; Margo tries her hand at nursing, fashion consulting, soap sculpting, hairdressing, and "losing her maidenhood"; Louisa becomes the proud owner of a boarding house populated by people far battier than she; and Larry writes a series of "smutty" novels, inspired by the carnal knowledge he has acquired on the island. Even Louisa's buttoned-up aunt, Hermione (Barbara Flynn), learns to relax when she comes for a visit, donning kaftans and imbibing vast quantities of ouzo. "I'm like a dog who wonders why she spent so many years barking," she says.

"Repressive regimes have no truck with eccentrics," observes William Sitwell.[8] And sure enough, all the Durrells' madcapping comes to an end once they get news of the Nazi encroachment in Albania. They free Gerry's menagerie, pack up their pink house, and tearfully say goodbye to their Grecian friends, returning to England at the end of the series for what they hope will be safety. Will the Durrells continue to indulge their eccentricity? The wistful tone of the series' ending suggests not. But they had four glorious years of it, as did we.

When *My Family and Other Animals* was originally published in 1956, many felt as if someone had thrown back the curtains and let in fresh air. It was just what a grim postwar Britain needed, suggesting that no matter how bleak present-day circumstances looked, Brits had the gumption, creativity, and humor to survive them. Sixty years later, *The Durrells in Corfu* enjoyed an unusually gushy reception in Britain, with TV critics praising the series as a "welcome vacation from our island of nightmares." The story of the Durrell family is once again what the country needs now, as it wrestles with the insanity of Brexit and its disastrous fallout. Meanwhile, there has been a wave of articles and books on the "decline" of British eccentricity, blaming its end on such forces as social media, a "health and safety fanaticism," and a political climate in which everyone is too afraid to say what he thinks. Could it be that this vital component of British identity, however mythical or overblown, is really gone—and is this also why *The Durrells* was so popular? As for America and eccentricity: the quality has never had much truck with us, perhaps because it requires two things Americans have never been much good at, leisure and a willingness to think in illogical, impractical ways. Yet the show's lesson is that our happiness depends on both.

MANNERS: JEEVES IN *JEEVES AND WOOSTER* (1990–1993)

Manners, says writer Mark Caldwell, "are what is left when serious issues of human relations are removed from consideration; yet without manners serious human relations are impossible."[9] Caldwell is right. Manners tend to strike Americans as trivial, old-fashioned, or even oppressive, yet as he suggests, they're vital to social harmony. Based on virtues like kindness, manners are what allow us to get through our days smoothly and pleasantly. Their purpose is not to stifle individual freedom, as many Americans assume, but to show respect and consideration for the needs, ideas, and opinions of others. Manners, in short, are the outward expression of moral character. And there is no *Masterpiece* figure who can teach us more about the value of good manners than Jeeves, the slick-haired and shiny-shoed valet from *Masterpiece*'s *Jeeves and Wooster*.

The series is based on the canon of thirty-five short stories and eleven novels by P. G. Wodehouse, published between 1916 and 1974. Wooster is a blithe and hapless gent with a knack for "landing in the soup" (which typically means that this wealthy young bachelor feels he's being dragooned into marriage); Jeeves is the wily and resourceful valet who always manages to rescue him. The stories are all sunlit silliness and innocence, there for us to read when we're suffering from boredom, a melancholy mindset, or drabness of soul. Reading even a page from the Jeeves and Wooster series makes us feel instantly better, charmed by the loopy characters, ridiculous plots, and jaunty inventiveness of language. "Mr. Wodehouse's idyllic world can never stale," said Evelyn Waugh in 1961. "He has made a world for us to live in and delight in."[10]

And Jeeves, as more than one critic has remarked, is perfect. No, really: he's *perfect*. Everything he says or does is utterly right, and no small part of this is his impeccable manners. It's a clever strategy: to make the man of lower social rank much more the gent than his employer, or for that matter, any of the bluebloods that populate Wodehouse's world. The potentially poisonous thing about manners is their entanglement with social class; manners often abet the cause of snobbery, excluding or ostracizing those who don't have the requisite knowledge of etiquette. Wodehouse completely upends this idea, making the servant a model of behavior for those whose upper-class status have veered them toward discourtesy or carelessness.

What makes Jeeves (played by Stephen Fry) such a mannerly model? To begin, he is consistently polite and cheerful, traits agreeable in themselves and useful in sustaining social harmony. He is also humble. Though far smarter than Bertie (Hugh Laurie), or any of Bertie's nitwit friends and relatives, Jeeves never flaunts his intelligence. He pursues erudition for its own sweet sake and uses his uncanny resourcefulness to help others. Like Hudson from *Upstairs, Downstairs* or Carson from *Downton Abbey*, Jeeves also rocks etiquette, instructing Wooster on what to wear, what to say, and generally on how to behave. Jeeves's ideas about etiquette are charmingly old-fashioned, and one of the running jokes in the series is his decided disapproval of Wooster's Jazz-Age tastes and sensibilities, deeming them vulgar.

Jeeves is also a master of tact, defined as an adroitness and sensitivity in dealing with others. Tact requires paying attention. One of its accomplishments is to find the pleasant or encouraging side of the truth. Unlike Bertie's Aunt Agatha, who believes in bald honesty and delivers her criticisms of Bertie with the force of a drilling machine, Jeeves speaks diplomatically, criticizing

Wooster in ways that never offend. He also excels at covering Wooster's mistakes without his master being quite sure it was done intentionally.

Jeeves does much good within his world, and like all those possessed of excellent manners, he does so by maneuvering delicately and cautiously in the right direction, without provoking anger. His behavior recalls Caldwell's comment that manners, while not having the power to "arbitrate fateful issues of right or wrong," can create good in their own "incremental, improvisational, indirect, and opportunistic way."[11]

Perhaps that's why Americans, who prefer the big and direct way of going about things, tend to have so little patience for manners. Jeeves, however, reveals the surprising magic of the quality, its natural polyvalence as well as its virtue. And played by the sublime Stephen Fry against Hugh Laurie's unsurpassable performance as Wooster, Jeeves also makes us laugh. Out loud. And often.

RESERVE: ELINOR DASHWOOD IN
SENSE AND SENSIBILITY (2008)

In a scene near the end of *Masterpiece*'s *Sense and Sensibility*, Elinor Dashwood and her younger sister, Marianne, are walking along the spectacular coastline of Devon, close to their cottage. Marianne, who has been Drama Queen through much of the story, impetuously pursuing the rakish Mr. Willoughby, says:

"Elinor, I look back on my conduct last autumn. I was a fool to myself and inconsiderate to everybody else."

"You cannot compare your conduct with his," her sister replies.

"No, but I can compare it with what it should have been." Pause. "I compare it with yours. I hope I am wiser now."

As Marianne knows, Elinor's admirable conduct in *Sense and Sensibility* stems from reserve. *Merriam Webster* defines the quality as "restraint, closeness, or caution in one's words and actions" or "forbearance from making a full explanation, complete disclosure, or free expression of one's mind." Whichever way you define it, reserve is not a quality Americans set store by. We pride ourselves on frankness. We indulge in big swirls of emotion and movement. And yet, would it be such a bad thing if Americans were to exercise a bit more reserve—especially in our current climate of outrage, grandstanding, and thoughtless commentary?

If we look at *Masterpiece*'s programming, we find that some of its most admirable characters—Christopher Foyle in *Foyle's War*, the older and wiser Branson in *Downton Abbey*, Denise Lovett in *The Paradise*—possess the quality of reserve. But the character who actually teaches us about its benefits and rewards is Elinor Dashwood.

Brilliantly adapted by Andrew Davies in 2008 from Jane Austen's novel, *Sense and Sensibility* is the story of two sisters, Elinor (Hattie Morahan) and Marianne Dashwood (Charity Wakefield), and their romantic relationships. Elinor personifies "sense" (i.e., common sense) while Marianne is all emotion, a capital-R Romantic. Elinor falls in love with the diffident Edward Ferrars (Dan Stevens) when he comes to visit his sister, but in keeping with her quiet personality, she safeguards herself by revealing very little to anyone about her feelings. Marianne, meanwhile, plunges head over heels for Willoughby (Dominic Cooper), swooning, gushing, and—when the relationship collapses after several weeks—spiraling into depression and illness. In the end, Elinor marries Edward, and Marianne marries the older and noble Colonel Brandon (Willoughby marries some rich bitch, eating his heart out over his mistake).

Many of those who first read Austen's novel are put off by Elinor's reserve, warming instead toward her more open and exuberant sister. Some even consider the novel a perversely unromantic book, suggesting as it does that a quiet, steady relationship based on long acquaintance is preferable to one based on passion. Like Marianne, though, the wise reader comes to see that self-containment has its virtues. Marianne's impulsive behavior exposes her to vicious gossip, worries her family, and, by way of one of those mysterious nineteenth-century illnesses, almost kills her. Elinor, meanwhile, quietly bears the burden of discovering that Edward, the pantywaist, had been secretly engaged to the odious Lucy Steele but couldn't find the nerve to tell her. Elinor is heartbroken by the discovery but tells no one, unwilling to upset her family or violate Edward's confidence.

Reserve helps you avoid trouble. But more importantly, it allows you to direct attention away from your own problems. While we may wonder at Elinor's stoicism, there is no denying that she is a loving, dutiful sister and daughter. Far more so than her high-strung mother, she takes care of everyone in the household. And she gains inner strength not only through service to those she loves but also acceptance of what she cannot change. Marianne, meanwhile, becomes more and more of a twit.

In Elinor, we learn that those who show reserve also tend to be calm, emotionally stable, self-sufficient, and observant. All these qualities make her the clear heroine of the novel, and Austen rewards her with the promise of a happy marriage to Edward. Andrew Davies gives her the very last shot of the film. In close-up, we see her radiant face as she watches her hapless husband chase a chicken around their garden. Elinor is Davies's girl, no question.

The British see reserve as one of their defining traits. They view it as essential to good manners, a courtesy we bestow on others by not burdening them with our emotions. Reserve acknowledges that our real selves are often not fit for display. Better to assume a veneer of cheerfulness and good will than to let others see how sad or overburdened or grumpy we really feel. Such behavior isn't hypocrisy; rather, it's a form of civility—a way of expressing our commitment to important social ideals in the face of our own weaknesses and failings. If *Sense and Sensibility* is about anything, it's about this. The series should be required viewing for all Americans.

WIT: *DOWNTON ABBEY* (2011–2016)

Scores of *Masterpiece* characters possess wit, from Miss Marple to Caligula. But the dowager countess from *Downton Abbey* is in a wit class all her own. Her fulltime job on that show was to deliver one dazzling riposte and *bon mot* after another.

Comedy, says Stephen Wagg, is "the great social organizer."[12] It provides pleasure not just in the joke but in the effervescent intimacy that a joke can generate. The dowager's wit is a vital part of *Downton Abbey*'s humor, along with slapstick (Molesley), sarcasm (Lady Mary, Mrs. Patmore), self-deprecation (Daisy), and the romantic comedy of Carson and Mrs. Hughes. But what is wit, exactly? Basically, it's the ability to use words in an amusing way. Wit differs from other types of humor in that it is an entirely verbal skill.

Such skill—possessed by the very few, hardly any of them living in the United States—requires cleverness. You can't be a dimwit or a halfwit and be witty. Benjamin Errett calls wit "the quick, instinctive, improvisational intelligence that allows us to say the right thing at the right time in the right place." Put another way, wit is a "speed game," making the countess's wit, at eighty-something, that much more admirable.[13] Wit also requires a mind that thinks in metaphors; it finds "similarity in dissimilar things or dissimilarity in similar things," as when the dowager quips, "Principles are like prayers: Noble of course, but awkward at a party."

However spontaneous and quick they may be, witty people pay close attention to the world around them. Those who have wit tend to be good listeners, studying conversation carefully so they know when to pounce. An elderly woman who spends most of her time sitting, the countess is always listening, and while her son, Lord Grantham, can sometimes be as thick as gunge, she misses nothing. To be a great wit, one must also have a vast sum of knowledge and worldly experience to draw from. "The highest wit," says an anonymous writer for *Littell's Living Age*, "is wisdom at play."[14] Like charm, wit is a skill that improves with age.

But whereas charm always seeks to please others, wit can offend. Deflating what it regards as hypocrisy, unjustified pride, and hollow ambition, it is aggressive and often hurtful. As much as we love her, there's no denying the dowager can be cruel. We enjoy it when she puts down rotters like Sir Richard Carlisle, that creep Lady Mary almost married. But we bristle when she pokes fun at Branson's ineptitude for small talk or his workingman's wardrobe. Still, we wouldn't change her. As Joseph Epstein observes, "We need wits on the scene. Without them, we fall into the grave danger of taking ourselves too seriously."[15]

Onscreen, wit draws one's attention to dialogue. It makes conversation performative, rendering it an art form. The best proof of this is in how the dowager's lines have traveled far beyond the confines of *Downton Abbey*. In America, they have made their way onto bumper stickers, tote bags, coffee mugs, cross-stitch patterns, and even the backs of women's underwear (see www.etsy.com). Here is a sampling:

- "Why does every day involve a fight with an American?"—*to Matthew Crawley after trying to sit in an American swivel chair and almost falling off it.*
- "Of course it would happen to a foreigner. No Englishman would dream of dying in someone else's house."—*on the Turk who died in Lady Mary's bed.*
- "I wonder your halo doesn't grow heavy. It must be like wearing a tiara around the clock."—*to do-gooder Isobel Crawley.*

These lines wouldn't be half as much fun if they weren't delivered by the inimitable Maggie Smith, whose timing, arched eyebrows, and matter-of-fact tone make each delivery a triumph. Her performance is enhanced by *Downton Abbey*'s winking camerawork. The camera shoots her in close-up as she delivers one of her zingers, showing how pleased she is with herself; or focuses on Carson, her devoted ally, who invariably smiles at her put-downs; or cuts to her victim looking foolish or devastated.

Wit can be a less-than-admirable quality, but when used well, it livens conversation and adds zest to social interaction. Can it be learned? In his recent book on the subject, Ben Errett tells us that Winston Churchill, a man legendary for his wit, was a reader of *Bartlett's Familiar Quotations* and sedulously read the joke columns in newspapers for comic material. "His magpie mind drew from books, film, media, and anywhere else he read, heard, or saw a line worth repeating," writes Errett.[16] One suspects something similar in the case of the dowager's creator, Julian Fellowes, who penned every wisecrack. Could it be that wit may not be as spontaneous as it seems but, rather, something that any of us, provided we're clever enough, can work up beforehand, stealing a line here or there as we choose? If so, the dowager gives us plenty of material to work with.

★ ★ ★

Charm, manners, reserve, wit—even cool and eccentricity—are qualities that ease and enhance social intercourse. We Americans pay little heed to such matters. As a society of go-getters addicted to work, achievement, success, and now a kind of therapeutic narcissism, we tend to be inwardly focused, inattentive to the feelings of others or to how we appear in public. Oh sure, we care about how our hair looks or whether we're keeping up with fashion trends. But we never consider developing attributes like wit or tact. Yet such is the contradictory nature of American society that when we see Lord Melbourne or Lady Violet on TV, we hanker to be them.

Our admiration for a British model of genteel, cultured personal behavior also cuts more deeply. It carries over from the characters to the actors who play them. We tend to believe, actually want to believe, that the actors are just as fascinating and delightful in real life as they are onscreen. Rufus Sewell, Bill Nighy, Maggie Smith . . . ; we adore these people, partly for the roles they play, partly for the skill with which they do so, partly for the charming image they, themselves, project. The British actors on *Masterpiece* not only seem more skilled and cultured than American actors, but more attractive as people. As we'll see now, our Anglophilia penetrates beyond the screen to the highly trained individuals who bring *Masterpiece*'s stories to life.

· 8 ·

Acting Up

$\mathcal{A}$ weekday morning in early December 1984. Nearly one hundred TV critics have gathered inside the ballroom at the Ritz-Carlton hotel in Boston, waiting to interview cast members of *The Jewel in the Crown*, *Masterpiece*'s epic, fourteen-part series about the final days of the British Raj in India. Everyone is jazzed about the production, extolling its superior cast, spectacular scenery, and unflinching portrait of the arrogance and inevitable corruption of British imperialism. While they agree that the acting is uniformly excellent, the one performance they can't stop talking about is that of Tim Pigott-Smith, who played the sadistic, racist police superintendent, Captain Ronald Merrick.

Pigott-Smith is in the hotel today. As he walks up to the stage, a journalist from the *Boston Globe* starts hissing; within seconds, they all do. The noise grows so loud that hotel staff members rush in to see if they need to call the police. But the actor, a boyish-looking man of thirty-six, shrugs his shoulders and smiles. Just the week before he'd been accosted on a London street by a woman who, brandishing her umbrella at him, said, "If we were in a restaurant right now, I'd come poison your food."

Pigott-Smith, who starred in *Masterpiece*'s production of *King Charles III* just before he died in 2017, was widely known as one of the nicest men in Britain's theatrical world. How did an affable actor like him transform into such a rotter? He studied the part for six months, going through the script scene by scene with the original novels beside him. Pursuing the theory that Merrick's racism stems from his own class inferiority, Pigott-Smith also spent hours talking to a criminal psychologist about men in law enforcement who abuse their power. And he devised twelve "Merrickisms"—thrusting his jaw out so his lips would form a sneer, "posing up" his "o" sounds to convey Merrick's efforts to sound like a gentleman—to make his character more vivid.

119

"By the end," he explains to his audience, "I could switch all this on; and, as an actor, if you can throw the physical switch, the mental process of the character will follow."[1]

This punctilious attention to character is the hallmark of British drama—and why actors have always been *Masterpiece*'s best asset. Critics may find fault with the script or cinematography, but they almost always point out the excellence of the performances. This was true in 1971, when reviewers complained about the contorted plot of *The First Churchills* but praised the acting of Sir John Neville and Susan Hampshire, and it's true now. As for the rest of us: we idolize these actors, bestowing our Anglophilia, every last drop of it, on people like Benedict Cumberbatch, David Oyelowo, and that other British monarch, Maggie Smith.

The pleasure American viewers take in watching *Masterpiece*'s performances goes beyond the skills and personalities of its actors, however. It's also about experiencing television as a kind of theater—of seeing performers who have worked at the Royal Shakespeare Company or trained at schools like the Royal Academy of Dramatic Arts, and who appear regularly on the London stage. *Masterpiece* based its original appeal on the assumption that British theater was the acme of cultural entertainment. That traditional appeal persists. And these days, as British actors continue to beat out their American peers for film and television roles, causing a new flurry of Anglophilia *and* a nationalistic defense of American talent, it is forcing Hollywood to take a cold, hard look in the mirror.

THE BRITISH ARE COMING

"There is something about Britain that smells of the theatre," write director Richard Eyre and dramatist Nicholas Wright in their masterful history of twentieth-century British drama.[2] One reason for theater's preeminence in England is simply that there has been so much of it. Seismic movements at several periods in English history have thrown up extraordinary riches: the Shakespearean decades of the 1580s–1610s; the witty, political drama of the Restoration era; the explosive melodrama of the late eighteenth and late nineteenth centuries; and the fervent, experimental period of the 1950s–1970s. British drama therefore encompasses several histories, each vividly different from one another. Plus, theater is everywhere in Britain. Almost every English town, no matter how small or godforsaken, has a repertory theater. London alone has roughly 230 playhouses, among them the Old Vic, once home to the English National Opera; the Barbican, London's venue for the Royal Shakespeare Company; and Shakespeare's Globe, a faithful reconstruction of the original Globe theater: all wooden benches and timber frames, and open to the evening sky.

What accounts for Britain's theatrical wealth? The ready answer is its nearly five-hundred-year-old devotion to Shakespeare. Eyre and Wright offer other explanations:

> Many of the characteristics of theatre coincide with those of the British nation: our love of ritual, processions, ceremonies, hieratic behavior and dressing up. Our parliamentary and legal systems depend, as does theatre, on adversarial conflict. And theatre is concerned with role-playing, which is, of course, second nature to a nation obsessed with the signs and behavior of class distinction and inured to the necessity of pretending to be what you aren't.[3]

Whatever the reasons, there's no question that the British seem to have an almost congenital love of drama, and that Americans, perceiving our own country to be deprived of a vital theatrical culture, admire them for it. While Anglophilia often takes the form of rural provincialism, expressing a fascination with the country's villages and rural landscapes, it is just as often a cosmopolitan impulse. British drama feeds that impulse, channeling our adulation of England toward its more urban and diverse attractions.

A weighty institution, British theater: small wonder, then, that so many actors attend drama school in order to learn the cornerstones of their craft. It was England, in fact, that established the world's first acting academy: the Dramatic College, started in 1904 by dramatist Herbert Beerbohm Tree. Tree founded the college to stop the exploitative employment of casual labor in the theater and to put an end to dilettante dallying with the art form. He also hoped that a drama school would keep theater "modern" by devising new techniques and approaches for every succeeding generation. As historian Simon Shepherd explains, Tree's motivations reflected "a serious, national commitment at the turn of the 20th century to the value of apprenticeship and craft vocation and the dignity of the artisan."[4]

Now known as the Royal Academy of Dramatic Arts (RADA), the school has graduated actors like Kenneth Branagh, Ralph Fiennes, Laurence Fox, Michael Gambon, Anthony Hopkins, Alan Rickman, and Mark Rylance (Gary Oldman was turned down, advised to enter a different line of work; so were Daniel Craig and Rosamund Pike). Britain boasts a bunch of other renowned schools as well. Topping the list are the National Youth Theatre, whose alumni include Daniel Day-Lewis; the London Academy of Music and Dramatic Art (John Lithgow, David Oyelowo, Donald Sutherland, Jim Broadbent); the Guildhall School of Music and Drama (Damian Lewis, Jude Law, Daniel Craig, Michelle Dockery, and Ewan McGregor); the Bristol Old

Vic Theatre School (Jeremy Irons and Patrick Stewart); the Guildford School of Acting (Bill Nighy); and the Central Royal School of Speech and Drama (Laurence Olivier, Judi Dench, and Vanessa Redgrave).

What thespian know-how do these schools impart? Technical skills, certainly: projecting and modulating one's voice; using facial expressions, gestures, and bodily movements to convey character; honing one's sense of timing. More importantly, students learn how to inhabit a wide range of characters. "Our training will ask an actor to really play against type at times, to play a role that they wouldn't necessarily be cast in in the profession, in order to work out and transform how they move towards that character. It's almost like putting on a second skin," says Joanna Reed, a member of the London Academy of Music and Dramatic Arts.[5]

That academic challenge pays off once British actors enter the professional world of theater, requiring they perform against type all the time. This gives them a more detached approach to the imitation game of acting than their peers across the pond. More importantly, it sharpens their imaginations and helps them maintain what is vital to any actor: a sense of play.

No wonder, then, that we find a startling vigor and variety to the performances on *Masterpiece*. Think of Claire Foy, who played the kindhearted and loyal heroine in *Little Dorrit* (2008), a Nazi-sympathizing brat in the remake of *Upstairs, Downstairs*, and a ruthless Anne Boleyn in *Wolf Hall*. Or consider James Norton, who starred in *Grantchester* as a gentle dreamboat of a vicar after portraying a vile rapist in *Happy Valley*, a role that earned him death threats. Or Derek Jacobi, whose career-defining role in *I, Claudius* demanded he be noble, tender hearted, and calculating all at once. Jacobi has played every type of villain and every manner of good man, including, on *Masterpiece*, the kindly bishop in *Les Misérables* and the well-meaning but weak-willed Grandfather Trent in *The Old Curiosity Shop* (2007). And while American actors tend to shy away from villainous roles because they're afraid of blackening their image, Brits go at them with gusto—from Siân Phillips, who played Livia in *I, Claudius* as the scheming matriarch from hell, to Ben Chaplin in *Press*, who portrays Duncan Allen, a tabloid editor, with the charisma of Satan.

Of course, the *sine qua non* of theatrical training in Britain is Shakespeare. Many *Masterpiece* actors—David Tennant, Judi Dench, Ralph Fiennes, Michael Gambon—have worked with the Royal Shakespeare Company, an organization that employs over a thousand actors who perform the Bard's plays at Stratford-upon-Avon and all over the world. According to Dench, this experience furnished her with "an invaluable toolbox of technical skills. . . . I wouldn't be the actress I am today if it weren't for the RSC."[6] Along with many other skills, Shakespeare requires actors to master pacing and cadence. More importantly, it challenges them to make a remote character relatable to a contemporary audience. Patrick Stewart, who jump-started his career with *Masterpiece*'s *I, Claudius*, says, "I think the experience that we get in making a 400-year-old text work is exactly what you need for giving credibility and believability to fantasy, science fiction, and the like." Translation: if you can make Hamlet, with all his iambic-pentameter, metaphor-heaped soliloquies, relatable to a modern audience, Jean Luc Picard is a walk in the park.

Unlike their American peers, actors in the UK have always moved fluidly among television, theater, and film. One reason is that all three industries are centered in London. Brits can therefore travel easily from studio to theater while their Yankee compeers have to shuttle between New York and Los Angeles. At the time of this writing, Claire Foy is performing at the Old Vic in a play called *Lungs* while also completing the shooting for the biopic *Louis Wain*, scheduled for release in 2020. Actors say they enjoy the different demands of each medium; and some, like *Downton Abbey*'s Penelope Wilton, firmly believe that of the three forms, television is the most demanding.

Until the mid-to-late 1990s, when Acorn TV and BBC America appeared on the scene, *Masterpiece* was essentially America's ticket counter to British drama. Now British stars like Benedict Cumberbatch, Tom Hiddleston, Martin Freeman, and Claire Foy are everywhere. What's more, they're taking on American roles, first in film (Rosamund Pike in *Gone Girl*, Christian Bale in *The Dark Knight*) and now on television. On any given night of channel surfing in the past several seasons, a viewer would likely have happened upon an English actor (or three) playing a born-and-bred Yankee: Damian Lewis in *Billions*, Ruth Wilson and Dominic West in *The Affair*, Rupert Friend in *Homeland*, Andrew Lincoln in *The Walking Dead*. It's a trend that has been causing Hollywood no small degree of consternation. "There is some sort of crisis in American acting," Michael Douglas mused gloomily to a magazine interviewer several years ago. Spike Lee, commenting on the "invasion" of black British actors, made some cogent remarks on the subject, too: "You want talented people. British actors training is very proper, whereas some of these other brothers and sisters, you know, they come in here, and they don't got that training." If "invasion" seems like a strong word, Lee may have felt he had good reason to use it: only a few weeks before, in December 2014, the docudrama *Selma* arrived, starring David Oyelowo as Martin Luther King Jr., Carmen Ejogo as Coretta King, Tom Wilkinson as Lyndon Johnson, and Tim Roth as Governor George Wallace. Every one of these actors is British. "Crisis or not," says one critic, "this is getting embarrassing."[7]

Since *Selma*'s release, a torrent of nervous essays has appeared in high-profile venues like the *New York Times* and the *New Yorker* trying to make sense of the "New British Invasion." The titles of these essays—"Why

British Actors Outclass Hollywood," "The Decline of the American Actor," and "British Actors Aren't Better Than Our Own"—suggest the mixture of envy, admiration, fear, and gloom that shapes current conversation on the topic. Film critic Terrence Rafferty, for example, argues that the American actor is in a "woeful state of decline." Blaming this partly on America's disregard for theatrical training, he takes a nostalgic look at Hollywood in the 1970s, when actors like Robert De Niro and Dustin Hoffman displayed a "creative, risk-taking spirit," born of Method training, that he thinks has since disappeared among American male stars. "What's becoming difficult to ignore in current American leading men," he says, "is a general absence of joy in their vocation."[8] For Rafferty, the "crisis" in American acting has less to do with a "British Invasion" than a Hollywood system that, through its schlocky scripts and lack of incentives to refine one's craft, has failed to nurture its actors. The upshot is that Hollywood stars, especially the men, have lost their ability to play. Rafferty is quick to point out that British actors have that ability in spades.

Other writers agree, expressing concern over Hollywood's "perverse predilection" for young stars. In their view, this leads to double trouble: 1) American actors become stars before they've had a chance to learn vital skills and 2) by the time they're forty, Hollywood is more or less done with them. In contrast to British film and television, which value older actors, Hollywood becomes a Nubian desert for those who hit middle age. What's more, if you're an actor in Britain, there is always the stage: at any given time, someone, somewhere, will be putting on a production of Shakespeare. And while the opportunity may not be as glamorous as starring in a feature film, it's a chance to act, to feed the soul. When he's seventy, Benedict Cumberbatch can play King Lear in Bampton. But Leonardo DiCaprio, who just turned forty-five at the time of this writing, may have a far tougher time finding work.

Other commentary on the British Invasion takes a very different tack. Kate Winslet, for example, quipped that having a "British accent is a one-way ticket to Hollywood stardom."[9] Some critics suggest we discount our own drama schools, pointing out that many aspiring American actors choose to study in England rather than stay here for their training. Others take issue with the assumption that a schooling in classical literature and theater is a prerequisite for good acting. "The idea is preposterous," argues a theater critic. And still others claim that our low opinion of American actors has less to do with their talent than the mass-marketed crap we see them in.[10]

In short, the current situation is a hot mess. Will American roles continue to go to Brits, or will a backlash here prevent it? Is it possible that this new concern over lack of theatrical training might lead drama schools to assume more prominence in American culture? Ditto, theater? Or is the "New British

Invasion" simply a fad, one that will soon die out and let Hollywood stardom continue *sans* Brittania? The answer is anyone's guess.

But what lies at the heart of it all is Anglophilia: its aspirations and fetishes, its impulse, always, to think in terms of absence. Simply put, we love England for what we think we lack. And no other institution has conditioned American Anglophilia more than *Masterpiece*. It awakened us to the richness of British drama and the larger cultural world of which it is a part—and left us feeling sadly inadequate.

COMMAND PERFORMANCES

What have been the program's top performances over the years? Trying to choose is fiendishly difficult: a write-down-a-name, cross-out-a-name affair. Yet judging by critical reviews and audience feedback, six actors and their roles stand out as especially masterful. Collectively, they also provide a fascinating look at the ways in which Anglophilia shapes our response to British acting.

Ian Richardson in House of Cards *(1990)*

Before Kevin Spacey, there was Ian Richardson. It was Richardson who appeared in the original *House of Cards* as a deliciously malevolent politician who reaches the highest position in office by sabotaging every one of his opponents.

House of Cards is the first series in a trilogy based on the novels by political insider Michael Dobbs, former chief of staff at Conservative Party headquarters. Firmly attuned to the era in which it was made, the four-episode BBC series depicts a 1980s political landscape of old-white-guy politicians, opinion polls, purloined documents, wiretaps, leaks to the press, and an obsessive media-mindedness, with clear parallels to the royal family and Thatcher administration. But its real interest is in the timeless, ruthless game of politics. And its champion player is Richardson's Francis Urquhart, parliamentary chief whip, whom screenwriter Andrew Davies adapted with Shakespeare's Richard III, Iago, and Macbeth in mind. It was Davies who came up with the idea of breaking the fourth wall by having his villain speak directly to the camera: a cheeky technique that the American version aped years later.

In the first episode, we learn that the country's prime minister has died and a new PM, Henry Collingridge, has taken over thanks to Urquhart's backroom manipulation. But when Urquhart visits his boss to see which great office of state will be his reward, he discovers that Collingridge plans to keep him right where he is. Urquhart takes the news calmly but storms underneath.

From that moment onward, he dedicates himself to destroying Collingridge and insinuating himself into the job. He systematically assembles a team of lackeys, all unaware of how they are being used. His ace lackey is a young journalist named Mattie Storin, whom he charms and seduces until she can no longer see the truth before her eyes. When she finally does confront him with her suspicions, he throws her off a building in a movement so quick and balletic we're left doubting the reality of what we saw.

Urquhart may be pure evil, but like the best of villains, he has impeccable manners. He drinks aged port, speaks flawless French, and adds "quite" to the end of his sentences like a grace note. Everything he does, he does effortlessly. This invests him with an almost weary evil, as if his black-hearted doings have less to do with ambition than with bored disgust at those not as smart, resourceful, or polished as he (i.e., everyone). These traits come to the fore when he interacts with the series' other male characters: the clueless Collingridge; the vulgar and buffoonish editor, Benjamin Landless; the horny political rival, Patrick Woolton; and most of all, the public relations consultant with a weakness for cocaine, Roger O'Neill. Urquhart has no weaknesses, but he ferrets out O'Neill's and blackmails him into pimping his girlfriend and terrorizing Storin. O'Neill does the work, but hates himself for it. He slips further into addiction, dying a squalid death in a bathroom stall off the motorway, rat poisoned by Urquhart.

A classically trained actor and founding member of the Royal Shakespeare Company, Richardson was mostly known before *House of Cards* for his theatrical roles (Americans may remember him as the toff in the Rolls-Royce who asks for a jar of *Grey Poupon* mustard). Following Davies's script, the actor based his performance of Urquhart on Richard III, the man who would stop at nothing to be king—and whose dazzling use of language, political brilliance, and intelligence make him an overwhelming presence. What else makes Richardson's performance so deliciously good? His appearance certainly helps. Tall and lean with a natural hauteur of being, Richardson moves with natural grace. He speaks in a honeyed voice: every consonant is clipped, every vowel perfectly sounded, every "r" rolled (soon after *House of Cards* began newspapers in Britain and America began referring to Richardson as "The Voice"). And on those rare occasions that require it, he can shift Urquhart's mood with electrifying rapidity, taking him from Uriah Heep humility—voice barely audible, head bowed—to full-on, "tiger-footed" rage. In the end, though, it is Richardson's face that makes his performance so memorable. No other actor (Michael Kitchen and Maggie Smith, excepted) does an arched eyebrow as well as he, nor masters such an enigmatic smile. Richardson's black, watery eyes can convey contempt, gleeful mischief, and emotional deadness all within less than a minute. Long after the words or camera shots of *House of Cards*, it's the actor's face we remember.

When Kevin Spacey starred in America's version of *House of Cards* twenty-three years later, it was inevitable that critics would compare him to Richardson. Reviewers in the UK loved Spacey in the role, arguing that he deepened the character by making him less an arch-villain (they also loved his southern accent). American reviewers, however, almost all insisted that Richardson delivered the better performance. "Kevin Spacey is great, but the late Ian Richardson . . . is doing something else altogether," writes James Fallows for the *Atlantic*.[11] What that something is, exactly, Fallows never says. The author also praises Richardson for his "Shakespearian grandeur," neglecting to mention that Spacey is himself a Shakespearian actor (in fact, he'd just completed a world tour playing Richard III on stage). In truth, both performances are a marvel. But it's revealing that our critics preferred the guy with the British accent.

Helen Mirren in Prime Suspect

On a January night in 1992, in a show called *Prime Suspect*, Helen Mirren's Jane Tennison charged onto *Mystery!*, angry as hell. Having been bypassed once again to lead a murder investigation, she says to her boss, "Look, I'm the only officer of my rank who is continuously overstepped, sidestepped, or whatever. What do I have to do to prove myself?" Her manner is composed, but we feel her smoldering rage. And we get it, having just seen her male colleagues: they're pigs, heedlessly in service to the chief inspector, who makes a game of nailing suspects in record time and then buys rounds of beers to celebrate his prowess.

There had never been a female character like Jane Tennison on television before nor a performance quite as intense. Mirren had been vaguely familiar to American audiences from a clutch of artsy films in the 1980s. But *Prime Suspect* would make her an acting legend and American celebrity, earning her two Emmy awards and four nominations, three BAFTA awards, and two Golden Globe nominations. In a retrospective several years ago, *Esquire* called her performance "the most sustained example of great acting in the history of television."[12] It would go on to inspire a small legion of other actresses playing female detectives, including Gillian Anderson in *The Fall*, Sarah Lancashire in *Happy Valley*, and, most of all, Kyra Sedgwick in the American series *The Closer*. Sedgwick's character, closely patterned on Tennison, also obsesses over cases, tramples feelings, and battles the old-boy network, though she's half the badass.

Prime Suspect was the first detective series to put a woman's life, professional and psychological, at center stage. American shows like *Cagney and Lacey* and *Police Woman* had featured female detectives, but they had simply aped the male action formulas of the 1980s. By contrast, *Prime Suspect*'s creator, Lynda La Plante, adopted a psychological and criminological point of view. What's more, she took the detective series into the new area of sexual politics. Jane Tennison inspired women of all professions with her "screw you" attitude. In America, she quickly emerged as a feminist icon. The early 1990s were, after all, a period of intense feminist backlash in the United States. Men were calling Hillary Clinton a "rogue feminist" and comparing her to Lady Macbeth. Meanwhile, the New Right, headed by Phyllis Schlafly, had started a "Stop ERA" campaign. "To many American women in 1992," said one critic for the *New Yorker*, "it seemed Tennison was fighting back on behalf of us."[13]

Prime Suspect showed Mirren doing her job with skill, style, and gusto. She mulled over case files when everyone else quit for the night, finding clues no one else saw. She played good cop and bad cop both, sweet-talking suspects into fessing up, but when that didn't work, getting down and dirty. By the end of Season 1, every single man in the department winds up signing a letter asking that she not be taken off the case. By the end of Season 3, she had become a detective superintendent and was on her way up the ladder to Scotland Yard. Yet Tennison is no role model. She wrecks her relationship with her live-in boyfriend (Tom Wilkinson) because she refuses to make time for him or his son. She treats her immediate family with appalling disregard, showing up late to her aged father's birthday party and then forcing everyone to watch the tape of her interview over again after they've just watched it live. She often lacks compassion, pressing grieving relatives for answers to her questions. And as the series progresses, she numbs her inner demons with alcohol. In the final episode, she accuses a murder suspect of "reeking of alcohol." He retorts, "That's not me, it's you."

Mirren was forty-six when *Prime Suspect* premiered. In 1992, it was rare to see a forty-something woman on the screen in such a major role—and one so deliberately unglamorized. At Mirren's insistence, *Prime Suspect* never tried to make the actress beautiful; she wore little makeup and a simple, short hairstyle. And as she aged (she was sixty when the show ended in 2006), we saw it. "You have to allow yourself to grow older in front of the camera— you have to not fight it," Mirren said in an interview. "With Tennison, I let myself do that . . . you see everything . . . the wrinkles, dark eyes, thinning hair, everything."[14] Her show-all portrayal created more opportunities for actresses, expanding their range of roles and lifting unspoken restrictions on their behavior and appearance.

What accounts for Mirren's excellence? On the one hand, it was the ice-cold precision she brought to the role. Gestures, movements, facial expressions: all were kept at a minimum, designed to reflect a woman who refused to show weakness. Yet Mirren could metamorphose in a moment, unleashing a fierce temper or bursting into sudden affection. And however tough her character could be, Mirren played her with a real and palpable vulnerability. We see it in Tennison's compulsive efforts to straighten her blazer, the child-like way she clutches a pillow when alone, her countless introspective gazes.

"I wanted to be a great performer. I mean *great*," Mirren has said of her younger self, sounding very much like her character. Onstage and off, Mirren is known for her intensity. "She reaches for life," said Jeremy Irons, Mirren's costar in *Elizabeth I*. Her approach to playing Tennison was to "go for it, move quickly, think about it later. . . . Of all the characters I've ever played, Jane is the one I've most allowed just to be. I walk out on the set and let it happen." Yet the actress would spend hours in the television studio reviewing herself on taped footage, fixing misspoken or mistimed words, adding a fretwork of vocal nuances here and there. "She is meticulous and exacting," says one of the series' directors, Philip Martin.[15]

During the seven seasons in which she played Jane Tennison, Mirren never gave a weak performance. One of her best scenes, in fact, occurs in the penultimate episode, when Tennison visits her father's home while he lies dying in the hospital. Donning her old constable's hat, she listens to Dusty Springfield's "Stay Awhile" in her childhood bedroom, swaying by herself with all the self-loving delight of a teenager, then slowly collapsing onto her bed, drunk and exhausted. The scene lasts less than a minute, but Mirren makes it unforgettable.

Today Mirren may be the most admired actress in the world: a woman whose talents are so complex and multifaceted they resist description. American women especially love her for what they perceive as her authenticity: her candor, independence, penchant for swearing, and spirited acceptance of old age (this is the L'Oreal spokeswoman who said that her moisturizer "probably does fuck all," but that she wears it because "it just makes me feel better"). Thanks to Mirren, it's the British woman, not the French one, who's now modeling how to be sexy and tough for the fifty-plus group of her American peers.

Damian Lewis in The Forsyte Saga (2002)

Thanks to series like *Band of Brothers*, *Homeland*, and *Billions*, Damian Lewis is widely reputed to be the English actor who plays American characters better than Americans. "I go get my groceries now in an American accent," he claims. But before Lewis mastered his Yonkers dialect or inhabited the psyche of an emotionally damaged marine, he played the tightly wound, tormented Soames Forsyte in *Masterpiece*'s *The Forsyte Saga*. It was that role—an English gentleman trapped by his Victorian proclivities and assumptions—that "transformed" Lewis as an actor, he claims. "I'd never played anyone so difficult."[16]

A prosperous partner in his family's law firm, Soames Forsyte is obsessed with two things: reputation and property. Disapproving of his younger brother, Jolyon Forsyte's, choice to abandon his family for the woman he loves, he arranges matters so Jolyon is left penniless. And when Soames marries the beautiful but poor Irene Heron, he oppresses her with his behavioral demands and jealousies, treating her as if she were some valuable object he paid for and now owns. "Damn Soames, with all his thousands in the bank and no soul," says Jolyon's daughter, June.

In playing such an unpalatable character, Lewis discovered what he calls the "argument of acting." It was Soames Forsyte who taught Lewis how to be a "champion" for his characters, be they overreaching monarchs (*Wolf Hall*), domestic terrorists (*Homeland*), or men who appear to lack a soul. Acting, for Lewis, is like a legal case. This idea of a performance as a contest, a dispute that can be won, appeals to his deeply competitive nature. (As one might expect from someone who has baronets and knights in his family, Lewis is legendary for his natural confidence.) The tougher the fight, the bigger the reward. "I will always find a defense for characters, and that's why it's fun playing people who are morally ambiguous," he says.[17]

For Soames, Lewis found one line of defense in his character's upbringing. Heir apparent to the Forsyte family, Soames has already inherited its dubious Victorian ideals: maintain a sense of order no matter what, bear your burdens stoically, and respect class distinctions. His idea of a successful marriage is patterned on what he sees as his mother's devotion to his father, a man she clearly doesn't love but somehow manages to make a home for. Soames cannot understand why Irene won't do the same, given that he has furnished her with a secure and comfortable life. In his mind, he is a good and tolerant husband.

Lewis's performance is thus a defense and dissection of the British gentleman, a characterization that allows us to see how this ideal shaped men like Soames to their very core, hardening their hearts even as it extolled virtues like gallantry and politeness. Yet Soames *does* love Irene—Lewis's other line of defense. In contrast to Eric Porter's truly frigid portrayal in the first *Forsyte Saga*, Lewis's Soames only *appears* to lack emotion. "You feel too much," his mother tells him. "You always have," reminding him that, as a boy, he had a kitten he loved so much he overfed it. Lewis lets us see that little boy beneath

Soames's air of arrogance and taut waistcoats. And while we pity Irene, the actor wins us over to Soames's side of the argument by making us feel his character's desire.

The climax of Lewis's performance is the most infamous scene in *The Forsyte Saga*: it's late at night, and for once, Irene's bedroom door is unlocked. She lies asleep. Soames approaches her tentatively, overwhelmed by her beauty. When she awakens and pushes him away, he grows angry and rapes her. The scene occurs in less than three minutes. But within that period, Lewis manages to convey desire, frustration, masculine resolve, self-justification, and regret all at the same time. At the end of it, while Irene lies crying in bed, he speaks to her tenderly, as if the rape had been an act of lovemaking. This isn't a case of cruel hypocrisy; rather, it's the deluded act of a man who desperately wishes his marriage to be a success and yet knows he is already defeated. She leaves him the next day.

It's no secret that *The Forsyte Saga* is grand soap opera. To balance all its melodramatic swirls, cast members had to act with a certain measure of nuance. Not surprisingly, given its roster of stars—Rupert Graves, Amanda Root, Ioan Gruffudd, Gina McKee—almost everyone did, and no one more than Lewis. His performance is a master class in the power of subtlety. To communicate Soames's emotional coldness, he speaks in a monotone voice but modulates it whenever Soames is in Irene's presence. To suggest Soames's social awkwardness, he averts his eyes when conversing, moves rigidly, gestures uncertainly, trails off his sentences. When Soames makes loves to Irene, Lewis has him approach her gingerly, as if she were some exquisite object that his touch might somehow mar. And as Irene grows more distant from him, he begins to interact with the things that stand in for her. Several scenes show Soames waiting outside Irene's bedroom, touching the knob gently, pressing into the door. After she leaves him, he lays out one of her ball gowns on a bed, picks it up tenderly, and dances with it. Played by the wrong actor, the scene could have been ludicrous. In Lewis's hands, it's indelible.

In 2008, when *Masterpiece* was relaunched, one of its biggest changes was to streamline its opening title sequence. Gone was the country house library, the trumpets, the wingchair. In their place was a new sequence featuring an open book and, behind its turning pages, the shadowy faces of six actors in their *Masterpiece* roles: Helen Mirren as Jane Tennison, Eamonn Walker as Othello, Colin Firth as Darcy in *Pride and Prejudice*, Keira Knightley as Lara in *Dr. Zhivago*, Gillian Anderson as Lady Dedlock in *Bleak House*, and Damian Lewis as Soames Forsyte. For several years, every time viewers turned on *Masterpiece*, they'd see these faces onscreen. Lewis was delighted. "I get more face recognition from people going 'You know, you're the guy who floats

across the front of *Masterpiece Theater.'* . . . I'm chuffed to bits. It's my proud-
est achievement."[18]

Lewis's comment may be flip, but there's no denying the sequence's undeniable power. It froze those actors into icons of great performances, feeding
our Anglophilia and our nostalgia at the same time, reminding us that however
much we may appreciate Lewis for his American transformations, we also
enjoyed him as a British actor in a distinctly British role.

Gillian Anderson in Bleak House

When American audiences tuned into *Masterpiece's Bleak House* in January of
2006, they knew actress Gillian Anderson mainly as the redheaded FBI agent,
Detective Scully, in *The X-Files*, a cultish sci-fi show about aliens. Anderson
had starred as Scully for nine years, and when she left the series, and America,
in 2002, she vowed not to do anything in television for a very long time.
Then she read the script of *Bleak House* and "fell in love with the character of
Lady Dedlock."

Bleak House is a fast-paced, fifteen-part miniseries about Victorian England's Courts of Chancery, adapted from Dickens's novel by Andrew Davies.
It's also a story about murder, secrets, power, and greed. There are subplots
galore, one of which involves Lady Dedlock, an aristocratic wife who harbors
a terrible secret: as a young woman, she slept with a man and had his illegitimate child. Entrapped by the mistakes of her past, she suffers every minute
because she cannot tell anyone, least of all her husband, the truth. As a consequence, she holds everything tightly within herself, "like a Ming vase with
a Munch scream" as a *New York Times* critic brilliantly put it.[19] A woman like
that is going be blackmailed. And blackmailed she is, by one of the ickiest
characters in Victorian literature: a lawyer whose name—Mr. Tulkinghorn—
couldn't be any more Dickensian-Symbolic. What happens? Well, let's just
say things don't end well for Lady Dedlock (whose name is also Dickensian
Symbolic), which is especially tragic because the illegitimate child she thought
was dead is actually the novel's heroine, the resourceful, kind, and plucky
Esther Summerson, desperate for a mother.

How do you play a character impenetrable to the world but really
cauterized by pain? NPR's Scott Simon asked Anderson in an interview. "I
owe much to the richness of Dickens's characterization . . . it's an immediate
template for an actor to work with," Anderson explained.[20] Following Dickens, Anderson gives a highly stylized, melodramatic performance at first. She
delivers her lines with bored hauteur, speaking more slowly than anyone in
the nineteenth century. In answer to her husband's question about whether
it is raining, she replies, "Yes . . . my love . . . and I am bored to death with

it. Bored to death with this place . . . bored to death with my life . . . bored to death with myself." Anderson seems to take an hour to get through those lines, but the delivery works because she is so sure of its calculated effect.

Soon enough, Tulkinghorn closes in on her secret, and as he does, Lady Dedlock's cool demeanor disappears. The scenes between her and Tulking-horn are among the best in *Bleak House*, putting two captains of composure in contest with each other. But as the series progresses, his composure gives way to cruelty, hers to fear. Terrified and guilt obsessed, she tragically under-estimates the depth of her husband's love and loyalty, choosing to flee in the middle of the night.

Before she does, she reveals the truth to Esther in a scene so heart-wrenching it would make anyone but Tulkinghorn cry. Andrew Davies admitted to being worried about the scene. "When I came to the moment in *Bleak House* where Lady Dedlock says to her daughter, 'I am your wretched, unhappy mother,' I thought 'Can we really do it like that?' Then I thought, 'Let's just try.' So basically I copied it out of the book and most people, including me, found it very moving. . . . People have always loved a bit of full-on emotional indulgence."[21] He's right. But Anderson also plays the scene with understatement, making it more emotional rather than less. She weeps but says very little and barely moves. All her suffering is in her face: pale, mysterious, and full of depth.

Her role as Lady Dedlock earned Anderson a bounty of accolades, in-cluding nominations for a BAFTA, a Golden Globe, and an Emmy award. Since then, she has become the American actress known for playing British characters impeccably: a Damian Lewis in reverse. In fact, almost all her roles since 2005—including Miss Havisham in *Great Expectations* and Stella Gibson in *The Fall*—have been British. Most of them have been in theater. As a con-sequence, Gillian Anderson has acquired all the aura of a great British thespian. It's not just the roles or her performances of them, however, that give her this aura. With her posh British accent (by now, permanent), her impeccable man-ners, and her famous reserve, Anderson seems bonafidedly British: a walking embodiment of Anglophilia.

Kenneth Branagh in *Wallander*

Kenneth Branagh achieved fame very early as an actor. Trained at RADA, he won its top acting prize and then shot out of the traps, immediately landing the part of Henry V with the Royal Shakespeare Company: the youngest actor in its history to do so (he was twenty-four). Three years later, he founded his own theater company. At twenty-nine, he earned an Academy Award nomi-nation for Best Director and Best Actor for *Henry V*, a film hailed by critics for "bringing Shakespeare to the masses." "The speed and enormity of his accomplishments were breathtaking," says biographer Mark White.[22]

But early fame can have its price. By the time he was thirty, Branagh had developed a reputation in England, not wholly unjustified, for being cocky and arrogant. Soon a Pandora's box of complaints opened up about him, with British critics attacking everything from his acting to his ambition to his appearance. "The British press, bored with the Ken-worship it invented, has lately gone in for Branagh-bashing," observed *Time* magazine in 1989.[23] It was a curious phenomenon, one that says more about the British press, perhaps, than about Branagh. But it worked its damage. While he whirred through a series of stunning accomplishments in his thirties and forties, he never reached the superstar height he had achieved earlier. Currently in his late fifties, Branagh still brings to each performance the intensity and assurance that has always defined his work. But coupled with those qualities, now, is a real and palpable sense of humility. In Branagh, we find an actor subdued by age and wisdom, and one who is all the better for it.

Nowhere is this more visible than in *Wallander*, the BBC miniseries in which Branagh plays the eponymous hero: an angsty, middle-aged detective who works to solve crimes like human trafficking and drug selling in southern Sweden. Over the years, Wallander has battled depression, diabetes, and drink. In many ways, he fits right into the pantheon of crime-drama detectives, good but guilt-ridden men who can't maintain personal relationships yet are filled with wistful family feeling. But Branagh brings an authenticity to the role—born, perhaps, of his own chastening—that distinguishes his detective from others.

Running on *Masterpiece Mystery!* from 2009 to 2016 for a total of four seasons, *Wallander* is based on the international bestsellers by the father of Nordic Noir, Henning Mankell. A Swedish version appeared on cable television from 2005 to 2013, starring native actor Krister Henriksson and earning superb critical reviews. Given that series' success as well as the novels' popularity, Mankell's film production company, Yellow Bird, decided to produce an English-language version. It was Mankell himself who suggested Branagh audition for the part, guessing he would play the detective with a more brooding intensity than Henrikkson. Mankell was right.

Wallander achieves much of its somber mood and resonance from the stark, flat expanses of the southern Swedish coast, with its shimmering fields and lonely trees outlined against big blue-gray skies, all of it shot with bleak sublimity by cinematographer Anthony Dod Mantle. But it is Branagh's performance that gives the series its noirish tragedy. Over four seasons, he takes Wallander from a man whose obsession with work makes him arrogantly thoughtless to someone who understands the root of his downfall but is powerless to change it.

Wallander confirms the Nietzschean belief that darkness will swallow you whole if you venture there too often. The evil and dolor he faces every day at work—the vicious assault of a colleague that leaves her in a coma, the self-immolation of a girl right before his eyes—has seeped into his psyche so completely that he can't escape it. It has cost him almost every important relationship in his life and left him little consolation. He buys a home with his new girlfriend (played exquisitely by Saskia Reeves) as a "fresh start," but within days it becomes clear that a life of tranquil domesticity is beyond his grasp. He reaches out to his estranged daughter (Jeany Spark) only to be swept into a case so completely that he leaves her waiting at restaurants. Meanwhile, Wallander is always exhausted by the certainty that whatever he does, it will never be enough. With each season, his face grows more wan and bloated. And then, in Season 4, he begins to change—only to discover he has a fatal disease.

In a genre known for its conventionality, Branagh somehow makes Wallander seem thoroughly authentic. He drinks water from the tap, exposes his flabby gut, wears the same rumpled clothes over and over, and at one point wipes his armpits on an office curtain. More important than these details is Branagh's choice to simply let Wallander *think*. Like other *Masterpiece* detectives, such as Morse and Endeavour, Wallander is a dogged crime fighter given more to deep thought than car chases. But he is far more introspected and isolated than these others. Much of the time, we see him turned inward, weighed down with the burden of facing, time after time, the grisly things that people do. "This is a man who is unafraid—and in fact temperamentally disposed—to think in a concentrated fashion about difficult subjects, to the exclusion of all else," explains Branagh. "So there is little room in his mind for small talk, superficiality. . . . He doesn't even have extra room for what might be therapeutic reflection. It's almost always about why people commit acts of violence. And complicated analysis and consideration of what drove him or her to it."[24]

Playing such a character requires a stripped-down mode of acting far different from Branagh's earlier, high-octane performances. As part of his preparation, Branagh meditated twice a day to "hear instincts" or "uniformed hunches." And he trained himself to let go of the big swirls of movement for which he once was famous. "I made myself get slower, heavier," he explained.[25]

During Season 4, where Branagh delivers his best performance, Wallander discovers he has early-onset Alzheimer's disease. All three episodes are a meditation on one man confronting a devastating illness. Their tone is elegiac, their slate-gray look stressing his inevitable decline. Now Wallander not only juggles inner demons but mortal fear. He goes quietly about his business of questioning suspects, but we sense the panic raging inside him. It's in his fleeting looks, his sudden and momentary gestures.

As all this occurs, Branagh brings a new gentleness to Wallander, born of the character's realization that love, the ability to show and receive it, could have helped him all along. He tries in the end to redeem his life—to be a good father, a good grandfather—but his efforts are up against a new kind of darkness. It's grace, half given.

Of all the countries in which it aired, *Wallander* had its biggest success in the States. Ratings for the show were consistently solid, and critics here adored it. "The best crime drama on television," *Newsweek* called it. Running through almost all the critical commentary is rapture over Branagh's performance, with some critics pointing out that while the plotlines often got "silly" or "far too convoluted," Branagh always redeemed *Wallander*. "Watch it to be amazed by what an actor like Branagh can do when given the space," advised *Esquire*. Tellingly, the article goes on to commend Branagh for "elevating" a genre that we Americans debased with "clichéd performances."[26]

Claire Foy in Wolf Hall

When *Wolf Hall* aired in 2015, most of the critical praise was heaped upon Mark Rylance for his masterful performance as the enigmatic Thomas Cromwell. But Claire Foy, twenty-nine at the time and with a fraction of Rylance's acting experience, was every bit as brilliant, as Anne Boleyn.

Boleyn is a mystery, a confusion of types. Witch, bitch, siren, feminist: she is all these and more, according to the historical record. In the view of some, she was a sorceress; to others, a tramp who bedded her own brother and seduced the king. Those who come to her defense claim she was a pawn, and yet others describe her as a master manipulator. In Foy's hands, Boleyn is, like Cromwell himself, determined. Knowing that her body is her currency, she wagers that she can pursue a lawful marriage to the king because of his need for an heir. "I was always desired," the pregnant Anne says to Cromwell, "but now I'm valued, you see? And that's different."

Boleyn is also witty, mysterious, intelligent, and voluptuous: traits we recognize because we see how Cromwell, a shrewd and discerning man, appreciates them himself. She may be responsible for the downfall of his mentor, Cardinal Wolsey, but he nevertheless appreciates her as a worthy opponent. Outsiders both, Cromwell and Boleyn have the sharpest political instincts of anyone in Henry's court, and one pleasure in watching *Wolf Hall* is to see how each comes to respect the other. When they first meet in episode one, Cromwell clearly despises Anne for helping to oust Wolsey; and she, used to getting her own way, regards him as an annoying obstacle. By the next episode, a kinship between them emerges. Discussing one lord who refuses to say what the king wishes to hear, Boleyn calls him "a fool." "Why?" asks Cromwell. She replies, "People should say whatever will keep them alive. You would, wouldn't you?" Cromwell doesn't respond, and we know why; she's right. Like her, he is a survivor.

By episode 5, however, Boleyn has failed to produce a male heir, and Henry's attention has turned to Jane Seymour. Rather than following Cromwell's advice to "keep silent and dutiful," Boleyn becomes more reckless and outspoken. By episode 6, Cromwell is trying her for adultery, forced to do so by the king and the letter of the law. All tight framing and close-ups, the series narrows its drama down to these two figures and their faces. In hers is terror, in his pity and resolve. *Wolf Hall*'s final scene is her execution, witnessed from Cromwell's perspective. We know what will happen, of course. But Foy's performance somehow makes history fragile again. Her face is ghastly pale as she walks up to the platform: her final speech, barely audible.

Foy is one of those actresses whose appearance and manner belie her power. Small in stature with porcelain skin and saucer blue eyes, she looks fragile and innocent. These features made her portrayal of the kind-hearted heroine in *Masterpiece*'s *Little Dorrit* that much more convincing; here, as Anne Boleyn, it serves as counterpoint to her toughness. We see that face and can't believe a woman that ruthless owns it. Foy is also a quiet actress, reserved and self-contained. "She has this amazing capacity to be still and transformative and communicative all at the same time," her *Crown* costar Matt Smith said. She uses body movements minimally; everything comes through her voice and face. In any given scene in *Wolf Hall*, especially toward the end, she rarely has more than several sentences at a time. She doesn't need words; her fear and desperation are there in her eyes. "It's hard to look at anyone else in a scene with her because those eyes always pull you back," said a reviewer for the *Guardian*. "She is a muted powerhouse."[27] So, too, is Mark Rylance, one of the most intuitive and self-contained actors in Britain. To see these two actors playing against each other is *Masterpiece* gold.

Foy's performance as Anne Boleyn landed her the center-stage part of Queen Elizabeth II in *The Crown*. That still, self-contained quality critics recognized in *Wolf Hall* became Foy's best asset in *The Crown*, eventually earning her the part of Janet Armstrong in the American film, *First Man*. The film's producers guessed rightly that Foy's quiet reserve was a perfect match for the stoic, deeply private character of Armstrong. Reserve is a deeply British trait, one that Americans notoriously lack. Foy not only models it for us but, in *The First Man*, uses it to turn an ordinary woman into an American heroine.

★ ★ ★

In the 1970s, *Masterpiece*'s actors performed their roles largely on sets. Shows such as *I, Claudius* and *The Six Wives of Henry VIII* were shot in BBC studios, where sets attempted to replicate the imperial palace in ancient Rome or the court of a Tudor king. Sometimes the production backgrounds were more sparing. The first season of *Upstairs, Downstairs*, for instance, used a collapsible set that the crew packed up after each rehearsal.

This arrangement is almost impossible to believe now. By the early 1980s, as *Masterpiece* expanded its reach in search of a popular audience, production began to sweep viewers away to some spectacular landscape or estate in England, Scotland, or some other part of Britain. This tactic wasn't simply to prettify its drama. The appeal went deeper than that, especially for audiences in the United States. *Masterpiece*'s locales gave, and continue to give, Anglophilic Americans a strong visual taste of what we are most seeking from its stories—England itself. Our final chapter takes us there.

· 9 ·

A *Masterpiece* Travel Guide

Remember watching *Downton Abbey*'s opening sequence, shown on *Masterpiece* almost ten years ago now? First we saw a telegraph machine clicking out news of the *Titanic* disaster, followed by shots of a train, a glimpse at a picturesque village, and a long view of a resplendent house. Seconds later we were following Daisy, the kitchen maid, and Thomas, the footman, as they made their way through its magnificent rooms. We passed housemaids Anna and Gwen, plumping pillows in the morning room. We saw Mrs. Hughes, the housekeeper, patrolling the grand hallways and Carson, the butler, cleaning silverware in his snug pantry. Then we traveled upstairs to an opulent bedroom where Lady Mary, looking like some disappointed princess, sat atop her bed, ringing the bell for service. "And they're off," quipped Thomas.

So was *Downton Abbey*. That spectacular, five-minute opening introduced us to a world we would come to cherish over the next six years. We loved it not only for its characters and their assorted dramas but also for the world itself: its rooms, estates, and landscapes.

Houses like Highclere Castle (the "real" Downton Abbey) and their environs play a starring role in *Masterpiece*'s drama. Its creators know viewers want to see Britain's bonny landscapes and handsome buildings as much as we want to immerse ourselves in the stories. We wish to be transported. And we are. Watching a *Masterpiece* production feels like armchair travel every time. Often, it inspires actual trips to the places where the series were filmed.

Although some programs, like *Sherlock*, take place in cities, the majority of *Masterpiece* productions are set in rural spaces. The reason is crystal clear: for millions of people, it is the countryside that represents British identity. The vast majority of those living in the UK may be urban, but the countryside retains its symbolic force. The country is Britain as it should be, an area

139

replete with pretty villages, historic sites, memorials, monuments, protected areas, and pubs with tables in the garden. Yet as cities, towns, and even villages keep growing to cater to the country's rapidly growing population, and with England already the most densely populated country in Europe, the English countryside is slowly diminishing.

Small wonder, then, that over the years, the BBC and other studios have produced so many dramas that present England as a peaceful, Arcadian space. For viewers in the UK, these dramas reflect a reassuring view of their country, verifying its ages-old history and natural beauty. For Americans, they have a slightly different attraction, as we'll see in a moment.

One feature of the British countryside that makes it so amenable to drama is its striking blend of the spectacular and picturesque. In the northwestern part of the country lies the Lake District, known for its fells and pristine bodies of water. Close by are the Yorkshire dales and moors, sublimely rugged and isolated. Central England has the Cotswolds region, defined by its rolling hills, dry stone walls, fertile pastures, wildlife parks, and endless walking routes. Southwestern England has Cornwall, with its dramatic coastlines and cliffs and traditional farms dotted with sheep. Southeastern England has the sparkling seaside town of Brighton and the Downs national parks.

Via *Masterpiece*, we see more than breathtaking landscapes, however. We also view the great estates, centuries-old villages, and historic buildings that form a vital part of Britain's heritage.

Heritage is a powerful word in Britain. The rise of a conscious appeal to heritage began there during the mid-nineteenth century, when writers like John Ruskin and William Morris promoted the concept to counteract the instabilities and rapid changes of modern life. In their writings, the remains of the past—architecture, ruins, antique objects, and monuments—took on a special meaning that persists to this day. Ensuring continuity with Britain's past, they strengthened a sense of national identity. They also provided an antidote to contemporary life, promising a kind of spiritual salvation for British citizens by inspiring veneration. For Ruskin, architectural remains were especially important, since the marring effects of industry had deprived nature of its ability to guard and shape England's national self. In old buildings and homes, England could still find that which connected forgotten and future ages with each other. "We may live without her," he said of architecture, "but we cannot remember without her."[1]

Ruskin's idea of heritage required civic responsibility: somebody, after all, had to clean the downspouts. Ever the enthusiast, Ruskin vigorously championed the need for a collective stewardship of England's buildings and lands. His ideas caught on quickly. By the 1860s, property owners began to see themselves as holding estates in trust for the nation. Preservation became a watchword, as did "inheritance" and "legacy." Sweeping the country was a new sense of duty to pass historic buildings and objects on to the nation's descendants, augmented by improvements of the present. Knowing this context, we can see why Downton Abbey's continuance means so much to Lord Grantham; for him, maintaining the estate isn't just about family inheritance or even the duty one owes to those who work on the estate. It's about nationhood.

Upholding Britain's new commitment to heritage, the National Trust was established in 1895 by three pioneering individuals: Octavia Hill (a Victorian all-star of social reform), Sir Robert Hunter, and Hardwicke Rawnsley. Its aim was not only to preserve important sites but also open them up for everyone to enjoy. Today, the National Trust maintains 780 miles of coastline; over 250,000 hectares of land; an estimated 500 historic houses, castles, parks, and gardens; and nearly one million works of art. It boasts 5.6 million members, 65,000 of whom are volunteers, and employs 1,500 tenant farmers. Many of the estates we see on *Masterpiece* are owned and operated by the National Trust, having been donated by private owners who could no longer afford to maintain them.

From its beginning, the trust has vigorously promoted the concept of "heritage tourism," knowing that concepts like tradition and ancestry can only be kept alive if people see and experience the places they celebrate. Plus, all that money from admission fees and souvenir sales helps keep those magnificent piles up and running. British television has shaped this tourism, inspiring millions of viewers in the UK to go see for themselves whether Lacock Village is really as twee as it looks in *Cranford* (it is) or whether Napoleon really owned Lord Grantham's desk at Highclere Castle (he did). And while they visit these locales to take lots of photos and see pretty things, they're also motivated by national pride; you can see it in their faces.

As outsiders, it's impossible for Americans to feel that same sense of pride. We're drawn to *Masterpiece*'s locales, rather, for their beauty, history, and in the case of villages, their storybook diminution compared to our own vast landscape. But there is something deeper at work for us, too—a vague, persistent longing for solidity and permanence, for a feeling of *home*. Nostalgia comes from the Greek *nostos* (return home) and algia (longing). Its yearning is not so much for the past as for a sense of rootedness and belonging. Historians tell us that nostalgia originally meant "homesickness," coined by an ambitious Swiss doctor named Johannes Hofer in 1688. Contrary to our intuition, nostalgia came from medicine, not from poetry or politics. Among its earliest victims were various displaced people of the seventeenth century: sailors, domestic servants working away from their families, and freedom-loving students who left their homes to study abroad. One could die from nostalgia if not treated. By the mid-nineteenth century, the disease had developed into the broader and more amorphous phenomenon we know it as today; as philosopher Svetlana Boym puts it, "nostalgia for one's local home had given way to nostalgia for *being at home* in the world."[2]

Are Americans particularly nostalgic? Nostalgia strikes those who feel uprooted, and Americans move incessantly—on average, a whopping 11.7 times during our lives (compared to four times for Europeans). This itch to leave, to relocate, involves several factors: the vastness of our landscape coupled with a common language; our obsession with finding new work opportunities; and (let's be frank) our relative indifference to our families. "The American DNA encodes wanderlust ambition," writes *New York Times* columnist Michael Powell, citing iconic figures like Huck Finn and Jay Gatsby. "Uprootedness is, and always has been, part and parcel of being American," says Arnold Rampersad, a professor at Stanford University. "It is the flip side of the defining aspect of Americanness, the capacity of its citizens to reinvent themselves." And Andrew Delbanco says, "There is a long and often sentimental tradition of celebrating the small town"—Andy Griffith's Mayberry—"as the right kind of place to grow up and become morally solid." At the same time, America "regards the small town as airless and imprisoning."[3]

All this wanderlust makes us a people of fractured geographies—and because we don't find the sense of home we're after in our small towns, we look for it in Britain.

Or maybe we just like seeing great real estate.

Whatever the reason, we Americans love the locales of *Masterpiece* drama. Below is a "travel guide" to twenty of them. Most of these places are rural; a few urban ones are included because they're so vital to our sense of England. How, after all, can you leave out 221B Baker Street?

As we'll see, filming on location is a tangled business. A single *Masterpiece* series might involve shooting in as many as thirty different places. Sometimes a fictional setting—say, Kensington Palace in *Victoria* or Pemberley in *Pride and Prejudice*—is represented by several different sites. More often than not, producers mix on-location filming with studio sets; Downton Abbey's kitchen, servant quarters, and upstairs bedrooms were all built at Ealing Studios in London while the rest of the estate—the library, morning room, great hall, dining room—was shot at Highclere Castle. All of this points to the fact that the places we see on *Masterpiece* are a complex compilation, as much image as they are reality.

No matter: the sites below, however masquerading or manipulated, are all essential to *Masterpiece* and to the country they inhabit, beckoning us to visit them for the shows we love and for their own splendid sake.

221B BAKER STREET

This is the legendary locale where Sherlock Holmes and Dr. Watson live, of course. But its history is complicated. When Arthur Conan Doyle wrote the Holmes stories, there was no 221B Baker Street (Baker Street existed, but its numbers only ran through the 100s). If you visit the address today, you'll find the *Sherlock Holmes Museum*. It's worth a trip if you happen to be in London, though the Sherlock Holmes Pub, brimming with Holmesiana, has an even better collection—and great French fries. The museum bears the famous 221B number by permission of the City of Westminster, although it actually lies between 237 and 241. Technically speaking, then, there is *still* no 221B Baker Street.

What, then, does a production company do? Granada opted to re-create the famous residence from scratch, constructing a full-scale outdoor replica of the street complete with shops, three-story residences, gas lamps, a post office, barber shop, a tailor, and even an undertaker. To date, it remains one of the largest TV sets ever built. The production team also designed a full-scale indoor replica, scouring the countryside for just the right period furniture and furnishings. Both the interior and exterior sets were open to the public as part of the Granada Studios tour between 1988 and 1999.

For the BBC *Sherlock*, Hartswood Studios filmed exterior shots of 221B Baker Street a half mile northeast of the museum, on quiet North Gower Street where you can visit "Speedy's Café," the tiny restaurant above which the famous detective and Watson live. In tribute to the series, it features the "Sherlock Holmes Special" as a breakfast item Monday through Saturday.

CASTLE HOWARD

Castle Howard made its television debut in the series that really should have been a *Masterpiece* production but wasn't: *Brideshead Revisited*. That was 1981, and since then, the estate has starred in a string of period dramas including *Masterpiece*'s *The Buccaneers* (1995), *Death Comes to Pemberley* (2013), and *Victoria* (2017–2019). Located in North Yorkshire, fifteen miles north of York, Castle Howard is one of England's most treasured houses. It's a baroque extravaganza, with coronets, cherubs, urns, and cyphers galore—not to mention a spectacular crowning dome. When it was completed in the early 1800s after nearly a hundred years of labor, some groused about its flamboyance, calling it "vulgar." But Horace Walpole, the man credited with writing Britain's first

Gothic novel, deemed it "sublime." Two spectacular gardens flank the estate, each with its own lake. In the warmer months, visitors can take boat trips on either lake and see breathtaking views of the house.

In *Victoria*, several of Castle Howard's rooms doubled for Kensington Palace in Season 1, including the Museum Room, Castle Howard Bedroom, and the Long Gallery. (In 1850, Victoria herself stopped at Castle Howard to rather disastrous effect. She got lost in the castle several times and her hubby, Prince Albert, kept pestering their host, the Earl of Carlisle, with questions about the sculpture collection.) In *Death Comes to Pemberley*, the castle served as the titular estate of Mr. Darcy (Matthew Rhys) and his feisty bride, Lizzie (Anna Maxwell Martin), still very much in love and starting a family. The production team said, not ironically, that they chose the castle because they were drawn to its "family feel" and "intimacy."

CHARTWELL

This was Winston Churchill's country home from 1922 until the time of his death in 1964. Twenty-five miles from London, it was a world unto itself for England's legendary leader, a place where he composed speeches, wrote books, and gathered advisors around his dining room table, serving plenty of brandy, to strategize against the Germans. But Churchill played at Chartwell, too. He built walled gardens (himself, at the rate of ninety bricks per hour), designed lakes and swimming pools, and landscape painted to his heart's content. For Churchill, Chartwell was the safe base from which he could enter into the messy, uncertain world of London politics. It was his retreat and harbor, and he delighted in playing the English squire while there.

In the summer of 1953, after he suffered a near-fatal stroke, Chartwell also became Churchill's sanatorium. His advisors wanted to keep him in London, but Clementine, his wife, wisely intuited that Chartwell would give him the privacy he needed to recuperate. So he spent the summer there without the British public knowing a thing about it. This moment in the great leader's life is the subject of *Masterpiece*'s *Churchill's Secret*, filmed at Chartwell House.

Relatively modest in comparison to England's other estates—no grand ballrooms, no long halls or priceless antique collections—Chartwell has "an intimate feel" that enhances the series' very private look at a larger-than-life figure. All exterior shots (of the house, gardens, and surrounding landscape) were filmed at the estate; interior spaces were re-created on a set. Hal Vogel, the series' executive producer, said, "We did have the opportunity to film inside but it just seemed easier to do it in the studio . . . it gives us more flexibility. So really, it was the grounds and being able to show the house, which we can't recreate." Lindsay Duncan, who played Clemmie Churchill, said, "I've never been quite so affected by a location . . . there were loads of visitors milling around . . . and I was really struck by the fact that they actually lived there. It's such an obvious thing to say but I thought, Churchill walked through that door."[4]

CHATSWORTH

Chatsworth is a stately home in Derbyshire, dating from the sixteenth century and located on the east bank of the River Derwent. Set in an expansive parkland, it is often voted by tourists as Britain's "Best Country House" because of its magnificent library, sculpture gallery, and muraled walls and ceilings.

Chatsworth has starred as the romantic backdrop in a cluster of period dramas, including the 2005 film *Pride and Prejudice*; Netflix's *The Crown* and *Peaky Blinders*; and most importantly, *Masterpiece*'s *Death Comes to Pemberley* (only fitting, given that Chatsworth is thought to have inspired Jane Austen's own description of Pemberley). The south and west facades of Chatsworth were used to depict Pemberley's famous exteriors. For the house's interior, the production crew filmed in Chatsworth's most spectacular first-floor rooms: the Painted Hall, Great Dining Room, Sculpture Gallery, and Oak Room.

Chatsworth is chock-a-block with priceless antiques, making filming there hard on the nerves. On the second day of shooting *Pemberley*, one crew member dropped a vase. Everyone's blood ran cold; they assumed it was one of Chatsworth's famous Ming vases, estimated at one million pounds each. Luckily, it turned out to be one of their own reproductions.

CORNWALL

"Cornwall is on everyone's lips these days. Those lingering shots of wild moorland, Grecian blue sea and soft pale sand in every episode of the BBC's *Poldark* have drawn visitors from around the world," says the *Guardian*.[5] Tourism in Cornwall has shot up by 20 percent since *Poldark* was launched in 2015 (although the smash comedy *Doc Martin* has something to do with this, too).

A large county located on England's southwestern tip, Cornwall has been a popular filming locale since the 1920s, ever since Alfred Hitchcock set his film *The Manxman* there. The county is unique in that it retains, to this day, a cloak of local tradition and a palpable sense of isolation. As a peninsula, it boasts wild moorland and hundreds of sandy beaches. Southern Cornwall has sandy coves and teeny-tiny harbor towns while northern Cornwall has lofty cliffs, sweeping bays, and what has to be the world's most spectacular surf.

Cornwall's centrality to the Poldark story started with the twelve novels by Winston Graham, published between 1945 and 2002. Graham made Cornwall the heart of his novels, entwining it with the character of Ross Poldark himself. Place and hero alike are wild, beautiful, and rugged—literally scarred, too, by the greed of those exploiting the landscape for its natural resources. When the BBC first decided to adapt the novels (the original *Poldark* aired on *Masterpiece* in 1975–1976), it also made Cornwall the star of the series, filming many scenes on location. The present-day remake, capitalizing on better equipment and a far bigger budget, goes even further. Cornwall dominates the drama. Most of the action, even the conversation, takes place outdoors, often against the backdrop of its breathtaking and rugged coastline. The series also packs in sunset views, aerial shots, and close-ups of every imaginable native flower (someone in that camera crew must be a serious gardener).

Specific locales in the new *Poldark* include Bodmin Moor, Botallack, Charlestown, Holywell Bay, Kynance Cove, Levant Mine, Padstow, and Porthcurno. The cast and crew loved filming there, crediting Cornwall as the factor "that really brought the story together." The only complaint, voiced by the cameramen, was that the sky was too blue (clouds apparently make better drama). But everyone else involved in the production loved it. "Standing on the cliff, looking at the views, you have to pinch yourself that you are really there," said Eleanor Tomlinson, who plays Poldark's wife, Demelza, on the series.[6]

GRANTCHESTER

Located beside the River Cam in South Cambridgeshire, roughly one hour from London, Grantchester is a quaint village known for its thatched cottages, medieval church, and pubs, including the Rupert Brooke Pub (named after the World War I poet). Grantchester also boasts the Orchard Tea Garden, a favorite haunt of the Bloomsbury Group back in the 1910s and 1920s, and, according to the *Daily Mail*, the world's highest concentration of Nobel Prize winners.

Nowadays, Grantchester is known for *Masterpiece*'s detective show of the same name, featuring not one but two hunky he-men of the cloth, Sidney Chambers and Will Davenport. Most of the scenes are shot in Grantchester, where author James Runcie also set the novels on which the series is based. The village is as storybookish as can be—too charming to be real and the very last place you'd expect to find so many violent murders. But then that's the point.

HOUGHTON LODGE

In the BBC's delightful, heartwarming adaptation of *David Copperfield*, starring Maggie Smith and Daniel Radcliffe, little David (Daniel Radcliffe) travels by foot from London to his aunt Betsey (Maggie Smith) in Dover. Tired and dirty, he sees her house from afar. It's a quirky, fairy-tale house: all bright-white walls and funny windows, surrounded by a garden brimming with cornflowers. This is Houghton Lodge.

A private residence located in Test Valley (also home to Highclere Castle), Houghton Lodge is a classic example of *cottage orné*, a genre of architecture that flourished between the 1790s and 1820s. A thoroughly Romantic conception, *cottage orné* was designed to celebrate a natural, easy way of living as opposed to the formality of baroque and neoclassical styles. Architects used it primarily for the rural retreats of the wealthy who, after the roads underwent improvement in the 1780s, suddenly discovered they could escape London more easily and for shorter periods of time. Houghton Lodge was built in 1790 by John Plaw—one of the pioneers of *cottage orné*—and probably intended as a fishing lodge. Anyone who visits the place now, with its lemony wallpaper, arched doorways, and 350-foot herbaceous border, would laugh at this snatch of history. "Some fishing lodge!" said Maggie Smith while filming there.

HOUSES OF PARLIAMENT

Otherwise known as the Palace of Westminster, this is the meeting place of the House of Commons and the House of Lords, forming the United Kingdom's parliament. Located in Westminster, London, it is one of England's most iconic buildings (its most famous feature is the clock tower, known as Big Ben) and has a long and complex history. The original structure was built in the eleventh century, though it suffered great damage in a fire of 1512. Two centuries later, it underwent a period of intense development only to catch fire again in 1834. During that year, on the night of October 16, two under-floor stoves ignited the wood paneling in the Lords Chamber. The fire quickly swept through the entire palace and destroyed many of its buildings. Artists J. M. W. Turner and John Constable witnessed the event, along with Charles

Dickens and thousands of other sightseers. Westminster Hall was saved, as were the Jewel Tower, the cloisters, and the crypt of St. Stephen's Chapel, but everything else had to be rebuilt. Victorian architect Sir Charles Barry, assisted by A. W. N. Pugin, designed the Houses' structures we see today. Executed in the Gothic Revival style, they were begun in 1837 and completed in 1860.

Masterpiece's 1990 trilogy *House of Cards* opens all nine of its episodes with a spectacular aerial view of the Houses of Parliament. The effect is to make us feel awed by their architectural grandeur—only to then have us see the rot in its political fabric. For interior shots of the Houses, the production crew used Manchester's town hall.

LACOCK

Lacock is a village in the county of Wiltshire, owned almost entirely by the National Trust. Its unpaved streets and centuries-old cottages give Lacock a wholly unspoiled appearance, making it the ideal place to film period drama. Many TV series and movies have used it, including both 1996 film versions of *Emma*; the BBC *Pride and Prejudice* (1995); *Masterpiece*'s *Moll Flanders* (1996) and *The Mayor of Casterbridge* (2003); *Harry Potter* (Lacock Abbey serves as Hogwarts); and *The Other Boleyn Girl* (2008). But *Masterpiece*'s *Cranford* (2008) is the drama that gave Lacock star billing.

Cranford is based on Elizabeth Gaskell's 1853 novel of the same name, an affectionate portrait of people and customs that were already becoming anachronisms by that time. Although Gaskell based *her* Cranford on Knutsford, the village where she grew up, the production crew chose Lacock because, in one producer's words, "It's like something you'd see in a painting." *Cranford* uses the iconic villages for almost all its settings, in fact. Its miniature feel (the central grid of Lacock is only four streets) perfectly suits the insular world of the story as do its stone walls and pristine surroundings. And what a treat it is to see actresses Imelda Staunton, Deborah Findlay, Eileen Atkins, and Judi Dench parade around the village in their crinolines and bonnets! (As Andrew Davies once remarked about *Cranford*, "People like bonnets. I don't think you can underestimate that.")

LAMBTON ESTATE

In 2013, *Masterpiece* launched *The Paradise*, a sumptuous adaptation of Émile Zola's novel about a department store. That store was created counter by counter on the Lambton Estate in County Durham, located in the northeastern part of England.

When producers first conceived of the show, they knew they needed a space with a fab interior. They visited the Lambton Estate one cold and rainy afternoon. The house had plaster falling off the walls and leaks in every room. "Still," recalls one producer, laughing, "we thought it had lots of potential!" It took a crew of nearly two hundred people six months to transform the estate into the lavish store we see in the series, including a team of architects who had to design drawings and obtain planning permissions before anyone could lift a paintbrush.

Renovation was an operose challenge. "When working on a historic building you can't use modern materials," said one producer. "You've got to use the same materials the house was built in, so we had to make a lime-based plaster for the walls. A modern-day plaster will dry in two or three days but a lime-based plaster isn't dry after three weeks. The walls were still wet when we were filming!" The same producer also recounts how the art department "went to lots of local auctions and bought items in multiples because we needed a well-stocked shop. If anyone was selling a collection of pipes, mugs, shaving brushes, anything—we bought them!" They then sprayed everything gold so that all the rooms would gleam onscreen. "I wanted the whole series to sparkle with 19th century bling," said art director Keith Dunne.[7]

LYME PARK, CHESHIRE

When Jane Bennett in Austen's *Pride and Prejudice* asks her sister Lizzie how she finally came to fall in love with Mr. Darcy, Lizzie replies, "It has been coming on so gradually, that I hardly know when it began. But I believe I must date it from my first seeing his beautiful grounds at Pemberley." She's only half kidding. In truth, she was blown away by Darcy's estate. So whatever locale serves as Pemberley in a film or TV series has to have the same slaying effect on viewers. Lyme Park does. Located in Cheshire, about twenty minutes from Manchester and right on the edge of the Peak District, Lyme Park is one of England's most breathtaking estates. Owned by the National Trust, it has an imposing house, a deer park, formal gardens, and a thirteen-hundred-acre estate. The house is a mixture of baroque and Palladian styles, balancing classical principles with lots of flash. Lyme Park is where Mr. Darcy, dripping wet and babelicious, emerged from that lake and made period-drama history. A statue of him, still in that lake, commemorates the moment. In addition to using Lyme Park for the exterior of the Pemberley house and grounds, the production crew employed twenty-three other locations and eight studio sets, including Sudbury Hall, located in Derbyshire, for internal scenes at Pemberley.

MANCHESTER

England's second largest city has long suffered a bad reputation. Once the primary site of British manufacturing, Manchester was indeed a dirty and depressing place during the nineteenth century, plagued by overcrowdedness, pollution, and poverty. But it is a vibrant city today, much more English in its feel and attitude than the international city of London. It is also a forty-five-minute drive from Haworth, birthplace of the Brontë sisters, and only an hour away from the Lake District, home of Beatrix Potter and William Wordsworth and one of the most enchanting places on God's Green Earth. *Masterpiece*'s *World on Fire* (2020), an ensemble-based, World War II drama about "ordinary lives caught up in extraordinary times," sets much of its action in Manchester. Specific sites include Castlefield railways, Rochdale Town Hall, the Police Museum, Victoria Baths, and the breathtaking John Rylands library. "Every time I come to film," says director Adam Smith, the city has transformed that little bit more."[8]

NETHER WALLOP

"We're all very ordinary in St. Mary Mead but ordinary people can sometimes do the most astonishing things," says Miss Marple in *The Murder at the Vicarage*. The fictional village of St. Mary Mead, located in southern England, was where the elderly spinster learned her sleuthing trade. In the ordered tranquility of that village, populated with cottages, village shops, and the Blue Boar pub, Marple saw all sides of human nature and solved more murders on average than a Scotland Yard detective. Christie didn't base St. Mary Mead on any particular locale; "It could be any of hundreds of English villages," she once explained. When the BBC and, later, ITV decided to produce their own versions of the Marple stories, they used the idyllic location of Nether Wallop, Hampshire.

Nether Wallop is the innermost village of the three villages known as "The Wallops," the other two being Over Wallop and Middle Wallop (only the English could invent such names). They are located in the Test Valley district of Hampshire, England. Brimming with thatched cottages and twee gardens, Nether Wallop repeatedly ranks as one of the prettiest villages in

England. The BBC and ITV series both feature local sites such as St. Andrew's Church (dating from the eleventh century), Five Bells Lane, and the Village Square. "Dane Cottage" in Five Bells Lane serves as Miss Marple's home in the BBC series starring Joan Hickson. Recently remastered, the series portrays the village in breathtakingly twee ways. The scenery couldn't be more verdant, the streets more tidy, the sky more blue. Punctuate this with dozens of vintage cars and actors outfitted in old-timey tweed, and the experience feels like entering a postcard.

OXFORD

To most Americans, Oxford is synonymous with its famous university. But for fans of *Masterpiece*'s *Inspector Morse*, *Inspector Lewis*, and *Endeavour*, it is the murder capital of Britain.

Dubbed the "city of dreaming spires," Oxford is the oldest university town in the English-speaking world, stemming back to 1096. Roughly sixty miles from London, it has long been featured in film and television series, including *Brideshead Revisited* and the Harry Potter series. But no other drama has given it the consistent, loving attention of *Morse*, *Lewis*, and *Endeavour*. Episodes of all three series feature gorgeous shots of the city: its milky brown rivers, Gothic-inspired buildings, town center, and college lawns. Specific locales include the Sheldonian Theatre, the five-star Randolph Hotel, the Bodleian Library, Radcliffe Square, the Ashmolean museum, Christ Church College, Oxford's iconic Bridge of Sighs, Magdalen College, Keble College, and St Edmund's Hall, and loads of pub gardens like The Crickateers. Each series captures the city's air of learnedness, its stunning variety of architecture, and its palpable sense of order and tranquility. But whereas *Morse* often spotlights its more ordinary, shabby locales, underlining the detective's estrangement from the posh world of the university, *Lewis* and *Endeavor* spend more time within its grand halls and offices.

Ever since *Morse*'s debut in 1987, Oxford has enjoyed a vibrant, television-based tourism. Those who wish to go on a "Morse Tour" or "Endeavour Tour" can visit the same locales featured in the series, stopping at The Crickateers or the Lamb and Flag for a pint. Most tourists tend to be devoted fans of all three series, especially of *Morse*. To appeal to these tourists in particular, guides make it a point of referring to the famous detective in the present tense, as if he were not only alive, but real. Lest we think this touch a bit excessive, we might consider some of the stories recounted by guides, including one about "a lady from America, who returns every few years, and will not allow me to mention the detective's death. She always leaves the tour early, before reaching Exeter College, where old Morse succumbed to his heart attack on screen."[9]

PENSHURST PLACE

One of the many pleasures of watching *Masterpiece*'s *Wolf Hall* is seeing the buildings that date back to the fourteenth and fifteenth centuries, Penshurst Place among them. Located in Kent, roughly ninety miles from London, Penshurst Place has stood in the historic village of Penshurst since the fourteenth century, when the awe-inspiring Baron's Hall was completed in 1341 as a country retreat for the Lord Mayor of London.

The stately home and gardens were once used as a hunting lodge for King Henry VIII (and a base for courting Anne Boleyn). Now they feature opulent staterooms—the Queen Elizabeth Room, the Tapestry Room, the Solar, the Long Gallery, and the Crypt—that have starred in many period dramas, including *Wolf Hall*, where they were Tudorized to lavish effect.

Scenes in *Wolf Hall* were also filmed at National Trust sites, Lacock Abbey in Wiltshire, Chastleton House in Oxfordshire, and Montacute House in Somerset. Filming on location, says producer Mark Pybus, leant centuries-old authenticity to the series. "The advantages of filming in a historic location are massive," he said. "It also helps the actors, if they're stepping into the buildings that Henry VIII and Thomas Cromwell walked around in, it helps bring a realness to the project."[10]

American fans, incidentally, may be delighted to learn that Penshurst also served as "Clampett Castle" in the 1960s TV show *The Beverly Hillbillies*.

SOMERSET

Somerset is a large county in southwestern England, bordering Bristol to the north, Wiltshire to the east, Dorset to the southeast, and Devon to the southwest. Its coast faces southeastern Wales. Many of England's most beautiful towns and villages are located in Somerset, including Bath and Exmoor. *Masterpiece*'s *Sanditon* (2019) used various locales in Somerset to depict the loose-moraled titular town of Jane Austen's last novel—where the young heroine, Charlotte, finds love, and the hero, Tom Parker, struggles to build a fashionable spa and resort.

SYON HOUSE

Dating back to the early 1500s, Syon House is one of the last great houses of London. It holds a treasury of art and priceless antiques within its grand classical interiors, making it a sumptuous backdrop for period dramas. It also boasts "The Great Conservatory," the first conservatory to be built from metal and glass on a large scale. While the park and gardens feel like deep countryside, Syon is barely nine miles from Charing Cross station in London. *Masterpiece's Poirot, Miss Austen Regrets* (2007), and *Downton Abbey* all used the house for exterior and interior shots. But it was *Masterpiece's Daniel Deronda* that really made a star of Syon House. As the estate of the villainous Henleigh Grandcourt, who marries poor and vain Gwendolyn Harleth, Syon pulses as a symbol of its owner's wealth and the heroine's entrapment in a gilded cage of her own making.

DERBYSHIRE AND WEST YORKSHIRE

Neighboring each other, these two broad areas of northern England are characterized by slopes of black rock, tough pale grass, and purple heather. Strong Atlantic winds drive clouds turbulently across the sky. Innumerable "becks," as Yorkshire people call their small streams, run fiercely down hilly beds, giving the landscape a thread of white throughout. Rain is frequent, mist is frequent, and in winter snow is frequent.

The Brontë sisters grew up in the small village of Haworth, west of Bradford in West Yorkshire. They were intimately familiar with this rugged, sublime landscape and made it a starring character in their fiction. True to the novels, *Masterpiece* filmed much of *Jane Eyre* (2006) and *Wuthering Heights* (2009) in the countryside of West Yorkshire and its neighboring area, Derbyshire. Haddon Hall, a nine-hundred-year-old house ("the most perfect house to survive from the middle ages," according to one producer), served as Rochester's home, Thornfield, in *Jane Eyre* (and in both Franco Zeffirelli's 2004 and Cary Fukunaga's 2010 film adaptations). Unlike many old English estates that were "modernized" in the nineteenth century, Haddon Hall hasn't been updated since the 1500s, so it really does feel like stepping back in time— way back in time. *Wuthering Heights* used several West Yorkshire locations for its settings, including Stockeld Park, Oakwell Hall, and Bramham Park, all spectacular eighteenth-century country houses.

WEST WYCOMBE HOUSE

This may be the most unique of all country houses featured in *Masterpiece*. "One of the most theatrical and Italianate houses in all England" is how the National Trust describes it. Built between 1740 and 1800, it was conceived as a pleasure palace for Sir Francis Dashwood, a notorious bon vivant. And according to Dashwood's biographers, it served its purpose.

West Wycombe House is quite small compared to England's other country villas. Yet it is culturally important—for it reflects a period of eighteenth-century English history when young male aristocrats, returning from their Grand Tours with newly purchased art of all kinds, built a country house to accommodate their collections. In room after room, they displayed the education and culture they had acquired on their travels. West Wycombe's gardens are also among the finest and most idiosyncratic in England, each wildly different from the other.

Virtually half of the *Masterpiece* canon, it seems, has been shot at West Wycombe. These series include *Daniel Deronda*, *Cranford*, *Downton Abbey*, *Sense and Sensibility*, *Little Dorrit*, a few episodes of *Endeavour*, *Agatha Christie's Marple* ("A Pocket Full of Rye"), and *Howards End*. You can see the house's gorgeous rooms in most of these series, but it is West Wycombe's weathered yellow exterior, shown in long shot, that will really take your breath away.

HIGHCLERE CASTLE

No *Masterpiece* travel guide could omit Highclere Castle. In no other period drama has one place figured so prominently.

"I have always enjoyed country houses," Julian Fellowes writes in his foreword to *The World of Downton Abbey*. "There is something about their completeness, with their different rooms and offices catering to almost every need, making up a microcosm of a complete world, that is very satisfactory to me."[11] Fellowes knew that he wanted to set his epic story of the Grantham family in such a house—but where to find it? He and the executive producer of *Downton Abbey*, Gareth Neame, toured all over England, looking at nearly thirty houses, until they found Highclere Castle.

Currently the country seat of the eighth Earl of Carnarvon and his wife, Lady Fiona Carnarvon, Highclere Castle is over six hundred years old and has a room count of close to three hundred. It is situated on a 6,000-acre estate in Berkshire, about 45 miles west of London that includes parkland designed by the famous landscape designer Capability Brown. Like other country houses,

Highclere Castle was once "the power hub of the neighborhood," as Fellowes describes it. It was remodeled in "High Elizabethan" style between 1839 and 1842 by the famous Victorian architect, Sir Charles Barry (who also designed the Houses of Parliament), and updated further in 1878.

A mixture of Gothic influences and Italianate effects, the castle is replete with arched entryways, strapwork designs, coffered ceilings, and marble pillars. It boasts an impressive array of state rooms, including a library filled with over 5,650 books, a south-facing drawing room, and a dining room presided over by van Dyck's famous painting of King Charles I (rumored to be valued at $16 million). Other priceless paintings and antiques fill the house. "It was slightly terrifying to be there," says actor Dan Stevens (who plays Matthew Crawley). "The stewards stood around and made sure we didn't carve our names into the dining room table."[12]

The main plot of the legendary TV series centers on whether Downton Abbey will suffer the same fate as dozens of other country houses in the twentieth century. These "monuments to the past," as Fellowes calls them, started their decline with the agricultural depression of the late nineteenth century. Compounding its effect were crippling taxation, fear of the future, and the devastation of two world wars. In the 1950s, country houses "could hardly be given away as presents," says Fellowes. One after another—roughly one thousand between 1945 and 1955—fell victim to a demolition ball. Others stood in showy disrepair: shabby and indecent. Rather than representing Britain's illustrious heritage, they were sorry reminders of its economic and political decline. For a few decades, it seemed like Highclere Castle might go that route, too.

But *Downton Abbey* rescued it, just as it did *Masterpiece*, PBS, and period drama. Ever since the series' first season, Highclere Castle has attracted roughly 1,500 visitors per day, many of them Americans, to tour its rooms and grounds for a minimum fee of twenty-seven dollars. The Carnarvons, especially Lady Carnarvon, have been very upfront about the economic necessity of this tourism. It costs $1.5 million to run Highclere Castle every year, not including major renovations or repairs. "We have to be a modern business in spirit, even if we have older traditions in other ways," says Carnarvon. Self-described as a "prudent Scottish accountant," she welcomes visitors so she can "pay for the roof."[13] Her frankness points to a rich irony: that while Americans may see homes like Highclere Castle as bastions of English stability, they are in fact highly precarious—and very dependent on American money to keep them running.

★ ★ ★

Surveying these places and the *Masterpiece* series that showcase them, we come to realize how much Britain's locales inform the drama we love. When Americans think of England, they see it in their mind's eye: Buckingham Palace and Big Ben on the winding streets of London, the white cliffs of Dover on the southern coast, the great manor houses and quaint villages everywhere. Americans see a society steeped in tradition, somehow impervious to the changes wrought by time. And the key word is *see*. A great deal of American Anglophilia is visual. The landscapes and buildings of England represent our idealization of a society that has persisted for centuries with its stalwart, cultured, and charming qualities. They represent the England we cherish, incarnating the traditions that seem so appealing to a newer society where constant change is the norm.

Little wonder, then, that *Masterpiece* has skillfully summoned an array of British locales to enrich the flavor of its dramas over the last fifty years. Nether Wallop, Highclere Castle, and 221B Baker Street are more than just settings—more, too, than imposing, if mute, characters. They are the England that Americans yearn for.

Conclusion

$\mathcal{F}$ifty years, 450-plus programs, 2,250-plus episodes, and 250 awards: these are *Masterpiece*'s achievements by the numbers, and they are a record to be proud of. Out of the thousands of TV shows produced in America since the 1950s, roughly thirty have reached the fifty-year mark. Most of these are soap operas, sports, or news programs. No other primetime dramatic series comes close to *Masterpiece*'s longevity nor has won as many Emmy, Peabody, or Golden Globe awards. On a less tangible level, few programs have cultivated as loyal a viewer following. Yet despite the best efforts of everyone involved in the program, and regardless of consistent proof that *Masterpiece* is a viable product with a devoted fan base, the program's future is far from certain.

In truth, *Masterpiece* now faces a multitude of dangers. There is the perennial threat of government cuts, which, however overblown or unlikely, creates a hostile atmosphere where those at PBS and *Masterpiece* often feel besieged. Another threat is *Masterpiece*'s new competition. For many years, the program was America's one-stop shopping center for British drama. Now everyone offers it, from Netflix and Amazon to more specialized venues like BritBox and Acorn. *Downton Abbey* spawned this competition by showing the TV industry just how popular Brit-based drama could be. Thus, in a bittersweet irony, the series that singlehandedly rejuvenated *Masterpiece* also complicated the conditions under which it operates. No doubt, *Masterpiece* benefits in many ways from the current, synergistic explosion of UK-based drama—*Fleabag, Peaky Blinders, The Crown, Black Mirror, Innocent, Skins, Killing Eve*; the list goes on and on. But now it must compete with venues that have far deeper pockets.

Compounding these difficulties is Britain's political and social turmoil, exacerbated by the Brexit decision of June 2016, where 52 percent of the nation agreed to leave the European Union in hopes of controlling its borders and making its own trade deals—or as others see it, losing the automatic free-movement and free-trade rights that come with bloc membership. The results of that decision have been parliamentary chaos and a highly polarized nation, with Britain lurching toward economic free fall. Within this environment, the mythic ideal of England as a country of stability and order, of rural tranquility and quaintness, has come under increasing attack. Period dramas have always been charged with glorifying and romanticizing Britain's past. Now, critics say the genre fuels Brexit fantasies of isolationism. Such accusations have left the BBC in a perceptible identity crisis, unsure of how to shape its public image or what kind of product it wishes to produce in the future.

The greatest threat facing *Masterpiece*, however, is television itself, or what many now call the "post-television landscape." The medium has always been volatile. But within the past ten years, it has undergone a revolution disrupting all that once defined it. That revolution is streaming. When Netflix arrived in 2010, trailing clouds of glory, it personalized TV content by offering customers the opportunity to handpick their favorite shows and create their own menu: Me TV! Since then, Americans have canceled their cable subscriptions by the droves, choosing instead to subscribe, on average, to five or six channels perfectly tailored to their interests. Since 2014, Netflix's subscriptions have risen from 34 million to 140 million. Amazon and Hulu follow closely on its tails, with powerhouses Disney and Apple having just joined the game. We've entered the streaming wars. Everyone is taking up arms, producing new shows at a mind-boggling rate. Reflecting on all this television in 2015, John Landgraf, chief executive of FX networks, introduced the concept of "Peak TV," arguing that the medium couldn't possibly sustain its growth of 390-plus original scripted shows per year. He was wrong. In 2018, Peak TV hit another peak with 495 shows. In 2019, it topped 530.

This surfeit of content can be maddening, as almost any subscriber to a streaming service will tell you. You decide to watch a show (let's say a British mystery) you like or have heard about, so you plop down on your couch, turn on your TV and load your streaming device. Then you stumble from Netflix to BritBox to Acorn, trying to remember which of the three services has the program. BritBox has the first two seasons, which you have already seen, but not the third. You finally find the third season on Amazon Prime, but it costs $2.99 per episode. You sigh, swear, bow to fate, and cough up $14.99 for the entire season. Before you have even begun watching, you're in a bad mood. As this scenario illustrates, the media industry has rushed headlong into a hyper-fragmented mess, with a jumble of on-demand services. An abundance of TV excellence awaits us, but it takes the navigation skills of Magellan to find it.

How do you survive in such a climate? Those at PBS and *Masterpiece* have both shown incredible pluck and resourcefulness. *Masterpiece* now has its own app so we can watch *Poldark* at breakfast or replay our favorite episodes of *Sherlock* at 3:00 a.m., with the proceeds going to the program rather than BritBox or Amazon Prime. PBS is embarking on the use of virtual reality for its concerts and interactive gaming for its children's shows. Knowing how much TV excellence is out there, it now promotes itself as one of the few venues dedicated to learning. And in a poignant irony, given how critics once slammed it for its "snob appeal," PBS has become one of the only services that cater to viewers in poor, rural areas who don't have access to Netflix or Hulu or even basic cable.

As it faces its fiftieth anniversary, then, *Masterpiece* has become exactly like a protagonist in one of its own dramas. Just like that of *Downton Abbey*, the world of television is transforming fast, with no one knowing where its changes will lead. There is no going back to the past, though in the rose-ate glow of a "post-television" nostalgia, *Masterpiece*'s former rituals—the Sunday-night appointment time, the introductions delivered by an urbane host, the viewing parties and measured watching and weeklong anticipation—all seem part of a simpler, more civilized world. Against this torrent of change, *Masterpiece* strives to maintain its core values, just like the Bellamys or the Granthams or the women of Cranford. It is loyal to its fans, trustworthy with its partners, unwavering in its public mission, and committed to excellence. And like that modest but masterful detective Christopher Foyle, or that perfectly mannered valet Jeeves, *Masterpiece* continues to project an image of quiet self-assurance. It sends the message that however much it may adapt to shifts in viewer tastes and habits, or to political changes in Britain, it is determined to be true to itself.

Throughout this history, I have identified *Masterpiece*'s appeal as being rooted in the idea of tradition, with all its charms, boons, strengths, and trouble spots. Those at *Masterpiece* spin it a bit differently. They say their drama is about "emotional truths." *Masterpiece* imparts wisdom about how to pursue a well-lived life: to show kindness, use imagination, strive for fairness, embrace change even as you cherish essential beliefs and customs, and remember that love, as Judi Dench puts it in *Cranford*, is "the final word." At heart, these "emotional truths" are why so many viewers, from Americans to Britons to South Cambodians, enjoy *Masterpiece* dramas like *Downton Abbey*. Other shows deliver such truths, too, of course. But not week after week, program after program, year after year for fifty years.

And while we can watch *Masterpiece*'s drama on any number of platforms any day of the week, we can also take occasional pleasure in seeing it the traditional way—on Sunday nights at 9:00 p.m. EST, enjoying the simplicity of tuning in to one station and knowing exactly what we'll find there: just as viewers did in 1971.

Appendix 1

Masterpiece Productions with Casts

1971–1972

The First Churchills	Susan Hampshire, John Neville, James Villiers
The Spoils of Poynton	Ian Ogilvy, Gemma Jones, Diane Fletcher
The Possessed	Rosalie Crutchley, Keith Bell, Joan Hickson
Pere Goriot	Michael Goodliffe, Angela Browne, Andrew Keir
Jude the Obscure	Robert Powell, Fiona Walker, Alex Marshall
The Gambler	Dame Edith Evans, Colin Redgrave, Maurice Roëves
Resurrection	Alan Dobie, Brian Murphy, Tina Mathews
Cold Comfort Farm	Rosalie Crutchley, Peter Egan, Alastair Sim
The Six Wives of Henry VIII	Keith Mitchell, Annette Crosbie, Dorothy Tutin
Elizabeth R	Glenda Jackson, Rosalie Crutchley, Robin Ellis
The Last of the Mohicans	Philip Madoc, Joanna David, Richard Warwick

1972–1973

Vanity Fair	Susan Hampshire, Roy Marsden, Richard Caldicott
Cousin Bette	Margaret Tyzack, Helen Mirren, Thorley Walters
The Moonstone	Colin Baker, Anna Cropper, Robin Ellis
Tom Brown's Schooldays	Iain Cuthberson, Richard Morant, Anthony Murphy
Point Counterpoint	Sheila Grant, Max Adrian
The Golden Bowl	Gayle Hunnicutt, Daniel Massey, Jill Townsend

1973–1974

Clouds of Witness	Ian Carmichael, Rachel Herbert, David Langton

The Man Who Was Hunting Himself	Donald Burton, Carol Austin, David Savile
The Unpleasantness at the Bellona Club	Ian Carmichael, John Quentin, Anna Cropper
The Little Farm	Michael Elphick, Barbara Ewing, Diane Keen
Upstairs, Downstairs I, II	Jean Marsh, Gordon Jackson, Angela Baddeley
The Edwardians	Anthony Hopkins, Georgia Brown, Robert Powell

1974–1975

Murder Must Advertise	Ian Carmichael, Peter Bowles, Gwen Taylor
Upstairs, Downstairs III	Jean Marsh, Gordon Jackson, Angela Baddeley
Country Matters	Keith Drinkel, Jane Lapotaire, Susan Fleetwood
Vienna 1900	Lynn Redgrave, Robert Stephens, Dorothy Tutin
The Nine Tailors	Ian Carmichael, Glyn Houston, Don Eccles

1975–1976

Shoulder to Shoulder	Georgia Brown, Siân Phillips, Patricia Quinn
Notorious Woman	Rosemary Harris, George Chakiris, Sinead Cusack
Upstairs, Downstairs IV	Jean Marsh, Gordon Jackson, Angela Baddeley
Cakes and Ale	Michael Hordern, Judy Cornwell, Mike Pratt
Sunset Song	Andrew Keir, Edith Macarthur, Vivien Heilbron

1976–1977

Madame Bovary	Francesca Annis, Denis Lill, Tom Conti
How Green Was My Valley	Siân Phillips, Stanley Baker, Rhys Powys
Five Red Herrings	Ian Carmichael, Glyn Houston
Upstairs, Downstairs V	Jean Marsh, Gordon Jackson, Angela Baddeley
Poldark I	Robin Ellis, Jill Townsend, Angharad Rees

1977–1978

Dickens of London	Roy Dotrice
I, Claudius	Derek Jacobi, Siân Phillips, George Baker
Anna Karenina	Nicola Pagett, Eric Porter, Stuart Wilson
Our Mutual Friend	Leo McKern, John McEnery
Poldark II	Robin Ellis, Jill Townsend, Angharad Rees

1978–1979

The Mayor of Casterbridge	Alan Bates, Anna Massey, Anne Stallybrass
The Duchess of Duke Street I	Gemma Jones, Donald Burton, Christopher Cazanove
Country Matters II	Pauline Collins, Joss Ackland, Morag Hood
Lillie	Francesca Annis, Denis Lill, Peter Egan

1979–1980

Kean	Anthony Hopkins, Robert Stephens, Cherie Lunghi
Love for Lydia	Mel Martin, Jeremy Irons, Rachel Kempson
The Duchess of Duke Street II	Gemma Jones, Christopher Cazanove
My Son, My Son	Michael Williams, Patrick Ryecart, Frank Grimes
Disraeli: Portrait of a Romantic	Ian McShane, Mary Peach, Margaret Whiting

1980–1981

Crime and Punishment	John Hurt, Siân Phillips, Anthony Bate
Pride and Prejudice	Elizabeth Garvie, David Rintoul, Natalie Ogle
Testament of Youth	Cheryl Campbell, Rupert Frazer, Joanna McCallum
Danger UXB	Anthony Andrews, Judy Geeson, Maurice Roëves
Thérèse Raquin	Kate Nelligan, Mona Washbourne, Kenneth Cranham

1981–1982

A Town Like Alice	Bryan Brown, Helen Morse, Gordon Jackson
Edward and Mrs. Simpson	Cynthia Harris, Edward Fox, Peggy Ashcroft
The Flame Trees of Thika	Hayley Mills, David Robb, Holly Aird
I Remember Nelson	Kenneth Colley, Geraldine James, Anna Massey
Love in a Cold Climate	Judi Dench, Michael Aldridge, Lucy Gutteridge
Flickers	Bob Hoskins, Frances de la Tour

1982–1983

To Serve Them All My Days	John Duttine, Belinda Lang, Frank Middlemass
The Good Soldier	Jeremy Brett, Susan Fleetwood, Robin Ellis
Winston Churchill— The Wilderness Years	Robert Hardy, Siân Phillips, Nigel Havers

On Approval   Penelope Keith, Jeremy Brett, Lindsay Duncan
Drake's Venture   John Thaw, Paul Darrow, Charlotte Cornwell
Private Schultz   Ian Richardson, Michael Elphick, Bille Whitelaw
Sons and Lovers   Eileen Atkins, Karl Johnson, Tom Bell

1983–1984

Pictures   Wendy Morgan, Peter McEnery, Anton Rodgers
The Citadel   Ben Cross, Clare Higgins
The Irish R.M. I   Peter Bowles, Faith Brook, Lise-Ann McLaughlin
The Tale of Beatrix Potter Penelope Wilton, Holly Aird
Nancy Astor   Lisa Harrow, Pierce Brosnan, Nigel Havers

1984–1985

The Barchester Chronicles Susan Hampshire, Donald Pleasance
The Jewel in the Crown   Dame Peggy Ashcroft, Art Malik, Judy Parfitt
All For Love   Joan Plowright, Alec McGowen, Geraldine McEwan
Strangers and Brothers   Shaughan Seymour, Sheila Ruskin, Nigel Havers

1985–1986

The Last Place on Earth   Martin Shaw, Susan Wooldridge
Bleak House   Diana Rigg, Denholm Elliot, Suzanne Burden
Lord Mountbatten:
   The Last Viceroy   Nicol Williamson, Janet Suzman, Ian Richardson
By the Sword Divided I   Julian Glover, Sharon Maughan, Rob Edwards
The Irish R.M. II   Peter Bowles, Bryan Murray

1986–1987

Paradise Postponed   Paul Shelley, Jill Bennett, Peter Egan
Goodbye, Mr. Chips   Roy Mardsen, Jill Maeger
Lost Empires   Colin Firth, Beatie Edney, John Castle
Silas Marner   Ben Kingsley, Patrick Ryecart, Jenny Agutter
Star Quality:
   Noel Coward Stories   Susannah York, Judi Dench, Tom Courtney
The Death of the Heart   Patricia Hodge, Nigel Havers, Robert Hardy
Love Song   Michael Kitchen, Constance Cummings

1987–1988

The Bretts	Barbara Murrary, Norman Rodwaym, Belinda Lang
Northanger Abbey	Peter Firth, Robert Hardy, Katharine Schlesinger
Sorrell & Son	Richard Pasco, Peter Chelsom, Gwen Watford
Fortunes of War	Kenneth Branagh, Emma Thompson, Ronald Pickup
The Day After the Fair	Hannah Gordon, Anna Massey, Sammi Davis
David Copperfield	Nolan Hemmings, Colin Hurley, Brenda Bruce
By the Sword Divided II	Rob Edwards, Sharon Maughan, Timothy Bentinck

1988–1989

A Perfect Spy	Ray McAnally, Peter Egan, Peggy Ashcroft
Heaven on Earth	R. H. Thomson, Cedric Smith, Huw Davies
A Wreath of Roses	Joanna McCullum, Fabia Drake, Trevor Eve
A Very British Coup	Ray McAnally, Alan MacNaughtan, Keith Allen
All Passion Spent	Wendy Hiller, Maurice Denham, Phyllis Calvert
Talking Heads:	
Bed Among the Lentils	Maggie Smith
Christabel	Stephen Dillane, Elizabeth Hurley, Geoffrey Palmer
The Charmer	Nigel Havers, Rosemary Leach, Bernard Hepton
The Bretts II	Belinda Lang, Norman Rodway, Barbara Murray

1989–1990

And a Nightingale Sang	Joan Plowright, Phyllis Logan, Tom Watt
Precious Bane	Janet McTeer, John McEnery, John Bowe
Glory Enough for All	R. H. Thomson, Robert Wisden, Michael Zelniker
A Tale of Two Cities	James Wilby, Serena Gordon, Sir John Mills
The Yellow Wallpaper	Stephen Dillane, Julia Watson, Dorothy Tutin
After the War	Adrian Lukis, Robert Reynolds, Serena Gordon
The Real Charlotte	Patrick Bergin, Jeananne Crowley, Joanna Roth
The Dressmaker	Joan Plowright, Billie Whitelaw
Traffik	Lindsay Duncan, Bill Paterson, Jamal Shah
Piece of Cake	Nathaniel Parker, Jeremy Northam, Boyd Gaines

1990–1991

The Heat of the Day	Patricia Hodge, Michael Gambon, Michael York
The Ginger Tree	Samantha Bond, Daisuke Rye, Fumi Dan
Jeeves and Wooster I	Hugh Laurie, Stephen Fry, Mary Wimbush
Scoop	Michael Maloney, Nicola Pagett, Denholm Elliot

A Room of One's Own	Eileen Atkins
House of Cards	Ian Richardson, Susannah Harker
Summer's Lease	John Gielgud, Susan Fleetwood, Michael Pennington

1991–1992

Portrait of a Marriage	Janet McTeer, Cathryn Harrison, David Haig
A Murder of Quality	Denholm Elliott, Joss Ackland, Glenda Jackson
Sleepers	Nigel Havers, Warren Clarke, Michael Gough
She's Been Away	Dame Peggy Ashcroft, Geraldine James, James Fox
Parnell and the Englishwoman	Trevor Eve, Francesca Annis, David Robb
Adam Bede	Iain Glen, Patsy Kensit, James Wilby
A Doll's House	Juliet Stevenson, Trevor Eve, David Calder
Clarissa	Sean Bean, Saskia Wickham, Lynsey Baxter
Henry V	Kenneth Branagh, Derek Jacobi, Simon Shepherd
A Perfect Hero	Nigel Havers, James Fox, Barbara Leigh-Hunt
Titmuss Regained	David Threlfall, Kristin Scott Thomas, Rosemary Leach

1992–1993

The Best of Friends	John Gielgud, Wendy Hiller, Patrick McGoohan
The Blackheath Poisonings	Christine Kavanagh, Ian McNeice, Zoë Wanamaker
The Black Velvet Gown	Janet McTeer, Geraldine Somerville, Bob Peck
Calling the Shots	Lynn Redgrave, Cyril Nri, Jack Sheperd
Selected Exits	James Arlon, Gavin Ashcroft, John Grillo
Jeeves and Wooster II	Hugh Laurie, Stephen Fry, Mary Wimbush
The Countess Alice	Wendy Hiller, Zoe Wanamaker, Duncan Bell
Doctor Finlay I	David Rintoul, Ian Bannen, Annette Crosbie
Hedda Gabler	Fiona Shaw, Brid Brennan, Susan Colverd
Impromptu	Judy Davis, Hugh Grant, Mandy Patinkin
Memento Mori	Maggie Smith, Michael Hordern, Renee Asherson
A Question of Attribution	James Fox, Gregory Floy, David Calder
Two Monologues (In My Defense and A Chip in the Sugar)	Alan Bennett
The Secret Agent	David Suchet, Cheryl Campbell, Peter Capaldi

1993–1994

Jeeves and Wooster III	Hugh Laurie, Stephen Fry
To Play the King	Ian Richardson, Susannah Harker
Middlemarch	Juliet Aubrey, Patrick Malahide, Douglas Hodge
The Best Intentions	Samuel Fröler, Pernilla August, Max von Sydow
Body and Soul	Kristin Scott Thomas, Sandra Voe, Anthony Valentine
A Foreign Field	Alec Guinness, Leo McKern, Edward Herrmann
Selected Exits	James Arlon, Gavin Ashcroft, John Grillo
Sharpe	Sean Bean, Daragh O'Malley, John Tams
Where Angels Fear to Tread	Helena Bonham Carter, Judy Davis, Rupert Graves

1994–1995

Jeeves and Wooster IV	Hugh Laurie, Stephen Fry
The Blue Boy	Emma Thompson, Adrian Dunbar, Phyllida Law
The Cinder Path	Lloyd Owen, Catherine Zeta-Jones, Polly Adams
Doctor Finlay II	David Rintoul, Ian Bannen, Annette Crosbie
Hard Times	Harriet Walter, Bill Paterson, Alan Bates
Martin Chuzzlewit	Paul Scofield, Pete Postlethwaite, Tom Wilkinson
The Rector's Wife	Lindsay Duncan, Jonathan Coy, Miles Anderson
Sharpe II	Sean Bean, Daragh O'Malley, Assumpta Serna

1995–1996

Much Ado about Nothing	Kenneth Branagh, Emma Thompson, Keanu Reeves
The Final Cut	Ian Richardson, Susannah Harker
Prime Suspect: The Lost Child	Helen Mirren, John Benfield, Richard Hawley
Prime Suspect: Inner Circles	Helen Mirren, John Benfield
Prime Suspect: Scent of Darkness	Helen Mirren, John Benfield
The Great Kandinsky	Richard Harris, Tom Bell, Dorothy Tutin
The Choir	David Warner, James Fox, Richenda Carey
Peacock Spring	Peter Egan, Jennifer Caron Hall, Hattie Morahan
Bramwell I	Jemma Redgrave, David Calder
Signs & Wonders	James Earl Jones, Jodhi May, David Warner
Interview Day	Tom Wilkinson, Maureen Lipman
The Politician's Wife	Juliet Stevenson, Trevor Eve, Ian Bannen

1996–1997

Moll Flanders	Alex Kingston, Daniel Craig, Nicola Walker
Broken Glass	Mandy Patinkin, Elizabeth McGovern
Bramwell II	Jemma Redgrave, David Calder
Nostromo	Brian Dennehy, Albert Finney, Colin Firth
A Royal Scandal	Richard E. Grant, Susan Lynch, Michael Kitchen
Breaking the Code	Derek Jacobi, Alun Armstrong, Blake Ritson
Persuasion	Amanda Root, Ciaran Hinds, Corin Redgrave
Rebecca	Charles Dance, Diana Rigg, Emilia Fox

1997–1998

The Mill on the Floss	Emily Watson, James Frain, Cheryl Campbell
The Tenant of Wildfell Hall	Toby Stephens, Tara Fitzgerald, Rupert Graves
The Moonstone	Greg Wise, Keeley Hawes
Bramwell III	Jemma Redgrave, David Calder
Rhodes	Martin Shaw, Frances Barber, Neil Pearson
Reckless	Francesca Annis, Robson Green, Michael Kitchen
The Wingless Bird	Claire Skinner, Anne Reid, Edward Atterton
The Woman in White	Tara Fitzgerald, Justine Waddell, Andrew Lincoln
The Painted Lady	Helen Mirren, Iain Glen, Franco Nero
Far From the Madding Crowd	Paloma Baeza, Jonathan Firth, Nathaniel Parker

1998–1999

King Lear	Ian Holm, Paul Rhys, Timothy West
Wuthering Heights	Robert Cavanah, Orla Brady, Matthew Macfadyen
A Respectable Trade	Emma Fielding, Ariyon Bakare, Warren Clarke
The Unknown Soldier	Paul Brooke, Olivia Caffrey, Tom Chadbon
The Prince of Hearts	Robson Green, Rupert Penry-Jones, Tara Fitzgerald
Our Mutual Friend	Paul McGann, Anna Friel, Steven Mackintosh
Bramwell IV	Jemma Redgrave, David Calder
Cider with Rosie	Juliet Stevenson, Dashiell Reece, Joe Roberts
Reckless: The Sequel	Francesca Annis, Robson Green, Michael Kitchen
Frenchman's Creek	Richard Bonehill, Jeremy Child, Tim Dutton
Great Expectations	Ioan Gruffudd, Justine Waddell, Charlotte Rampling
Goodnight, Mr. Tom	John Thaw, Nick Robinson, Annabelle Apsion

1999–2000

A Rather English Marriage	Albert Finney, Tom Courtenay, Joanna Lumley
Aristocrats	Siân Phillips, Alun Armstrong, Ben Daniels
Lost for Words	Thora Hird, Pete Postlethwaite, Penny Downie
Shooting the Past	Lindsay Duncan, Timothy Spall, Liam Cunningham
Bramwell V	Jemma Redgrave, David Calder
Madame Bovary	Frances O'Connor, Greg Wise, Hugh Bonneville
All the King's Men	David Jason, Maggie Smith, William Ash
The Turn of the Screw	Jodhi May, Colin Firth, Caroline Pegg
David Copperfield	Daniel Radcliffe, Trevor Eve, Maggie Smith
Seeing Red	Sarah Lancashire, Richard Dillane, Stuart Richman
Monsignor Renard	John Thaw, Joachim Paul Assbock, John Axon

2000–2001

Oliver Twist	Sam Smith, Robert Lindsay, Julie Walters
Cora Unashamed (The American Collection)	Regina Taylor, Cherry Jones, Ellen Muth
Her Majesty Mrs. Brown	Judi Dench, Billy Connolly, Geoffrey Palmer
The Railway Children	Jack Bluemenau, Clare Thomas, Jemima Rooper
Stiff Upper Lips	David Artus, Kevin Furlong, Nicholas Selby
The American (The American Collection)	Matthew Modine, Diana Rigg, Aisling O'Sullivan
Bramwell VI	Jemma Redgrave, David Calder
Anna Karenina	Helen McCrory, Douglas Henshall, Stephen Dillane
Wives and Daughters	Francesca Annis, Justine Waddell, Bill Paterson
The Song of the Lark (The American Collection)	Alison Elliott, Maximilian Schell, Tony Goldwyn
Take a Girl Like You	Sienna Guillory, Rupert Graves, Robert Daws
Talking Heads: Miss Fozzard Finds Her Feet	Patricia Routledge

2001–2002

The Merchant of Venice	Henry Goodman, Peter De Jersey, Mark Umbers
The Ponder Heart (The American Collection)	Peter MacNicol, JoBeth Williams, Angela Betti
The Cazalets	Hugh Bonneville, Stephen Dillane, Lesley Manville
My Uncle Silas	Albert Finney, Sue Johnston, Joe Prospero
The Murder of Stephen Lawrence	Marianne Jean-Baptiste, Hugh Quarshie, Leon Black

Othello	Eamonn Walker, Christopher Eccleston, Keeley Hawes
Bertie & Elizabeth	James Wilby, Juliet Aubrey, Eileen Atkins
Love in a Cold Climate	Elisabeth Dermot Walsh, Javier Alcina, Rosamund Pike
Lucky Jim	Stephen Tomkinson, Robert Hardy, David Ryall
A Death in the Family (The American Collection)	Annabeth Gish, John Slattery, Austin Wolff
The Way We Live Now	David Suchet, Matthew Macfadyen, Cillian Murphy
Innocents	Tim Pigott-Smith, Madhav Sharma, Emma Cuniffe
The Road from Coorain	Juliet Stevenson, Richard Roxburgh, Katherine Slattery

2002–2003

Almost a Woman (The American Collection)	Wanda De Jesus, Miriam Colon, Cliff De Young
The Forsyte Saga	Damian Lewis, Ioan Gruffud, Gina McKee
My Uncle Silas II	Albert Finney, Sue Johnston, Joe Prospero
The Hound of the Baskervilles	Richard Roxburgh, Ian Hart, Richard E. Grant
Me & Mrs. Jones	Robson Green, Caroline Goodall, Keeley Hawes
Foyle's War	Michael Kitchen, Honeysuckle Weeks, Anthony Howell
Daniel Deronda	Hugh Dancy, Romola Garai, Hugh Bonneville
The Jury	Derek Jacobi, Antony Sher, Helen McCrory
White Teeth	Om Puri, Phil Davis, Naomie Harris

2003–2004

Our Town (The American Collection)	Paul Newman, Jane Curtin, Jake Robards
Warrior Queen	Alex Kingston, Steven Waddington, Emily Blunt
Goodbye, Mr. Chips	Martin Clunes, Victoria Hamilton, Conleth Hill
Doctor Zhivago	Keira Knightly, Sam Neill, Hans Matheson
The Forsyte Saga II	Damian Lewis, Ioan Gruffud, Gina McKee

2004–2005

The Lost Prince	Daniel Williams, Gina McKee, Bill Nighy
Talking Heads: The Hand of God	Eileen Atkins, David Haig, Thora Hird

Henry VIII	Ray Winstone, Joss Ackland, Helena Bonham Carter
Pollyanna	Amanda Burton, Kenneth Cranham, Georgina Terry
He Knew He Was Right	Oliver Dimsdale, Laura Fraser, David Tennant
Island at War	Saskia Reeves, Owen Teale, Laurence Fox

2005–2006

Sherlock Holmes and the Case of the Silk Stocking	Rupert Everett, Ian Hart, Anne Carroll
Kidnapped	James Anthony Pearson, Iain Glen, Adrian Dunbar
The Virgin Queen	Anne-Marie Duff, Tom Hardy, Kevin McKidd
Bleak House	Anna Maxwell Martin, Carey Mulligan
My Family and Other Animals	Matthew Goode, Imelda Staunton, Russell Tovey
Carrie's War	Keeley Fawcett, Jack Stanley, Karen Meagher
Under the Greenwood Tree	Keeley Hawes, James Murray, Terry Mortimer

2006–2007

Casanova	Rose Byrne, David Tennant, Peter O'Toole
To the Ends of the Earth	Benedict Cumberbatch, Jared Harris, Sam Neill
Jane Eyre	Ruth Wilson, Toby Stephens, Lorraine Ashbourne
Dracula	Dan Stevens, David Suchet, Marc Warren
The Wind in the Willows	Matt Lucas, Mark Gatiss, Lee Ingleby
The Secret Life of Mrs. Beeton	Anna Madeley, JJ Feild, Jim Carter

2007–2008

The Amazing Mrs. Pritchard	Jane Horrocks, Steven Mackintosh, Jodhi May
The Complete Jane Austen	Felicity Jones, Sally Hawkins, Hattie Morahan
A Room with A View	Elaine Cassidy, Rafe Spall, Laurence Fox
My Boy Jack	David Haig, Daniel Radcliffe, Kim Cattrall
Cranford	Judi Dench, Eileen Atkins, Imelda Staunton

2008–2009

The Last Enemy	Benedict Cumberbatch, Anamaria Marinca
God On Trial	Stephen Dillane, Eddie Marsan, Dominic Cooper
Filth: The Mary Whitehouse Story	Julie Walters, Alun Armstrong, Hugh Bonneville

The Unseen Alistair Cooke (doc)	Alistair Cooke, William F. Buckley, Lauren Bacall
Tess of the d'Urbervilles	Gemma Arterton, Eddie Redmayne, Hans Matheson
Wuthering Heights	Tom Hardy, Charlotte Riley, Andrew Lincoln
Oliver Twist	William Miller, Adam Arnold, Tom Hardy
David Copperfield (encore)	Daniel Radcliffe, Trevor Eve, Maggie Smith
Little Dorrit	Claire Foy, Matthew Macfadyen, Tom Courtenay
The Old Curiosity Shop	Derek Jacobi, Toby Jones, Sophie Vavasseur

2009–2010

Endgame	William Hurt, Chiwetel Ejiofor, Jonny Lee Miller
Place of Execution	Greg Wise, Juliet Stevenson, Lee Ingleby
Collision	Douglas Henshall, Kate Ashfield, Paul McGann
Return to Cranford	Judi Dench, Imelda Staunton, Michelle Dockery
Emma	Romala Garai, Jonny Lee Miller, Tamsin Greig
The 39 Steps	Rupert Penry-Jones, Lydia Leonard, David Haig
The Diary of Anne Frank	Ellie Kendrick, Kate Ashfield, Iain Glen
Small Island	David Oyelowo, Benedict Cumberbatch, Naomie Harris

2010–2011

Lennon Naked	Christopher Eccleston, Andrew Scott, Rory Kinnear
Framed	Trevor Eve, Eve Myles, Robert Pugh
Downton Abbey I	Maggie Smith, Hugh Bonneville, Michelle Dockery
Any Human Heart	Matthew Macfadyen, Jim Broadbent, Hayley Atwell
Upstairs, Downstairs	Keeley Hawes, Ed Stoppard, Adrian Scarborough
South Riding	Anna Maxwell Martin, David Morrissey, Penelope Wilton

2011–2012

Worricker: Page Eight	Bill Nighy, Rachel Weisz, Tom Hughes
A Song of Lunch	Emma Thompson, Alan Rickman
Downton Abbey II	Maggie Smith, Hugh Bonneville, Michelle Dockery
Great Expectations	Douglas Booth, Ray Winstone, Gillian Anderson
The Mystery of Edwin Drood	Matthew Rhys, Freddie Fox, Tamzin Merchant
Birdsong	Eddie Redmayne, Clemence Poesy, Matthew Goode

2012–2013

Upstairs, Downstairs II	Keeley Hawes, Ed Stoppard, Adrian Scarborough
Downton Abbey III	Maggie Smith, Hugh Bonneville, Michelle Dockery
Mr. Selfridge	Jeremy Piven, Ron Cook, Amanda Abbington

2013–2014

The Paradise	Joanna Vanderham, Emun Elliot, Patrick Malahide
Downton Abbey IV	Maggie Smith, Hugh Bonneville, Michelle Dockery
Mr. Selfridge II	Jeremy Piven, Ron Cook, Amanda Abbington
Breathless	Jack Davenport, Catherine Steadman, Shaun Dingwall

2014–2015

The Paradise II	Joanna Vanderham, Emun Elliot, Patrick Malahide
Worricker: Turks & Caicos	Bill Nighy, Winona Ryder, Christopher Walken
Worricker: Salting the Battlefield	Bill Nighy, Helena Bonham Carter, Ralph Fiennes
Downton Abbey V	Maggie Smith, Hugh Bonneville, Michelle Dockery
Mr. Selfridge III	Jeremy Piven, Ron Cook, Amanda Abbington
Wolf Hall	Mark Rylance, Damian Lewis, Claire Foy
Poldark	Aidan Turner, Eleanor Tomlinson, Jack Farthing

2015–2016

Home Fires	Francesca Annis, Samantha Bond, Ed Stoppard
Indian Summers	Julie Walters, Henry Lloyd-Hughes, Jemima West
Downton Abbey VI	Maggie Smith, Hugh Bonneville, Michelle Dockery
Mr. Selfridge IV	Jeremy Piven, Ron Cook, Amanda Abbington

2016–2017

Churchill's Secret	Michael Gambon, Romola Garai, Matthew Macfadyen
Indian Summers II	Julie Walters, Henry Lloyd-Hughes, Jemima West
Poldark II	Aidan Turner, Eleanor Tomlinson, Jack Farthing
The Durrells in Corfu	Keeley Hawes, Josh O'Connor, Milo Parker
Victoria	Jenna Coleman, Tom Hughes, Adrian Schiller
To Walk Invisible: The Brontë Sisters	Finn Atkins, Charlie Murphy, Chloe Pirrie
King Charles III	Tim Pigott-Smith, Oliver Chris, Charlotte Riley

Home Fires II	Francesca Annis, Samantha Bond, Ed Stoppard
My Mother and Other Strangers	Hattie Morahan, Owen McDonnell, Michael Nevin

2017–2018

Poldark III	Aidan Turner, Eleanor Tomlinson, Jack Farthing
The Collection	Richard Coyle, Mamie Gummer, Frances de la Tour
The Durrells in Corfu II	Keeley Hawes, Josh O'Connor, Milo Parker
Victoria II	Jenna Coleman, Tom Hughes, Adrian Schiller
The Child in Time	Benedict Cumberbatch, Kelly Macdonald, Stephen Campbell Moore
Little Women	Maya Hawke, Kathryn Newton, Emily Watson
Man in an Orange Shirt	Julian Morris, Vanessa Redgrave, Oliver Jackson-Cohen

2018–2019

The Miniaturist	Anya Taylor-Joy, Romola Garai, Alex Hassell
The Durrells in Corfu III	Keeley Hawes, Josh O'Connor, Milo Parker
Poldark IV	Aidan Turner, Eleanor Tomlinson, Jack Farthing
Victoria III	Jenna Coleman, Tom Hughes, Adrian Schiller
Mrs. Wilson	Ruth Wilson, Iain Glen, Fiona Shaw
Les Misérables	Dominic West, David Oyelwo, Lily Collins

2019–2020

The Durrells in Corfu IV	Keeley Hawes, Josh O'Connor, Milo Parker
Poldark V	Aidan Turner, Eleanor Tomlinson, Jack Farthing
Press	Charlotte Riley, Ben Chaplin, Al Weaver
The Chaperone	Elizabeth McGovern, Haley Lu Richardson, Victoria Hill
Sanditon	Crystal Clarke, Rose Williams, Theo James
Howards End	Matthew Macfadyen, Hayley Atwell, Tracey Ullman
World on Fire I	Jonah Hauer-King, Helen Hunt, Zofia Wichlacz

Appendix 2

Mystery! *Productions with Casts*

1980–1981

She Fell Among Thieves	Eileen Atkins, Malcolm McDowell, Michael Jayston
Rumpole of the Bailey I	Leo McKern, Jonathan Coy, Julian Curry
Rebecca	Jeremy Brett, Joanna David, Anna Massey
The Racing Game I	Mike Gwilym, Mick Ford, James Maxwell
Sergeant Cribb I	Alan Dobie, William Simons, David Waller

1981–1982

Dr. Jekyll and Mr. Hyde	David Hemmings
Malice Aforethought	Hywel Bennett, Cheryl Campbell, Belinda Carroll
Rumpole of the Bailey II	Leo McKern, Jonathan Coy, Julian Curry
The Racing Game II	Mike Gwilym, Mick Ford, James Maxwell
Sergeant Cribb II	Alan Dobie, William Simons, David Waller

1982–1983

Sweeney Todd	Freddie Jones, Heather Canning, Russell Hunter
Dying Day	George Hearn
Father Brown	Kenneth More
Melissa	Peter Barkworth, Moira Redmond, Joan Benham
Quiet as a Nun	Maria Aitken, Renée Asherson, Brenda Bruce
Sergeant Cribb III	Alan Dobie, William Simons, David Waller
Agatha Christie Stories I	Maurice Denham, Angela Easterling, Christopher Wren
Miss Morison's Ghosts	Hannah Gordon, Wendy Hiller

| *The Limbo Connection* | James Bolan, Rosalind Ayres, Michael Culver |
| *We, the Accused* | Ian Holm, Angela Down, Elizabeth Spriggs |

1983–1984

| *Reilly, Ace of Spies* | Sam Neill, Ian Charleson, Michael Aldridge |
| *Shades of Darkness* | Eileen Atkins, Alfred Lynch, Gareth Thomas |

1984–1985

Rumpole's Return	Leo McKern, Peggy Thorpe-Bates, Patricia Hodge
Rumpole of the Bailey III	Brenda Blethyn, Sylvia Coleridge, Emlyn Williams
Agatha Christie's Partners in Crime I	Graham Crowden, Dulcie Gray, Tim Woodward
Praying Mantis	Jonathan Pryce, Cherie Lunghi, Carmen Du Sautoy
Agatha Christie Stories II	Andrew Bicknell, Elizabeth Garvie, Amanda Redman
The Adventures of Sherlock Holmes I	Jeremy Brett, David Burke, Edward Hardwicke
The Woman in White	Ian Richardson, Jenny Seagrove, Deirdra Morris

1985–1986

Adam Dalgliesh Mysteries: Death of an Expert Witness	Roy Marsden, Cyril Cusack, Barry Foster, Chloe Franks
My Cousin Rachel	Geraldine Chaplin, Christopher Guard, John Shrapnel
Agatha Christie's Miss Marple I	Joan Hickson, Andrew Cruikshank, Keith Drinkel
The Adventures of Sherlock Holmes II	Jeremy Brett, David Burke, Edward Hardwicke
Charters and Caldicott	Robin Bailey, Michael Aldridge, Caroline Blakiston
Agatha Christie's Partners in Crime II	Graham Crowden, Dulcie Gray, Tim Woodward

1986–1987

| *Adam Dalgliesh Mysteries: Shroud for a Nightingale* | Roy Marsden, Joss Ackland, Sheila Allen |
| *Brat Farrar* | Mark Greenstreet, Dominique Barnes, Angela Browne |

Agatha Christie's Miss Marple II	Joan Hickson, Andrew Cruikshank, Keith Drinkel
Agatha Christie's The Secret Adversary	James Warwick, Francesca Annis, George Baker
The Return of Sherlock Holmes I	Jeremy Brett, David Burke, Edward Hardwicke
Cover Her Face	Roy Marsden, Phyllis Calvert, Mel Martin

1987–1988

Lord Peter Wimsey	Edward Petherbridge, Harriet Walter, Richard Morant
Agatha Christie's Miss Marple III	Andrew Cruikshank, Keith Drinkel, Frederick Jaeger
Inspector Morse I	John Thaw, Kevin Whately, James Grout
Rumpole of the Bailey IV	Leo McKern, Peggy Thorpe-Bates, Patricia Hodge
Adam Dalgliesh Mysteries: The Black Tower	Roy Marsden, Patrick Malahide, William Simons

1988–1989

Cause Célèbre	Helen Mirren, Harry Andrews, David Suchet
The Return of Sherlock Holmes II	Jeremy Brett, David Burke, Edward Hardwicke
Inspector Morse II	John Thaw, Kevin Whately, James Grout
Agatha Christie's Miss Marple IV	Joan Hickson, Andrew Cruikshank, Keith Drinkel
Game, Set and Match	Ian Holm, Mel Martin, Anthony Bate

1989–1990

Campion I	Peter Davison, Brian Glover, Andrew Burt
Rumpole of the Bailey V	Leo McKern, Peggy Thorpe-Bates, Patricia Hodge
Agatha Christie's Poirot I	David Suchet, Hugh Fraser, Philip Jackson
Adam Dalgliesh Mysteries: A Taste for Death	Roy Marsden, Dame Wendy Hiller, Bosco Hogan
Inspector Morse III	John Thaw, Kevin Whately, James Grout

1990–1991

Agatha Christie's Poirot: The Incredible Theft	David Suchet, Hugh Fraser, Philip Jackson

Mother Love	Diana Rigg, James Wilby, Fiona Gillies
Campion II	Peter Davison, Brian Glover, Andrew Burt
Agatha Christie's Poirot II	David Suchet, Hugh Fraser, Philip Jackson
The Dark Angel	Peter O'Toole, Beatie Edney, Jane Lapotaire
Die Kinder	Miranda Richardson, Frederic Forrest, Hans Kremer
The Man from the Pru	Jonathan Pryce, Anna Massey, Susannah York
Inspector Morse IV	John Thaw, Kevin Whately, James Grout

1991–1992

Adam Dalgliesh Mysteries:	
Devices and Desires	Roy Marsden, Harry Burton, Gemma Jones
The Casebook of Sherlock Holmes	Jeremy Brett, David Burke, Edward Hardwicke
Artists in Crime	Simon Williams, Ursula Howells, Edward Judd
Prime Suspect I	Helen Mirren, John Benfield, Tom Bell
Agatha Christie's Poirot III	David Suchet, Hugh Fraser, Philip Jackson
Inspector Morse V	John Thaw, Kevin Whately, James Grout

1992–1993

Maigret I	Michael Gambon, Barbara Flynn, Ciaran Madden
Agatha Christie's Poirot IV	David Suchet, Hugh Fraser, Philip Jackson
Prime Suspect II	Helen Mirren, John Benfield, Tom Bell
Sherlock Holmes:	
The Master Blackmailer	Gwen Ffrangcon-Davies, Robert Hardy, Nickolas Grace
Inspector Morse VI	John Thaw, Kevin Whately, James Grout
Rumpole of the Bailey VI	Leo McKern, Peggy Thorpe-Bates, Patricia Hodge

1993–1994

The Inspector Alleyn Mysteries I	Patrick Malahide, William Simons, Belinda Lang
Agatha Christie's Poirot V	David Suchet, Hugh Fraser, Philip Jackson
Sherlock Holmes:	
The Last Vampyre	Jeremy Brett, Edward Hardwicke, Juliet Aubrey
Maigret II	Michael Gambon, Barbara Flynn, Ciaran Madden
Agatha Christie's Poirot VI	David Suchet, Hugh Fraser, Philip Jackson

1994–1995

Agatha Christie's Poirot VI	David Suchet, Hugh Fraser, Philip Jackson
Cadfael	Derek Jacobi, Mark Charnock, Peter Copley
A Dark-Adapted Eye	Helena Bonham Carter, Celia Imrie, Sophie Ward
Gallowglass	John McArdle, Paul Rhys, Michael Sheen
Inspector Morse VII	John Thaw, Kevin Whately, James Grout
The Inspector Alleyn	
Mysteries II	Patrick Malahide, William Simons, Belinda Lang
Prime Suspect III	Helen Mirren, John Benfield, Tom Bell

1995–1996

Gallowglass	John McArdle, Paul Rhys, Michael Sheen
Agatha Christie's	
Poirot VII	David Suchet
Memoirs of Sherlock Holmes	Jeremy Brett, Edward Hardwicke
Inspector Morse IX	John Thaw, Kevin Whately
Chandler & Company	Catherine Russell, Barbara Flynn, Peter Capaldi
A Mind to Murder	Roy Marsden, Mairead Carty, Sean Scanlan

1996–1997

Oliver's Travels	Alan Bates, Sinead Cusack
Agatha Christie's	
Poirot VIII	David Suchet
Original Sin	Roy Marsden, Ian Bannen, Cathryn Harrison
Inspector Morse X	John Thaw, Kevin Whately
Cadfael II	Derek Jacobi, Michael Culver, Julian Firth

1997–1998

Into the Blue	John Thaw, Tom Towndrow, Vida Garman
Hetty Wainthropp	
Investigates I	Patricia Routledge, Derek Benfield, Dominic Monaghan
Deep Secrets	Colin Salmon, Amanda Donohoe, Sophie Okonedo
The Sculptress	Pauline Quirk, Caroline Goodall, Christopher Fulford
Cadfael III	Derek Jacobi, Michael Culver, Julian Firth
The Ice House	Frances Barber, Kitty Aldridge, Corin Redgrave
Inspector Morse XI	John Thaw, Kevin Whately

An Unsuitable Job for a Woman	Helen Baxendale, Annette Crosbie, Struan Rodger

1998–1999

Touching Evil	Robson Green, Nicola Walker, Shaun Dingwall
The Life and Crimes of William Palmer	Keith Allen, Jayne Ashbourne, Judy Cornwell
Cadfael IV	Derek Jacobi, Michael Culver, Julian Firth
The Heat of the Sun	Trevor Eve, Susannah Harker, Michael Byrne
Inspector Morse XII	John Thaw, Kevin Whately
A Certain Justice	Roy Marsden, Ricci Harnett, Britta Smith
Hetty Wainthropp Investigates II	Patricia Routledge, Derek Benfield, Dominic Monaghan

1999–2000

Second Sight	Clive Owen, Claire Skinner
An Unsuitable Job for a Woman II	Helen Baxendale, Annette Crosbie, Struan Rodger
Mrs. Bradley Mysteries (pilot)	Diana Rigg, Neil Dudgeon
Touching Evil II	Robson Green, Nicola Walker, Shaun Dingwall
Trial by Fire	Juliet Stevenson, Jim Carter
Lady Audley's Secret	Neve McIntosh, Juliette Caton, Steven Mackintosh
Hetty Wainthropp Investigates III	Patricia Routledge, Derek Benfield, Dominic Monaghan
Murder Rooms: The Dark Beginnings of Sherlock Holmes	Ian Richardson, Charles Edwards

2000–2001

The Wyvern Mystery	Naomi Watts, Derek Jacobi, Iain Glen
Hetty Wainthropp Investigates IV	Patricia Routledge, Derek Benfield, Dominic Monaghan
Touching Evil III	Robson Green, Nicola Walker, Shaun Dingwall

The Last Morse	(documentary)
Inspector Morse:	
Remorseful Day	John Thaw, Kevin Whately
Second Sight II	Clive Owen, Claire Skinner

2002

Forgotten	Paul McGann, Amanda Burton, Zara Turner
Murder Rooms:	
The Dark Beginnings of	
Sherlock Holmes II	Ian Richardson, Charles Edwards
The Inspector Lynley	
Mysteries	Nathaniel Parker, Sharon Small
Skinwalkers (An American	
Mystery Special)	Wes Studi, Adam Beach

2003

Dead Gorgeous	Fay Ripley, Helen McCrory
Mrs. Bradley Mysteries I	Diana Rigg, Neil Dudgeon
Hetty Wainthropp	
Investigates V	Patricia Routledge, Derek Benfield, Dominic Monaghan
The Inspector Lynley	
Mysteries II	Nathaniel Parker, Sharon Small
Coyote Waits (An American	
Mystery Special)	Wes Studi, Adam Beach

2004

A Thief of Time (An	
American Mystery	
Special)	Wes Studi, Adam Beach
Foyle's War II	Michael Kitchen, Honeysuckle Weeks, Anthony Howell
The Inspector Lynley	
Mysteries III	Nathaniel Parker, Sharon Small
Death in Holy Orders	Martin Shaw, Jesse Spence, Alan Howard

2005

Malice Aforethought	Ben Miller, Barbara Flynn, Megan Dodds
Agatha Christie's Marple	Geraldine McEwan
The Inspector Lynley	
Mysteries IV	Nathaniel Parker, Sharon Small
Foyle's War III	Michael Kitchen, Honeysuckle Weeks, Anthony Howell
The Murder Room	Martin Shaw, Janie Dee, Samantha Bond

2006

Jericho	Robert Lindsay, David Troughton, Ciaran McMenamin
Agatha Christie's Marple II	Geraldine McEwan
Inspector Lewis	Kevin Whately, Laurence Fox
The Inspector Lynley	
Mysteries V	Nathaniel Parker, Sharon Small

2007

The Sally Lockhart Mysteries: The Ruby in the Smoke	Billie Piper, Matt Smith, Julie Walters
Jericho II	Robert Lindsay
Foyle's War IV	Michael Kitchen, Honeysuckle Weeks, Anthony Howell
Agatha Christie's Marple III	Geraldine McEwan
Inspector Lynley VI	Nathaniel Parker, Sharon Small

2008

Inspector Lewis I	Kevin Whately, Laurence Fox
Foyle's War V	Michael Kitchen, Honeysuckle Weeks, Anthony Howell
Inspector Lynley VII	Nathaniel Parker, Sharon Small
The Sally Lockhart Mysteries: Shadow in the North	Billie Piper, Jared Harris, David Harewood

2009

Wallander	Kenneth Branagh, Richard McCabe, Tom Hiddleston
Agatha Christie's	
Poirot IX	David Suchet
Agatha Christie's	
Marple IV	Julia McKenzie
Inspector Lewis II	Kevin Whately, Laurence Fox

2010

Foyle's War VI	Michael Kitchen, Honeysuckle Weeks, Anthony Howell
Agatha Christie's	
Marple V	Julia McKenzie
David Suchet on the	
Orient Express	(documentary)
Agatha Christie's Poirot X:	
Murder on the Orient	
Express	David Suchet
Inspector Lewis III	Kevin Whately, Laurence Fox
Wallander II	Kenneth Branagh, Richard McCabe, Jeany Spark
Sherlock I	Benedict Cumberbatch, Martin Freeman

2011

Agatha Christie's	
Poirot XI	David Suchet
Agatha Christie's	
Marple VI	Julia McKenzie
Zen	Rufus Sewell, Catarina Murino
Inspector Lewis IV	Kevin Whately, Laurence Fox
Case Histories	Jason Isaacs, Amanda Abbington

2012

Sherlock II	Benedict Cumberbatch, Martin Freeman, Rupert Graves
Endeavour (pilot)	Shaun Evans, Roger Allam, Anton Lesser
Inspector Lewis V	Kevin Whately, Laurence Fox
Wallander III	Kenneth Branagh, Richard McCabe, Saskia Reeves

2013

Inspector Lewis VI	Kevin Whately, Laurence Fox
Endeavour I	Shaun Evans, Roger Allam, Anton Lesser
The Lady Vanishes	Tuppence Middleton, Tom Hughes, Julian Rhind-Tutt
Silk	Maxine Peake, Rupert Penry-Jones, Neil Stuke
Foyle's War VII	Michael Kitchen, Honeysuckle Weeks, Anthony Howell

2014

Sherlock III	Benedict Cumberbatch, Martin Freeman, Rupert Graves
The Escape Artist	David Tennant, Sophie Okenado, Toby Kebbell
Endeavour II	Shaun Evans, Roger Allam, Anton Lesser
Agatha Christie's Poirot XII	David Suchet
Agatha Christie's Marple VII	Julia McKenzie
Inspector Lewis VII	Kevin Whately, Laurence Fox
Death Comes to Pemberley	Matthew Rhys, Anna Maxwell Martin, Matthew Goode

2015

Grantchester	James Norton, Al Weaver, Robson Green
Arthur & George	Martin Clunes, Arsher Ali, Charles Edwards

2016

Sherlock: The Abominable Bride	Benedict Cumberbatch, Martin Freeman
Grantchester II	James Norton, Al Weaver, Robson Green
Wallander IV	Kenneth Branagh, Richard McCabe, Jeany Spark
Endeavour III	Shaun Evans, Roger Allam, Anton Lesser
Inspector Lewis VIII	Kevin Whately, Laurence Fox

2017

Sherlock IV	Benedict Cumberbatch, Martin Freeman, Rupert Graves

Grantchester III	James Norton, Al Weaver, Robson Green
Prime Suspect: Tennison	Stefani Martini, Sam Reid, Blake Harrison
Endeavour IV	Shaun Evans, Roger Allam, Anton Lesser

2018

Unforgotten I	Nicola Walker, Sanjeev Bhaskar
Unforgotten II	Nicola Walker, Sanjeev Bhaskar
Endeavour V	Shaun Evans, Roger Allam, Anton Lesser

2019

Unforgotten III	Nicola Walker, Sanjeev Bhaskar
Endeavour VI	Shaun Evans, Roger Allam, Anton Lesser
Grantchester IV	Tom Brittney, Robson Green, Al Weaver

2020

Baptiste I	Tcheky Karyo, Tom Hollander, Jessica Raine
Grantchester V	Tom Brittney, Robson Green, Al Weaver
Van der Valk I	Marc Warren, Luke Allen-Gale, Darrell D'Silva
Endeavour VII	Shaun Evans, Roger Allam, Anton Lesser
Unforgotten IV	Nicola Walker, Sanjeev Bhaskar

Notes

INTRODUCTION

1. For other accounts of the show's origins, see Eaton, *Making Masterpiece*, 11–13.
2. For a fascinating discussion of British influence on American television, see Miller, *Something Completely Different*.
3. See Stewart, "How Should Public TV."
4. Telephone interview with author, December 27, 2016.
5. Qtd. in Harris, "The Future of Tradition."
6. See Baker, "A Little Bones Trouble."
7. For McGovern's story, see Eaton, *Making Masterpiece*, 48.
8. Lyons, "What You Should Watch."
9. *Brideshead Revisited*, the Grand Dame of British costume drama, originally aired on WNET's *Great Performances* series. *Pride and Prejudice* was scooped up by A&E, *Masterpiece Theatre*'s big competitor in the 1990s. Rebecca Eaton passed on it, thinking "the world didn't need" another adaptation of the novel. She was wrong.

CHAPTER 1

1. For an extensive discussion of responses to Minow's "wasteland" speech, see Baughman's "Minow's Viewers." See also Minow's 1991 book *How Vast the Wasteland Now?* for his own retrospective look at the speech and Adlai Stevenson's "Letter to Minow." For the complete audio recording of the speech, see https://www.american rhetoric.com/speeches/newtonminow.htm.
2. Qtd. in Leopold, "Revisiting the Vast Wasteland."
3. Qtd. in Baughman, "Minow's Viewers," 453.
4. White with Jauch, "President's Speech to NET Affiliates," 3.
5. Carnegie Commission, *Public Television*, 1.

6. For a full description of Reith's vision of the BBC, see Briggs, *The BBC*, 53–56. Readers should note that BBC radio was launched in 1922, BBC television in 1936.

7. Qtd. in Ledbetter, *Made Possible by*, 41.

8. Callard, *Aspiration*, 2.

9. For a fascinating, well-researched discussion of the early pressures facing PBS, see Ledbetter, *Made Possible by*.

10. Callard, *Aspiration*, 5.

11. See O'Connor, "But How Do You?"; Moss, "A Different Suspense"; and the *Masterpiece* file on *The First Churchills*.

12. Qtd. in Ledbetter, *Made Possible by*, 147.

13. For a full discussion of the difference between reflective and restorative nostalgia, see Boym, *The Future of Nostalgia*, ch. 4 and 5.

14. Qtd. in Newcomb, "Anthology Dramas," 1002.

15. Thomson, *Television*, 143.

16. *Masterpiece* file on *Spoils of Poynton*.

17. Bianculli, *The Platinum Age of Television*, 111.

18. Qtd. in "The Forsyte Saga," *New Yorker*, Jan 10, 1970, 16.

19. For an in-depth picture of *The Forsyte Saga*'s reception in America, see Miller, *Something Completely Different*, ch. 4.

20. Qtd. in Allen, *To Be Continued*, 4.

21. See Miller, *Something Completely Different*, 82, for a full discussion of fans' responses to *The Forsyte Saga*.

22. See Nussbaum, "Tune in Next Week"; Carr, "Barely Keeping Up in TV's Golden Age"; Patterson and McLean, "Move Over Hollywood."

23. Adams, "Is Television a Medium without a Past?"

CHAPTER 2

1. See O'Connor, "*Upstairs, Downstairs*" and Carmody, "Domestic Drama."

2. Joan Wilson was the executive producer of *Masterpiece Theatre* from 1973 to 1985, following Christopher Sarson, who held the role from 1971 to 1973. Rebecca Eaton became executive producer after Wilson's death in 1985 and retired in 2019, succeeded by Susanne Simpson.

3. Qtd. in Eaton, *Making Masterpiece*, 29.

4. Floyd, *Backstairs with Upstairs, Downstairs*, 7.

5. Qtd. in Floyd, 13.

6. Floyd.

7. For a sampling of reviews that praised the show's historical accuracy, see Baum, "Farewell to Upstairs, Downstairs"; O'Connor, "BBC Ships PBS Another Great Hit"; and Gantz, "The Empire Strikes Back."

8. Telephone interview with author, December 27, 2015.

9. *Masterpiece* press release.

10. Floyd, *Backstairs with Upstairs, Downstairs*, 63.

11. O'Connor, "A Fond Cheerio" and "Departing Is Such Sweet Sorrow"; Henry, "A Farewell to Eaton Place."

12. See Eaton, *Making Masterpiece*, xv–xvi.

13. Drew, "Downton Abbey."

14. Rabinowitz, "Pride and Privilege," and Swanson, "Review: Downton Abbey."

15. Telephone interview with author, December 29, 2015.

16. Irving, "In Defense."

17. Stevens, "Why I left Downton Abbey."

18. Fellowes, Jessica, *The World*, 11.

19. Jenkins, "The End of the British Invasion"; interview with author, December 18, 2015.

20. Collins, "Downton-Abbey Cheat Sheet."

21. Interview with author, June 27, 2019.

22. Day-Lewis's comment appeared in "Why Do Americans Love Downton Abbey So Much? *New Statesman*, September 5, 2013. See Schama, "Why Americans Have Fallen" for Schama's comments. Cumberbatch's remark is on BBC America's website, Anglophenia (https://www.bbcamerica.com/anglophenia).

23. PR interview with Fellowes and Smith.

24. Stanley, "A Transatlantic Romance Continues."

CHAPTER 3

1. See Cooke, "How Alistair Cooke Evokes."

2. See Boorstin, *The Daniel J. Boorstin Reader*, 71.

3. For more information on the concept of middlebrow, see Rubin, *The Making of Middlebrow Culture*.

4. See Irving, "In Defense of Sentimentality."

5. For a fascinating and detailed account of the Stanford controversy, see Lindenberger, *The History in Literature*.

6. Both comments are quoted in Lindenberger, 41.

7. Brennan, "*Masterpiece*," 108.

8. *Masterpiece* file on *Our Town*.

9. See Gilbert, "PBS Adaptation."

10. Qtd. in Nicholson, "Is Dominic West?"

11. Qtd. in *Daily Telegraph*, "Thandie Newton."

12. Qtd. in Wallace, "Five Steps."

CHAPTER 4

1. Qtd. in Laity, "My Favourite Film."

2. Qtd. on IMDb, *Sense and Sensibility* entry.

3. See Cooper, "Sense and Sensibility."

4. Qtd. in Leggott and Taddeo, *Upstairs and Downstairs*, 79.

5. *Masterpiece* welded *Bleak House* into eight one-hour episodes instead.

6. See the BBC interview with Davies on *Bleak House* at www.bbc.com.

7. See Lopate, "Adapt This."

8. Dickens, *The Personal History and Experience of David Copperfield*, 28.

9. For a more thorough appraisal of Lynch's book, see Joshua Rothman's elegant and moving review "The History of 'Loving' to Read."

10. See Blitzer, "Elementary."

11. For a full, lively account of the production of *Sherlock Holmes*, read Peter Haining's *The Television Sherlock Holmes*.

12. See Haining for further information on the handbook.

13. Qtd. in Haining, 187.

14. Qtd. in Haining, 182.

15. See Oliver, "Jeremy Brett."

16. See Oliver.

17. Qtd. in Haining, 161.

18. Qtd. in Haining, 169.

19. Much of this description of Gattis's pitch to the Sherlock Holmes Society is taken from Matthew Boström's elegantly written and informative book *From Holmes to Sherlock*.

20. Qtd. in Bostrom, 2.

21. See Hale, "The Latest Sherlock"; Swanson, "Review of *Sherlock*, Season One"; Rosenberg, "Sherlock Holmes Meets the 21st Century."

22. See Martin, "Who Is the Greatest?"

23. See Nussbaum's "Fan Friction" for a fascinating analysis of *Sherlock* and its fans.

24. Qtd. in Frost, "'Sherlock' Writer Mark Gatiss."

25. Interview with author, June 2011.

26. Interview with author, July 2011.

27. See Carr, "Andrew Davies Hints."

28. See Rosseinsky, "Everything You Need to Know."

29. Interview with author, June 2011.

30. Interview with author, June 2011.

CHAPTER 5

1. See Tiedemann and Marsico, "America's Declining Interest"; Curry, "How Ignorance of American History"; and Boot, "Americans' Ignorance of History."

2. Qtd. in Lowenthal, *The Past Is a Foreign Country*, 48.

3. For these ideas, I am indebted to Lowenthal, ch. 3.

4. Sullivan is quoted in Roberts, *American Exceptionalism*, 174; for the Emerson quote, see Lowenthal, *The Past Is a Foreign Country*, 113; for Marsh, see Lowenthal, 108.

5. See Ravitch, "Decline and Fall."

6. Qtd. in Ravitch.

7. See Birnbaum, "Thomas Mallon."

8. For a sampling of thought-provoking essays on the uses and meanings of historical fiction, see Wood, "Invitation to a Beheading" and Greenblatt, "How It Must Have Been."

9. Qtd. in MacFarquhar, "The Dead Are Real."

10. Mallon, "History, Fiction, and the Burden of Truth."

11. McNamara, "*I, Claudius* Left Its Bloody, Sinister Mark on TV Drama."

12. Sontag, *Notes on Camp*, 11.

13. O'Connor, "Tour of Rome with *I, Claudius*."

14. Qtd. in Brennan, *Masterpiece*, 68.

15. Brown, "TV's *I, Claudius* Will Test the Boundaries of Public Broadcasting."

16. Qtd. in Brennan, *Masterpiece*, 68.

17. Qtd. in Brennan, 69.

18. Qtd. in Brennan, 29.

19. Qtd. in McGovern, "Glenda Jackson."

20. McGovern.

21. McGovern.

22. Leonard, "Virgin Territory."

23. Lowry, "Mr. Selfridge"; Wagner, "Jeremy Piven."

24. Qtd. in Lowry, 27.

25. Interview with author, June 2015.

26. Interview with author, June 2015.

27. Qtd. in Gritten, "His Machiavellian Godfather."

28. See Mantel, "Booker Winner Hilary Mantel."

CHAPTER 6

1. Chandler, *The Simple Art of Murder*, 1–18.

2. Qtd. in Miller, *Mystery!*, 2.

3. Gilbert, "The (Final) Problem with Sherlock."

4. Qtd. in Parker, "Wes Anderson Is under Edward Gorey's Spell."

5. Qtd. in Miller, *Mystery!*, 3.

6. Eaton, *Making Masterpiece*, 71.

7. McNamara, "A Pocket Full of Miss Marple."

8. Suchet and Wansell, *Poirot and Me*, 31.

9. Qtd. in Miller, *Mystery!*, 141.

10. Suchet and Wansell, *Poirot and Me*, 42.

11. Suchet and Wansell, 45.

12. Suchet and Wansell, 47.

13. Qtd. in Miller, *Mystery!*, 44.

14. Qtd. in Miller, 80.

15. Koch, "A Fond Farewell."

16. Qtd. in Miller, *Mystery!*, 81.

17. Qtd. in Miller, 80.
18. Koch, "A Fond Farewell."
19. McNamara, "Lamenting the End."
20. *Radio Times*, "Anthony Horowitz on the Dark Truth."
21. See Listrom, "*Grantchester*'s Holy Sleuths Are Brimming with Bromance and Charm."

CHAPTER 7

1. Hughes, "Rufus, the New Sunday Night Heartthrob."
2. Qtd. in Hughes.
3. Schwartz, "The Rise and Fall."
4. Dinerstein, "Why Cool Matters."
5. Mikul, *Eccentropedia*.
6. Qtd. in Sykes, "The Death of the English Eccentric."
7. Qtd. in Mahdawi, "Eccentric Women."
8. Qtd. in Sykes, "The Death of the English Eccentric."
9. Caldwell, *A Short History of Rudeness*, 2.
10. Qtd. in Leithauser, "Plenty of Room."
11. Caldwell, *A Short History of Rudeness*, 187.
12. Wagg, *Because I Tell a Joke or Two*, 4.
13. Errett, *Elements of Wit*, 47–49.
14. Qtd. in Errett, 4.
15. Epstein, "Wit," 55.
16. Errett, 5.

CHAPTER 8

1. Qtd. in London, "How an Actor."
2. See Eyre and Wright, *Changing States*, 2.
3. Eyre and Wright, 4.
4. Shepherd, *Cambridge Introduction*, 3.
5. Qtd. in Labrecque, "What Does the Latest."
6. Labrecque.
7. See Rafferty, "The Decline of the American Actor," on the decline of the American male actor for Douglas's comment, Lee's comment, and his own comment about "embarrassment."
8. See Rafferty.
9. Qtd. in Lusher, "Kate Winslet."
10. Veltman, "British Actors."
11. See Fallows, "Before You Watch."
12. Qtd. in "Command Performance."

13. Ibid.

14. Ibid.

15. Ibid.

16. See Collins, "Damian Lewis' Transformations."

17. See Collins.

18. See Collins.

19. See Leonard, "Charles in Charge."

20. Simon, "Gillian Anderson Paying a Visit."

21. Interview with the author, June 2011.

22. See White, *Kenneth Branagh*, 74.

23. See White.

24. See "Kenneth Branagh" page on the "Jane Austen's World" website (https://jane austensworld.wordpress.com/2010/10/02/kenneth-branagh-is-back-as-wallander-pbs -masterpiece-mystery-series-2/).

25. See "Kenneth Branagh."

26. See "Wallander Review."

27. Raeside, "Claire Foy."

CHAPTER 9

1. Qtd. in Baucom, *Out of Place*, 44.

2. Boym, *The Future of Nostalgia*, 7.

3. See Powell, "The American Wanderer," for all three comments.

4. See "Filming at Chartwell," *Masterpiece* website (https://www.pbs.org/video /masterpiece-churchills-secret-filming-chartwell/).

5. See *Telegraph*, "48 Hours In."

6. See "Filming in Cornwall," *Masterpiece* website.

7. See the BBC webpage on *The Paradise* (https://www.bbc.co.uk/programmes /p00vhpsv).

8. See Scullard, "The Manchester Family Story."

9. See "The Oxford of Inspector Morse."

10. See National Trust website, "Houses Packed with History Star in Wolf Hall" (https://www.nationaltrust.org.uk/lists/explore-places-with-tudor-history).

11. Fellowes, *The World of Downton Abbey*, 6.

12. Qtd. in Fellowes, 71.

13. See Haughney, "A Castle Becomes a Cash Register."

Bibliography

Adams, Erik. "Is Television a Medium without a Past?" *TV Club*, August 23, 2017. https://tv.avclub.com/is-television-a-medium-without-a-past-1798230245.

Ahmend, Tufayel. "How British Television Drama Is Taking Over the Entertainment World." *Newsweek*, April 9, 2016. https://www.newsweek.com/british-television-drama-itv-sky1-445406.

Allen, Robert C. *To Be Continued. . . .* London: Routledge, 1995.

Alterman, Eric. "The Decline of Historical Thinking." *New Yorker*, February 4, 2019. https://www.newyorker.com/news/news-desk/the-decline-of-historical-thinking.

Baker, Russell. "A Little Bones Trouble." *New York Times*, May 14, 1991.

Baucom, Ian. *Out of Place*. Princeton: Princeton University Press, 1999.

Baughman, James L. "Minow's Viewers: Understanding the Response to the Vast Wasteland Address." *Federal Communications Law Journal* 55 (2003).

Baum, Jeffrey. "Farewell to *Upstairs, Downstairs*." *Star Ledger*, May 11, 1977.

Bell, Ian A., and Graham Daldry. *Watching the Detectives*. New York: St. Martin's Press, 1990.

Benfey, Christopher. "Renaissance Men." *New York Times*, October 29, 2009. http://www.nytimes.com/2009/11/01/books/review/Benfey-t.html.

Bianculli, David. *The Platinum Age of Television*. New York: Anchor Books, 2017.

Birnbaum, Robert. "Thomas Mallon." *Morning News*, July 11, 2007. https://themorningnews.org/article/thomas-mallon.

Blake, Meredith. "Review: PBS' 'Victoria' Is Good, but Not as Royally Entertaining as 'The Crown.'" *Los Angeles Times*, January 14, 2017. https://www.latimes.com/entertainment/tv/la-et-st-victoria-review.

Blitzer, Jonathan. "Elementary." *New Yorker*, January 26, 2015. https://www.newyorker.com/magazine/2015/02/02/elementary?verso=true.

Blythe, Catherine. *The Art of Conversation*. New York: Gotham Books, 2009.

Boorstin, Daniel. *The Daniel J. Boorstin Reader*. New York: Modern Library, 1995.

Boot, Max. "Americans' Ignorance of History Is a National Scandal." *Washington Post*, February 20, 2019. https://www.washingtonpost.com/opinions/americans-ignorance

-of-history-is-a-national-scandal/2019/02/20/b8be683c-352d-11e9-854a-7a14d
7fec96a_story.html.

Boström, Mattias. *From Holmes to Sherlock*. New York: The Mysterious Press, 2013.

Boym, Svetlana. *The Future of Nostalgia*. New York: Basic Books, 2001.

Bradley, Laura. "As *Sherlock's* Future Remains Unclear, Benedict Cumberbatch Swipes at Martin Freeman." *Vanity Fair*, April 23, 2018.

Brennan, Timothy. "*Masterpiece Theatre* and the Uses of Tradition." *Social Text* 12 (Autumn 1985): 102–12.

Briggs, Asa. *The BBC: The First Fifty Years*. Oxford: Oxford University Press, 1986.

BritMovieTours. "BBC Sherlock Locations Tour by London Black Taxi." Accessed October 16, 2019. https://britmovietours.com/bookings/bbc-sherlock-locations-tour/.

———. "Inspector Morse, Lewis and Endeavour Tour of Oxford." Last modified September 1, 2019. https://britmovietours.com/bookings/inspector-morse-tour/.

Brookins, Julia. "The Decline of History Majors: What Is to Be Done?" *Perspectives on History*, May 10, 2016. https://www.historians.org/publications-and-directories/perspectives-on-history/may-2016/the-decline-in-history-majors.

Brown, Les. "TV's 'I, Claudius' Will Test the Boundaries of Public Broadcasting." *New York Times*, November 6, 1977.

Brown, Maggie. "*Foyle's War* Returns—in a World of Prefabs and Rations." *Guardian*, March 9, 2013. https://www.theguardian.com/tv-and-radio/2013/mar/10/foyles-war-returns-crime-cold-war.

Caldwell, Mark. *A Short History of Rudeness*. New York: Picador USA, 2000.

Callard, Agnes. *Aspiration: The Agency of Becoming*. Oxford: Oxford University Press, 2018.

Carmody, Nick. "Domestic Drama." *Pittsburgh Post-Gazette*, January 24, 1974.

Carnegie Commission. *Public Television, a Program for Action: The Report and Recommendations of the Carnegie Commission on Educational Television*. New York: Bantam, 1967.

Carr, David. "Barely Keeping Up in TV's Golden Age." *New York Times,* March 9, 2014. https://www.nytimes.com/2014/03/10/business/media/fenced-in-by-television-excess-of-excellence.html.

Carr, Fiora. "Andrew Davies Hints at Second Series for Jane Austen Adaptation *Sanditon*." *RadioTimes*. August 20, 2019. https://www.radiotimes.com/news/2019-08-20/andrew-davies-hints-at-second-series-for-jane-austen-adaptation-sanditon/.

Caughie, John. *Television Drama: Realism, Modernism, and British Culture*. Oxford: Oxford University Press, 2000.

Causey, Michael. "An Interview with Thomas Mallon." *Washington Independent Review of Books*, September 4, 2019. https://www.washingtonindependentreviewofbooks.com/index/php/features/an-interview-with-thomas-mallon.

Chandler, Raymond. *The Simple Art of Murder*. New York: Vintage Books, 1988.

Cieply, Michael, and Brooks Barnes. "Oscar's Heart May Be in Hollywood, but His Accent Is British." *New York Times*, February 11, 2016. https://www.nytimes.com/2016/02/12/movies/oscars-heart-may-be-in-hollywood-but-his-accent-is-british.html.

Clark, Donald. "Kenneth Branagh: 'The Life of an Actor? Strange Men Phone and Offer You Money.'" *Irish Times*, February 8, 2019. https://www.irishtimes.com /culture/film/kenneth-branagh -the-life-of-an-actor-strange-men-phone-and-offer -you-money-1.3782915.

Collins, Lauren. "Damian Lewis' Transformations." *New Yorker*, January 11, 2016. https://www.newyorker.com/magazine/2016/01/18/blue-blood-blue-collar.

Collins, Sean. "Downton-Abbey Cheat Sheet." *Rolling Stone*, January 4, 2013. https:// www.rollingstone.com/movies/movie-news/downton-abbey-season-three-cheat -sheet-172332/.

"Command Performance: The Reign of Helen Mirren." *New Yorker*, October 2, 2006. https://www.newyorker.com/magazine/2006/10/02/command-performance-3.

Conway, Michael. "The Problem with History Classes." *Atlantic*, March 16, 2015. https://www.theatlatic.com/education/archive/2015/03/the-problem-with-his tory-classes/387823/.

Cooke, Alistair. "How Alistair Cooke Evokes the World of Masterpieces. *New York Times*, January 19, 1986. https://www.nytimes.com/1986/01/19/arts/how-alistair -cooke-evokes-the-world-of-the-masterpieces.html.

Cooper, Gladys. "Sense and Sensibility." *Telegraph*, January 4, 2008. https://www .telegraph.co.uk/culture/books/3670277/Sense-and-Sensibility-or-pain-and-pre judice.html.

Cornish Times. "Poldark Creates New Tourist Industry for County." May 28, 2019. http://www.cornish-times.co.uk/article.cfm?id=124717&searchyear=2019.

Croghan, Carmen. "Dated or Delightful? Inspector Morse." *Telly Visions*, January 4, 2017. https://blogs.weta.org/tellyvisions/2017/01/04/dated-or-delightful-inspec tor-morse.

Curry, Robert. "How Ignorance of American History Feeds Demagogues Who Hate the Constitution." *Federalist*, June 13, 2019. https://thefederalist.com/2019/06/13 /ignorance-american-history-feeds-demagogues-hate-constitution/.

Daily Telegraph. "Thandie Newton: British TV Docs Not Have Enough Roles for Black Actors Because There Are So Many Period Dramas." March 19, 2017. https:// www.telegraph.co.uk/news/2017/03/19/thandie-newton-british-tv-does-not -have-enough-roles-black-actors/.

Davies, Andrew. "*Emma* 3: Austen's Horrible Heroine." *The Telegraph*, November 3, 1996. https://www.telegraph.co.uk/culture/4706153/Austens-horrible-heroine .html.

———. *The Television Series*. Manchester: Manchester University Press, 2005.

Davies, Serena. "Telegraph Pick: *Sense and Sensibility* (BBC1)." *Telegraph*, January 3, 2008. https://www.telegraph.co.uk/culture/3674554/Telegraph-pick-Sense-and -Sensibility-BBC1.html.

Deresiewicz, William. *A Jane Austen Education*. New York: Penguin, 2011.

Dickens, Charles. *The Personal History and Experience of David Copperfield the Younger*. London: Chapman and Hall, 1872.

Dinerstein, Joel. *The Origins of Cool in Postwar America*. Chicago: University of Chicago Press, 2017.

————. "Why Cool Matters." Ted Talk. https://www.youtube.com/watch?v=-kboK01-OOk.

Drew, Richard. "'Downton Abbey': The Best TV Show You Might Never See." *Atlantic*, January 5, 2011. https://www.theatlantic.com/entertainment/archive/2011/01/downton-abbey-the-best-tv-show-you-might-never-see/68858/.

Eaton, Rebecca. *Making Masterpiece: 25 Years Behind the Scenes at Masterpiece Theatre and Mystery! on PBS*. New York: Viking, 2013.

Epstein, Joseph. "Wit." *The Ideal of Culture: Essays*. Edinburgh, VA: Axios Press, 2018.

Errett, Benjamin. *Elements of Wit: Mastering the Art of Being Interesting*. New York: Tarcher Perigee, 2014.

Eyre, Richard, and Nicholas Wright. *Changing States: A View of British Theatre in the Twentieth Century*. London: Bloomsbury, 2000.

Fallows, James. "Before You Watch the New House of Cards, Do Yourself a Favor and See the Original." *Atlantic*, February 12, 2014. https://www.theatlantic.com/entertainment/archive/2014/02/before-you-watch-the-new-em-house-of-cards-em-do-yourself-a-favor-and-see-the-original/283795/.

Fellowes, Jessica. *Downton Abbey: A Celebration*. New York: St. Martin's Press, 2015.

————. *The World of Downton Abbey*. New York: St. Martin's Press, 2011.

————. *A Year in the Life of Downton Abbey*. New York: St. Martin's Press, 2014.

Fellowes, Jessica, and Matthew Sturgis. *The Chronicles of Downton Abbey*. New York: St. Martin's Press, 2012.

Floyd, Patty Lou. *Backstairs with Upstairs, Downstairs*. New York: St. Martin's Press, 1988.

Free Tours by Foot. "Sherlock Holmes in London Tour." Accessed October 16, 2019. https://freetoursbyfoot.com/sherlock-holmes-tour-london/.

Frost, Caroline. "'Sherlock' Writer Mark Gatiss Tells Complaining Fans: 'Go Read a Children's Book.'" *Huffpost*, January 16, 2017. https://www.huffingtonpost.co.uk/entry/sherlock-writer-mark-gatiss-defends-complicated-script_uk.

Furland, Akuce, "Civility vs. Civilité." *Atlantic*, October 2001. https://www.theatlantic.com/magazine/archive/20001/10/civility-vs-civilit/302304.

Gantz, Jeffrey. "The Empire Strikes Back." *Boston Phoenix*, March 24, 1987.

Geary, James. *Wit's End*. New York: W.W. Norton & Company, 2019.

Gilbert, Matthew. "PBS Adaptation Brings New Dimension to 'Jane Eyre.'" *Boston Globe*, January 19, 2007. http://archive.boston.com/ae/tv/articles/2007/01/19/pbs_adaptation_brings_new_dimension_to_jane_eyre/.

Gilbert, Sophie. "The (Final) Problem with Sherlock." *Atlantic*, January 17, 2017. https://www.scribd.com/article/336835877/The-Final-Problem-With-Sherlock.

————. "How 'Sherlock' Turned into a Superhero." *Atlantic*, January 17, 2017. https://www.theatlantic.com/entertainment/archive/2017/01/sherlock-the-final-problem-review/513311/.

Goldsworthy, Kerryn. "Austen and Authenticity." *Australian Humanities Review*, July 1996. http://australianhumanitiesreview.org/1996/07/01/austen-and-authenticity/.

Gopnik, Adam. "Are Liberals on the Wrong Side of History?" *New Yorker*, March 20, 2017. https://www.newyorker.com/magazine/2017/03/20/are-liberals-on-the-wrong-side-of-history?verso=true.

Gordon, Ken. "Alexa and the Age of Casual Rudeness." *Atlantic*, April 23, 2018. https://www.theatlantic.com/family/archive/2018/4/alexa-manners-smart-speakers-command/5586523.

Graham, Alison. "Why Endeavour Is the Most Comforting Show on TV." *Radio-Times*, February 24, 2019. https://www.radiotimes.com/news/tv/2019-02-24/endeavour-itv-review/.

Green, Benny. "'I, Claudius' Review." *Punch*, October 4, 1977.

Greenblatt, Stephen. "How It Must Have Been." *New York Review of Books*, November 5, 2009. https://www.nybooks.com/articles/2009/11/05/how-it-must-have-been/.

Grey, Tobias. "Kenneth Branagh on Life Lessons from William Shakespeare." *Wall Street Journal*, May 7, 2019. https://www.wsj.com/articles/kenneth-branagh-on-life-lessons-from-william-shakespeare-11557234416.

Gritten, David. "His Machiavellian Godfather." *Written By*, April 2015.

Gross, Lottie. "Has the 'Poldark Effect' Ruined Cornwall?" *Telegraph*, July 14, 2019. https://www.telegraph.co.uk/travel/destinations/europe/united-kingdom/england/cornwall/articles/the-poldark-effect/.

Gussow, Mel. "Jeremy Brett, an Unnerving Holmes, Is Dead at 59." *New York Times*, September 14, 1995. https://www.nytimes.com/1995/09/14/obituaries/jeremy-brett-an-unnerving-holmes-is-dead-at-59.html.

Haining, Peter. *The Television Sherlock Holmes*. London: W. H. Allen, 1986.

Hale, Mike. "'Agatha Christie's Poirot' Comes to an End." *New York Times*, July 25, 2014. https://www.nytimes.com/2014/07/26/arts/television/agatha-christies-poirot-comes-to-an-end.html.

———. "The Latest Sherlock Hears a Who." *New York Times*, October 21, 2010. https://www.nytimes.com/2010/10/22/arts/television/22sherlock.html.

———. "Review: 'Wolf Hall,' the Mini-Series, Unspools Its Power Plays on PBS." *New York Times*, April 2, 2015. http://www.nytimes.com/2-15/04/03/arts/television/review-wolf-hall-the-mini-series-unspools-its-power-on-pbs.html.

———. "A War Ended, but, It Turns Out, Crime Didn't." *New York Times*, April 29, 2010. https://www.nytimes.com/2010/04/30/arts/television/30foyle.html.

———. "War Is Over, but Enemies Are Afoot in London." *New York Times*, September 13, 2013. https://www.nytimes.com/2013/09/14/arts/television/in-foyles-war-the-hero-switches-to-intelligence-work.html.

Hards, Shannon. "Poldark Effect Will Continue in Cornwall after BBC Series Ends, Claims Tourism Boss." *Cornwall Live*, May 23, 2019. https://www.cornwalllive.com/news/celebs-tv/ poldark-effect-continue-cornwall-after-2888528.

Hardwick, Mollie. *The World of Upstairs, Downstairs: An Illustrated Social History from the Turn of the Century to the Great Depression*. New York: Holt, Rinehart and Winston, 1976.

Harris, Lee. "The Future of Tradition." *Hoover Institution: Policy Review*, June 1, 2005. https://www.hoover.org/research/future-tradition.

Haughney, Christine. "A Castle Becomes a Cash Register." *New York Times*, May 24, 2013. https://www.nytimes.com/2013/05/26/fashion/trying-to-turn-a-castle-into-a-cash-register.html.

Henry, George. "A Farewell to Eaton Place." *Star Ledger*, April 28, 1977.

Hill, Rose. "Poldark Power: From TV to Tourism." BusinessForSale.com. Accessed October 16 2019. https://uk.businessesforsale.com/uk/search/hotels-and-holiday -accommodation-businesses-for-sale/articles/poldark-power-from-tv-to-tourism.

Hodge, Gavanndra. "Claire Foy Steps into the Spotlight." *Wall Street Journal*, January 9, 2019. https://www.wsj.com/articles/claire-foy-steps-into-the-spotlight -11547038970.

Hodges, Michael. "Endeavor: On the Trail of Morse's Oxford." *RadioTimes*, March 4, 2018. https://www.radiotimes.com/travel/2018-03-04/endeavour-on-the-trail -of-morses-oxford/.

Hughes, Tammy. "Rufus, the New Sunday Night Heartthrob Actor Sets Pulses Racing as Dashing Lord Melbourne in the First Episode of New Drama Victoria." *Daily Mail*, August 29, 2016. https://www.dailymail.co.uk/tvshowbiz/article-3764296 /Rufus-new-Sunday-night-heart-throb-Actor-sets-pulses-racing-dashing-Lord -Melbourne-episode-new-drama-Victoria.html.

Hutcheon, Linda. *A Theory of Adaptation*. New York: Routledge, 2006.

Inspector Morse's Oxford. Directed by Stephen Gammond. London: Baker Street Studios, 2012.

Irving, John. "In Defense of Sentimentality." *New York Times*, November 25, 1979. https://www.nytimes.com/1979/11/25/archives/in-defense-of-sentimentality -dickens.html.

James, P. D. *Talking About Detective Fiction*. New York: Alfred A. Knopf, 2009.

Jenkins, Mark. "The End of the British Invasion." *Slate*, May 3, 2002. https://slate .com/culture/2002/05/the-end-of-the-british-invasion.html.

Klemesrud, Judy. "From Sherlock to Modern Villain." *New York Times*, May 26, 1985. https://www.nytimes.com/1985/05/26/arts/from-sherlock-to-modern-villain .html.

Koch, John. "A Fond Farewell to 'Inspector Morse.'" *Boston Globe*, February 22, 2001. https://www.chicagotribune.com/news/ct-xpm-2001-02-22-0102220019 -story.html.

Labrecque, Jeff. "What Does the Latest British Invasion Say about the State of American Acting?" *Entertainment Weekly*, January 28, 2015. https://ew.com/article /2015/01/28/selma-british-actors/.

Laity, Paul. "My Favourite Film: *Sense and Sensibility*." *Guardian*, December 25, 2011. https://www.theguardian.com/film/2011/dec/26/favourite-film-sense-and -sensibility.

Lardner, James. "James Lardner on Television." *New Yorker*, November 12, 1977.

Ledbetter, James. *Made Possible by . . . the Death of Public Broadcasting in the United States*. New York: Verso, 1997.

Leggott, James, and Julia Taddeo, eds. *Upstairs and Downstairs: British Costume Drama Television from* The Forsyte Saga *to* Downton Abbey. Lanham, MD: Rowman & Littlefield, 2014.

Leithauser, Brad. "Plenty of Room for Stupidity: On P.G. Wodehouse." *New Yorker*, March 26, 2014. https://www.newyorker.com/books/page-turner/plenty-of-room -for-stupidity-on-p-g-wodehouse.

Leonard, John. "Charles in Charge." *New York Magazine*, January 12, 2006. http://nymag.com/nymetro/arts/tv/reviews/15525/.

———. "Virgin Territory." *New York Magazine*, April 13, 2006. http://nymag.com/arts/tv/reviews/16720/.

Leopold, Wendy. "Revisiting the Vast Wasteland." Northwestern University. https://www.northwestern.edu/newscenter/stories/2011/05/newt-minow-vast-wasteland-symposium.html.

Levere, Jane. "'Foyle's War' Creator Anthony Horowitz Discusses New Season." *Forbes*, September 15, 2013. https://www.forbes.com/sites/janelevere/2013/09/15/foyles-war-creator-discusses-new-season/#7c7d52b62e68.

Levine, Lawrence W. *Highbrow Lowbrow*. Cambridge, MA: Harvard University Press, 1990.

Lindenberger, Herbert. *The History in Literature: On Value, Genre, Institutions*. New York: Columbia University Press, 1990.

Listrom, Tom. "Grantchester's Holy Sleuths Are Brimming with Bromance and Charm." *The Guardian*, November 3, 2014.

London, Michael Billington. "How an Actor Made Himself Into the Villain Everyone Loves to Hate." *New York Times*, February 17, 1985. https://www.nytimes.com/1985/02/17/arts/how-an-actor-made-himself-into-the-villain-everyone-loves-to-hate.html.

Lopate, Phillip. "Adapt This." http://philliplopate.com/2011/08/adapt-this/.

Lowenthal, David. *The Past Is a Foreign Country*. Cambridge: Cambridge University Press, 1999.

Lowman, Rob. "Kenneth Branagh Offers a Bittersweet Goodbye to 'Wallander.'" *Los Angeles Daily News*, August 28, 2017. https://www.dailynews.com/2016/05/06/kenneth-branagh-offers-a-bittersweet-goodbye-to-wallander/.

Lowry, Brian. "TV Review: Mr. Selfridge." *Variety*, March 19, 2013. https://variety.com/2013/tv/reviews/tv-review-mr-selfridge-1200325470/.

Luce, Edward. "US Declining Interest in History Presents Risk to Democracy." *Financial Times*, May 2, 2019. https://www.ft.com/content/e19d957c-6ca3-11e9-80c7-60cc53e6681d.

Lusher, Adam. "Kate Winslet Claims That Being English Is a One-Way Ticket to a Hollywood Acting Career." *Independent*, December 7, 2015. https://www.independent.co.uk/arts-entertainment/films/features/kate-winslet-claims-that-being-english-is-a-one-way-ticket-to-a-hollywood-acting-career-a6764061.html.

Lynch, Deidre Shauna. *Loving Literature: A Cultural History*. Chicago: University of Chicago Press, 2015.

Lyons, Margaret. "What You Should Watch: Carol and the Durrells in Corfu." *New York Times*, October 14, 2016. https://www.nytimes.com/2016/10/14/arts/television/carol-the-simpsons-what-to-watch.html.

MacFarquhar, Larissa. "The Dead Are Real: Hilary Mantel's Imagination." *New Yorker*, October 8, 2012. https://www.newyorker.com/magazine/2012/10/15/the-dead-are-real.

Mahdawi, Arwa. "Eccentric Women: Why They Are More Important than Ever in Our Oppressive Era." *Guardian*, November 20, 2018. https://www.theguardian

.com/lifeandstyle/2018/nov/20/eccentric-women-why-they-are-more-important
-than-ever-in-our-oppressive-era.

Mallon, Thomas. "Does History Based on Fact Have a Responsibility to the Truth?
New York Times, October 27, 2015. https://www.nytimes.com/2015/11/01
/books/review/does-fiction-based-on-fact-have-a-responsibility-to-the-truth.html.

———. "History, Fiction, and the Burden of Truth." University of Albany. Accessed
September 14, 2016. https://www.albany.edu/history/hist_fict/Mallon/Mallons
.htm.

———. "Writing Historical Fiction." *American Scholar* 61, no. 4 (Fall 1992): 604–10.

Maloney, Allison. *The World of Glamour and Romance*. London: Simon and Schuster
UK, 2014.

Mantel, Hilary. "Booker Winner Hilary Mantel on Historical Fiction." *Guardian*, October 16, 2009. https://www.theguardian.com/books/2009/oct/17/hilary
-mantel-author-booker.

———. "How I Came to Write Wolf Hall." *Guardian*, December 7, 2012. http://
www.theguardian.com/books/2012/dec/07/bookclub-hilary-mantel-wolf-hall.

Martin, Judith. "Miss Manners on Rudeness in the Age of Trump." *Atlantic*, February 16, 2017. https://www.theatlantic.com/entertainment/archive/2017/02
/alternative-virtues-for-the-trump-era/516498/.

———. "Republic of Manners." *Atlantic*, November 2007. https://www.theatlantic
.com/magazine/archive/2007/11/republic--of-manners/306311/.

Martin, Tim. "Who Is the Greatest Ever Sherlock Homes?" *Telegraph*, December
31, 2014. https://www.telegraph.co.uk/culture/tvandradio/10543095/Sherlock
-is-Benedict-Cumberbatch-the-greatest-ever-Holmes.html.

Martinson, Jane. "Kenneth Branagh: Playing Wallander Left Me in 'Permanent State
of Anxiety.'" *Guardian*, June 24, 2015. https://www.theguardian.com/media
/2015/jun/24/kenneth-branagh-wallander-interview-conspiracy.

McClurg, Jocelyn. "The Secret to Agatha Christie's Enduring Appeal? We Solve the
Mystery." *USA Today*, November 12, 2017. https://www.usatoday.com/story
/life/books/2017/11/12/secret-agatha-christies-enduring-appeal-we-solve
-mystery/832612001/.

McElroy, Ruth. *Contemporary Crime Drama*. London: Routledge, 2017.

McGovern, Joe. "Glenda Jackson: The Best Actress Who Walked Away." *Entertainment*, February 1, 2016.

McLean, Craig. "Kenneth Branagh Interview for Wallander." *Telegraph*, January 8, 2010. https://www.telegraph.co.uk/culture/tvandradio/6947587/Kenneth
-Branagh-interview-for-Wallander.html.

McNamara, Mary. "Critic's Notebook: 'I, Claudius' Left Its Bloody, Sinister Mark on
TV Drama." *Los Angeles Times*, May 6, 2012. https://www.latimes.com/entertain
ment/la-xpm-2012-may-06-la-ca-critics-notebook-claudius-20120506-story.html.

———. "Lamenting the End of Foyle's War, a TV Masterpiece." *Los Angeles Times*,
February 3, 2015. https://www.latimes.com/entertainment/tv/la-et-st-foyles-war
-20150203-column.html.

———. "A Pocket Full of Miss Marple." *Los Angeles Times*, July 3, 2009. https://
www.latimes.com/archives/la-xpm-2009-jul-03-et-miss-marple3-story.html.

Menand, Louis. "What Jane Austen Doesn't Tell Us." *New York Review of Books*, February 1, 1996. https://www.nybooks.com/articles/1996/02/01/what-jane -austen-doesnt-tell-us/.

Mikul, Chris. *Eccentropedia: The Most Unusual People Who Have Ever Lived*. New York: Headpress, 2012.

Millard, Rosie. "Sex and Sensibility Works Wonders, Dear Jane." *Times*, December 30, 2007. https://www.thetimes.co.uk/article/sex-and-sensibility-work-wonders -dear-jane-nlx526qv7lh.

Miller, Jeffrey S. *Something Completely Different: British Television and American Culture*. Minneapolis: University of Minnesota Press, 2000.

Miller, Ron. *Mystery! A Celebration*. San Francisco: KQED Books, 1996.

Minow, Newton. *How Vast the Wasteland Now?* Los Angeles: Gannett Media Center, 1991.

Mirren, Helen. *In the Frame: My Life in Words and Pictures*. New York: Atria Books, 2007.

Mitchison, Amanda. "Benedict Cumberbatch on Playing Sherlock Holmes." *Guardian*, July 16, 2010. https://www.theguardian.com/tv-and-radio/2010/jul/17 /benedict-cumberbatch-sherlock-holmes.

Moore, Thomas. *The Re-Enchantment of Everyday Life*. New York: HarperCollins, 1996.

Morris, Steven. "'Poldark Is Brilliant for Cornwall': County Opens Arms as TV Tourists Swoon." *Guardian*, September 4, 2016. https://www.theguardian.com /tv-and-radio/2016/sep/04/poldark-is-brilliant-for-cornwall-county-opens-arms -as-tv-tourists-swoon.

Mortimer, Ian. "Why Historians Should Write Fiction." *Wordpress*, November 23, 2011. https://ihrconference.wordpress.com/2011/11/23/why-historians-should -write-fiction/.

Moss, Martin. "A Different Suspense." *Star Ledger*, January 13, 1971.

Naidu, Sam. *Sherlock Holmes in Context*. London: Palgrave Macmillan, 2017.

Naseem, Saba. "How Much U.S. History Do Americans Actually Know? Less Than You Think." *Smithsonian*, May 28, 2015. https://www.smithsonian.com/history /how-much-us-history-do-americans-actually-know-less-you-think-180955431/.

National Trust. "Poldark's Filming Locations." Accessed October 16, 2019. https:// www.nationaltrust.org.uk/lists/poldarks-filming-locations.

Newcomb, Horace, ed. "Anthology Dramas." *Encyclopedia of Television*. Chicago: Fitzroy Dearborn Publishers, 1997: 246–249.

Nicholson, Rebecca. "Is Dominic West the Authentic Voice of a Working-Class Hero?" *Guardian*, December 15, 2018. https://www.theguardian.com/comment isfree/2018/dec/15/is-dominic-west-the-authentic-voice-of-a-working-class-hero.

———. "Victoria Series Three Review—Sit Back and Enjoy the Soapy Ride." *Guardian*, March 24, 2019. https://amp.theguardian.com/tv-and-radio/2019 /mar/24/victoria-review-itv-queen-victoria-prince-albert-series-three.

Nijhuis, Michelle. "Waiting for Cumberbatch." *New Yorker*, October 29, 2015. http:// www.newyorker.com/culture/culture-desk/waiting-for-benedict-cumberbatch.

Nussbaum, Emily. "Fan Friction." *New Yorker*, January 20, 2014. https://www.new yorker.com/magazine/2014/01/27/fan-friction.

———. "Queens Boulevard." *New Yorker*, May 4, 2016. http://www.newyorker .com/magazine/2015/05/04/queens-boulevard.

———. "Tune in Next Week: The Curious Staying Power of the Cliffhanger." *New Yorker,* July 22, 2012. https://www.newyorker.com/magazine/2012/07/30/tune -in-next-week.

Oates, Chris. "American TV's British Invasion." *Salon*, April 2, 2013. https://www .salon.com/2013/04/02/are_you_with_me_doctor_who_exploring_the_british _tv_phenomenon_partner/.

O'Connor, John. "BBC Ships PBS Another Great Hit." *New York Times*, January 21, 1974.

———. "But How Do You Keep Up Good Television?" Review of *The First Churchills. The New York Times*, January 22, 1971.

———. "Departing Is Such Sweet Sorrow." *New York Times*, April 4, 1977: 38–39.

———. "A Fond Cheerio to 165 Eaton Place." *New York Times*, May 1, 1977. https://www.nytimes.com/1977/05/01/archives/tv-view-a-fond-cheerio-to -165-eaton-place.html.

———. "Reviews/Television; Inspector Morse Is Back on 'Mystery.'" *New York Times*, December 15, 1988. https://www.nytimes.com/1988/12/15/arts/reviews -television-inspector-morse-is-back-on-mystery.html.

———. "Review/Television: Of Inspector Morse and His Personifier." *New York Times*, April 22, 1993. http://www.nytimes.com/193/04/22/arts/review-television -of-inspector-morse-and-his-personifier.html.

———. "TV Tour of Rome with 'I, Claudius.'" *New York Times,* November 3, 1977. https://www.nytimes.com/1977/11/03/archives/tv-tour-of-rome-with-i -claudius.html.

———. "*Upstairs, Downstairs* Is Too Good to Miss." *New York Times*, January 20, 1974. https://www.nytimes.com/1974/01/08/archives/tv-upstairs-downstairs-is -too-good-to-miss.html.

O'Donovan, Gerard. "Branagh in Stupendous Form as Wallander Bows Out: Review." *Telegraph*, June 2016. https://www.telegraph.co.uk/tv/206/06/05/branagh -on-stupendous-form-as-wallander-bos-out-review-/.

O'Grady, Megan. "Why Are We Living in a Golden Age of Historical Fiction?" *New York Times*, May 7, 2019. https://www.nytimes.com/2019.05/07/t-magazine /historical-fiction-books.amp.html.

Oliver, Myrna. "Jeremy Brett; TV Series Sherlock Holmes." *Los Angeles Times*, September 14, 1995. https://www.latimes.com/archives/la-xpm-1995-09-14-me -45667-story.html.

Owen, Jannette. "Foyle's War Rallies for a Seventh Series." *Guardian*, April 9, 2010. https://www.theguardian.com/tv-and-radio/tvandradioblog/2010/apr/09/foyles -war.

"The Oxford of Inspector Morse." *Country Life*, August 18, 2018. https://www .countrylife.co.uk/out-and-about/theatre-film-music/oxford-inspector-morse -dreaming-spires-dead-bodies-lots-lots-pubs-182670.

Parker, James. "Wes Anderson Is under Edward Gorey's Spell." *Atlantic,* March 2019. https://www.theatlantic.com/magazine/archive/2019/03/edward-gorey -american-goth/580444/.

Parrill, A. Sue. "Pride and Prejudice on A&E: Visions and Revisions." *Literature/Film Quarterly* 27, no. 2 (1999): 142–49.

Patterson, John, and Gareth McLean. "Move Over Hollywood." *Guardian,* May 19, 2006. https://www.theguardian.com/film/2006/may/20/features.weekend.

Pin, Emile Jean, and Jamie Turndorf. *The Pleasure of Your Company.* New York: Praeger, 1985.

Porter, Lynnette. *Sherlock Holmes for the 21st Century.* Jefferson: McFarland & Company, 2012.

Powell, Michael. "The American Wanderer, In All His Stripes." *New York Times,* August 23, 2008. https://www.nytimes.com/2008/08/24/weekinreview/24powe.html.

Priestman, Martin. *Crime Fiction.* Cambridge: Cambridge University Press, 2003.

Puterbaugh, Parke. "The British Invasion: From the Beatles to the Stones. The Sixties Belonged to Britain." *Rolling Stone,* July 14, 1988. https://www.rollingstone.com /music/music-news/the-british-invasion-from-the-beatles-to-the-stones-the-six ties-belonged-to-britain-244870/.

Queenan, Joe. "Why America's Anglophiles Are Missing the Point of the Royal Wedding." *Time,* April 28, 2011. http://content.time.com/time/magazine/article /0,9171,2068118,00.html.

Rabinowitz, Dorothy. "'Endeavour' Review: Hope Meets Uncertainty." *Wall Street Journal,* July 26, 2018. https://www.wsj.com/articles/endeavour-review-hope -meets-uncertainty-1532643505.

———. "Pride and Privilege." *Wall Street Journal,* January 7, 2011. https://www.wsj .com/articles/SB10001424052748704405704576064551170158190.

Radio Times. "Anthony Horowitz on the Dark Truth behind Foyle's War." January 4, 2015. https://www.radiotimes.com/news/2015-01-04/anthony-horowitz-on-the -dark-truth-behind-foyles-war/.

———. "Foyle's War: Anthony Horowitz on the Show's Dark, Discerning and Absolutely True Storylines." January 4, 2015. https://www.radiotimes.com /news/2015-01-04/anthony-horowitz-on-the-dark-truth-behind-foyles-war/.

Raeside, Julia. "Claire Foy: Wolf Hall's Perfectly Complex Anne Boleyn." *Guardian,* February 26, 2015. https://www.theguardian.com/tv-and-radio/2015/feb/26 /claire-foy-wolf-hall-perfect-anne-boleyn.

Rafferty, Terrence. "The Decline of the American Actor." *Atlantic,* July 2015. https://www.theatlantic.com/magazine/archive/2015/07/decline-american-actor /395291/.

Ravitch, Dianne. "The Decline and Fall of Teaching History." *New York Times,* November 17, 1985. https://www.nytimes.com/1985/11/17/magazine/decine-and -fall-of-teaching-history.html.

Richards, Antony J. *Inspector Morse on Location.* Sawston: Irregular Special Press, 2016.

Rideal, Rebecca. "Forget *The Crown,* ITV's Endeavour Is the Period Drama of Our Time." *New Statesman America,* February 8, 2019. https://www.newstatesman.com /culture/tv-radio/2019/02/forget-crown-itv-s-endeavour-period-drama-our-time.

Roberts, Timothy. *American Exceptionalism*. New York: Routledge, 2017.

Rosenberg, Alyssa. "Sherlock Holmes Meets the 21st Century." *Atlantic*, October 19, 2010. https://www.theatlantic.com/entertainment/archive/2010/10/sherlock-holmes-meets-the-21st-century/64788/.

Rosseinsky, Kate. "Sanditon: Everything You Need to Know about ITV's New Jane Austen Adaptation." *Evening Standard*, August 23, 2019. https://www.msn.com/en-gb/entertainment/tv/sanditon-everything-you-need-to-know-about-itvs-new-jane-austen-adaptation/ar-AAGiAkK.

Rothman, Joshua. "The History of 'Loving' to Read." *New Yorker*, February 3, 2015. https://www.newyorker.com/culture/cultural-comment/history-loving-read.

Rozen, Leah. "'Sherlock' vs. 'Sherlock': Robert Downey Jr. or Benedict Cumberbatch." *BBC America*, 2011. http://www.bbcamerica.com/anglophenia/2011/12/sherlock-vs-sherlock-robert-downey-jr-or-benedict-cumberbatch/.

Rubin, Joan Shelley. *The Making of Middlebrow Culture*. Chapel Hill: University of North Carolina Press, 1992.

Russell, John. "It's Not Easy Being Queen: Writer Daisy Goodwin on 'Victoria' Season 1." *TV Insider*, March 3, 2017. https://www.tvinsider.com/112952/victoria-daisy-goodwin-pbs/.

Russello, Gerald J. "Liberalism: The Great Anti-Tradition." *American Conservative*, April 22, 2019. https://www.theamericanconservative.com/articles/liberalism-the-great-anti-tradition/.

Scaggs, John. *Crime Fiction*. New York: Routledge, 2005.

Schama, Simon. "Why Americans Have Fallen for Snobby Downton Abbey." *Newsweek*, January 16, 2012. https://www.newsweek.com/why-americans-have-fallen-snobby-downton-abbey-64157.

Scheck, Frank. "Author Hilary Mantel on the Page-to-Stage Transition of 'Wolf Hall.'" *Hollywood Reporter*, April 3, 2015. http://www.hollywoodreporter.com/news/author-hilary-manetel-page-stage-786230.

Schulman, Michael. "Cover Story: The Mind-Bending Benedict Cumberbatch." *Vanity Fair*, November 2016.

———. "Superfans: A Love Story." *New Yorker*, September 9, 2019. https://www.newyorker.com/magazine/2019/09/16/superfans-a-love-story.

Schwartz, Benjamin. "The Rise and Fall of Charm in American Men." *Atlantic*, June 2013. https://www.theatlantic.com/magazine/archive/2013/06/when-men-lost-their-charm/309303/.

Scullard, Vickie. "The Manchester Family Story." *Manchester Evening News*, October 30, 2019.

Sennett, Richard. "Charismatic De-Legitimation: A Case Study." *Theory and Society* 2 (1975): 171–81.

Shepherd, Simon. *The Cambridge Introduction to Modern British Theatre*. London: Cambridge University Press, 2009.

Simon, Scott. "Gillian Anderson Paying a Visit to 'Bleak House.'" NPR, January 21, 2006.

Smith, Lesley. "'Foyle's War': After the War, What Next?" *Pop Matters*, September 16, 2013. https://www.popmatters.com/foyles-war-after-the-war-what-next-2495724021.html.

Solomon, Robert C. *In Defense of Sentimentality*. Oxford: Oxford University Press, 2004.

Sontag, Susan. *Notes on Camp*. New York: Penguin Modern, 2018.

Stanley, Alessandra. "A Transatlantic Romance Continues." *New York Times*, January 2, 2014. https://www.nytimes.com/2014/01/03/arts/television/downton-abbey-returns-for-a-fourth-season.html.

Stevens, Dan. "Why I Left Downton Abbey." *Telegraph,* March 7, 2016. https://www.telegraph.co.uk/culture/tvandradio/downton-abbey/9765334/Dan-Stevens-Why-I-left-Downton-Abbey.html.

Stewart, David. "How Should Public TV Follow Up the Success of *The Forsyte Saga?*" *Current*, April 14, 1997. https://current.org/1997/04/how-should-public-tv-follow-up-the-forsyte-saga-success-2/.

Stewart, Matthew. "The 9.9 Percent Is the New American Aristocracy." *Atlantic*, June 2018. https://www.theatlantic.com/magazine/archive/2018/06/the-birth-of-a-new-american-aristocracy/559130/.

Stewart, Susan. *On Longing*. Durham, NC: Duke University Press, 1993.

Stohr, Karen. *On Manners*. New York: Routledge, 2012.

Strausbaugh, John. "Have Our Manners Gone to Hell?" *American Heritage*, September 1991. http://www.americanheritagecom/have-our-manners-gone-to-hell-0.

Suchet, David, and Geoffrey Wansell. *Poirot and Me*. London: Headline Publishing, 2013.

Sullivan, Margaret C. "Andrew Davies: Putting the Sex Back in Sense and Sensibility." *Austen Blog.com*, May 29, 2006. https://austenblog.com/2006/05/29/andrew-davies-putting-the-sex-back-in-sense-and-sensibility/.

Swanson, Peter. "Review: Downton Abbey." *Slant*, January 8, 2011. https://www.slantmagazine.com/tv/downton-abbey-season-one/.

———. "Review of Sherlock: Season One." *Slant*, October 22, 2010. https://www.slantmagazine.com/tv/sherlock-season-one/.

Sykes, Tom. "The Death of the English Eccentric." *Daily Beast*, April 14, 2017. https://www.thedailybeast.com/the-death-of-the-english-eccentric.

Tamarkin, Elisa. *Anglophilia: Deference, Devotion, and Antebellum America*. Chicago: University of Chicago Press, 2008.

Teeman, Tim. "Hilary Mantel on 'Wolf Hall,' Kate Middleton, and Plans for New Novels." *Daily Beast*, April 8, 2015. http://www.thedailybeast.com/articles/2015/04/08/hilary-mantel-on-wolf-hall-kate-middleton-and-plans-for-new-novels.html.

Telegraph. "48 Hours in Cornwall." April 17, 2019. https://www.msn.com/engb/lifestyle/travel/48-hours-in-cornwall-an-insider-guide-to-englands-wild-west/ar-BBW1BfH.

Thomas, Liz. "Case of Emma Fatigue Sees BBC Viewers Turn Off in Millions." *Daily Mail*, October 21, 2009. https://www.dailymail.co.uk/tvshowbiz/article-1221804/Case-Emma-fatigue-sees-BBC-viewers-turn-millions.html.

Thomson, David. *Television: A Biography*. London: Thames and Hudson, 2016.

Tiedemann, Jennifer, and Karen Marsico. "Americans' Declining Interest in History Is Hitting Museums Like Colonial Williamsburg Hard." *Federalist*, August 22, 2017. https://www.thefederalist.com/2017/8/22/americans-declining-interest-history -hitting-colonial-williamsburg-hard-not-one/.

Travers, Peter. "Kenneth Branagh Embodies the Bard in Mesmerizing 'All Is True.'" *Rolling Stone*, May 9, 2019. https://www.rollingstone.com/movies/movie-reviews /all-is-true-movie-review-kenneth-branagh-832318/.

Vanacker, Sabine, and Catherine Wynne. *Sherlock Holmes and Conan Doyle*. London: Palgrave Macmillan, 2013.

Veltman, Chloe. "British Actors Aren't Better Than Our Own." *Wall Street Journal*, March 24, 2007. https://www.wsj.com/articles/SB117467810369547113.

Virtue, Graeme. "Endeavour: It's Inspector Morse with a Moustache—and Surprisingly Great." *Guardian*, February 12, 2019. https://www.theguardian.com /tv-and-radio/2019/feb/12/endeavour-its-inspector-morse-with-a-moustache -and-surprisingly-great.

———. "*Grantchester*'s Holy Sleuths Are Brimming with Bromance and Charm." *Guardian*, November 3, 2014.

Visit Cornwall. "15 Poldark Film Locations." Accessed October 16, 2019. https:// www.visitcornwall.com/poldark/blog/poldark-film-locations.

Visit London. "Sherlock Holmes' London." Accessed October 16, 2019. https:// www.visitlondon.com/things-to-do/sightseeing/one-day-itineraries/sherlock -holmes-london.

Wagg, Stephen. *Because I Tell a Joke or Two: Comedy, Politics, and Social Difference*. London: Routledge Press, 1998.

Wagner, Curt. "Jeremy Piven Does Quick Change for 2 Famous Roles." *Chicago Tribune*, April 1, 2014. https://www.chicagotribune.com/redeye/ct-redeye-xpm -2014-04-01-48894873-story.html.

Wallace, Kelly. "Five Steps Toward Making Theatre More Diverse." *Playbill*, December 8, 2019. http://www.playbill.com/article/5-steps-toward-making-theatre -more-diverse.

"Wallander Review: He's Back, and He's Still Got It." *Guardian*, May 23, 2016. https://www.theguardian.com/tv-and-radio/2016/may/23/wallander-review -back-and-still-got-it.

Walsh, Bernard. "'Foyle's War' Returns with Crimes of Espionage." Associated Press, September 12, 2013. https://www.yahoo.com/entertainment/news/foyles-war -returns-crimes-espionage-184533755.html.

Weiss, Joanna. "Andrew Davies Has Adapted to Jane Austen's Sensibility." *Boston Globe*, January 6, 2008. http://archive.boston.com/ae/tv/articles/2008/01/05 /andrew_davies_has_adapted_to_jane_austens_sensibility/.

Wells, Tish. "1940s Drama 'Foyle's War' Returns on PBS." *Miami Herald*, September 11, 2013. https://www.mcclatchydc.com/news/nation-world/national /article24755458.html.

Wertheimer, Ron. "Television Review: So Many Knots, Inspector, and Time Is Running Out." *New York Times*, February 22, 2001. https://www.nytimes

.com/2001/02/22/arts/television-review-so-many-knots-inspector-and-time-is-running-out.html.

White, John F., with Dan Jauch. "President's Speech to NET Affiliates." New York City, April 22, 1968 (copy of speech in White files, National Public Broadcasting Association).

White, Mark. *Kenneth Branagh*. London: Faber and Faber, 2005.

Wiegand, David. "'Foyle' Brilliantly Explores Moral Gray Areas of War." *San Francisco Chronicle*, January 21, 2003. https://www.sfgate.com/entertainment/article/Foyle -brilliantly-explores-moral-gray-areas-of-2675884.php.

Williams, Alex. "Americans Are Barmy Over Britishisms." *New York Times*, October 10, 2012. https://www.nytimes.com/2012/10/11/fashion/americans-are-barmy -over-britishisms.html.

Wollaston, Sam. "Foyle's War: Our Girl—TV review." *Guardian*, March 24, 2013. https://www.theguardian.com/tv-and-radio/tvandradioblog/2013/mar/25/foyles -war-our-girl-tv-review.

———. "Wolf Hall Review—'Event Television: Sumptuous, Intelligent and Serious'." *Guardian*, January 22, 2015. http://www.theguardian.com/tb-and-radio/2015 /Jan/22/wolf-hall-review-slabs-of-guilt-lifted-triumphantly-from-the-bookshelf.

Wollaston, Sue. "Endeavour Review—as Comforting as Cheese on Toast." *Guardian*, February 5, 2018. https://www.theguardian.com/tv-and-radio/2018/feb/05 /endeavour-review-as-comforting-as-cheese-on-toast.

Wood, James. "Invitation to a Beheading." *New Yorker*, May 7, 2012. http://www .newyorker.com/magazine/2012/05/07/invitation-to-a-beheading.

Young, Samantha. "Based on a True Story: Contemporary Historical Fiction and Historiographical Theory." *Otherness: Essays and Studies* 2, no. 1 (August 2011).

Zafar, Aylin. "Are Americans Over Being Polite?" *Time*, March 18, 2012. https:// newsfeed.time.com/2012/03/18/are-americans-over-being-polite/.

Index

About the Author

Nancy West is professor of English at the University of Missouri and the author of *Kodak and the Lens of Nostalgia* (2000) and *Tabloid, Inc.: Crimes, News, Narratives* (2010). Her books have led to appearances on PBS's *American Experience* and the BBC's *Genius of Photography* as well as keynote speeches at the National Gallery of Art in Washington, DC, the London School of Design, and the Amon Carter Museum. She is a regular contributor to *Written by Magazine*, the *Atlantic*, the *Chronicle of Higher Education*, and the *Los Angeles Review of Books*. She is currently writing a memoir, set in the 1970s, about the Manhattan film scene.